Red Squirrels

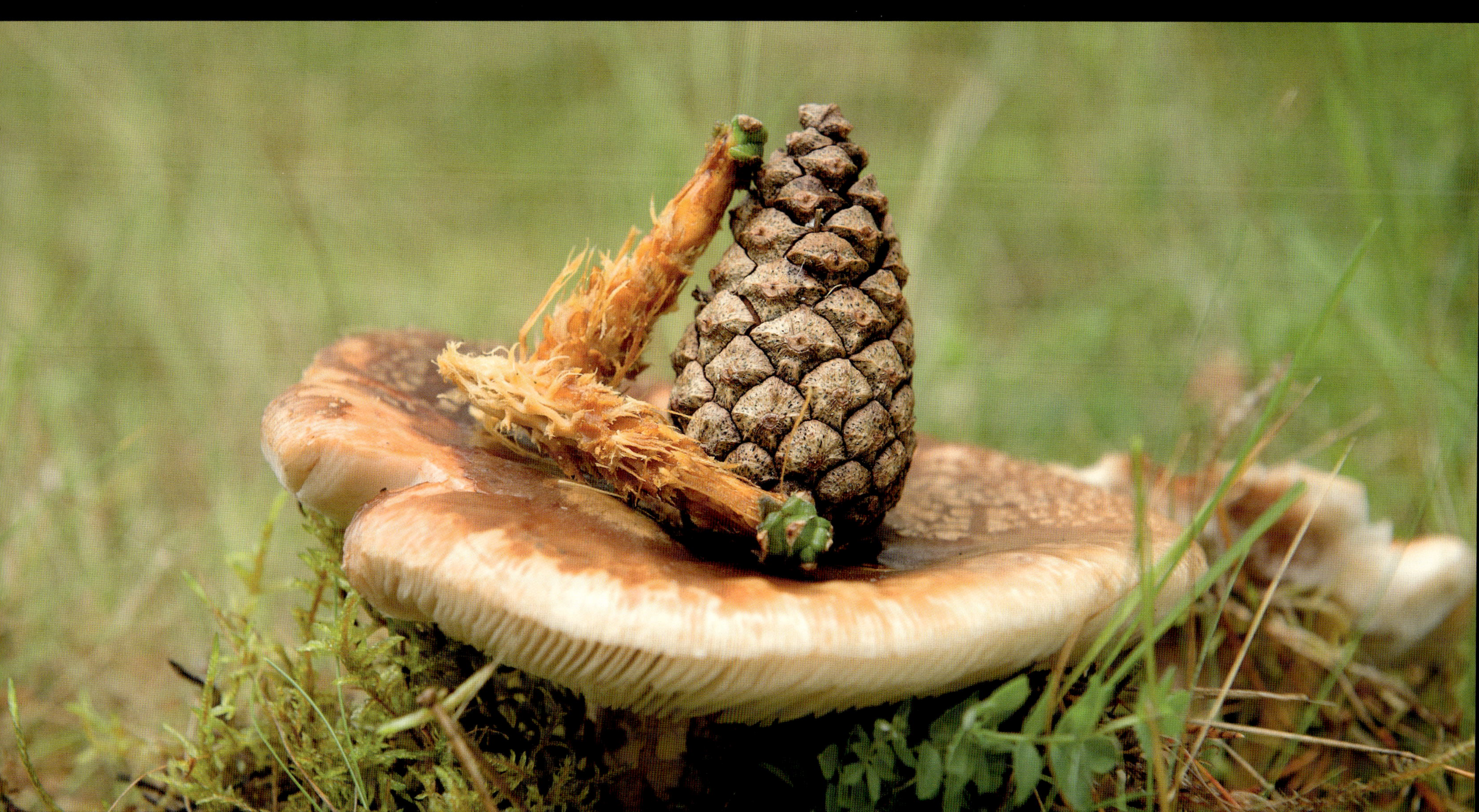

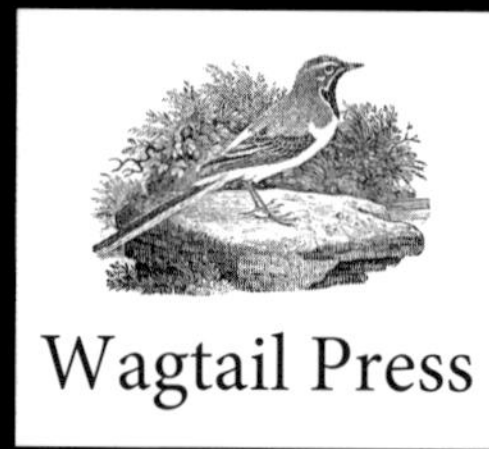

Wagtail Press

Book design by Will Nicholls & Gemma Wilkinson
Printed By ELANDERS LTD
All photographs © Will Nicholls

ISBN : 978-0-9559395-2-5

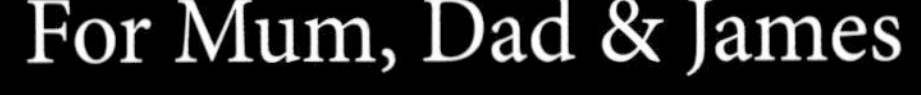

For Mum, Dad & James

Foreword by
Steve Backshall

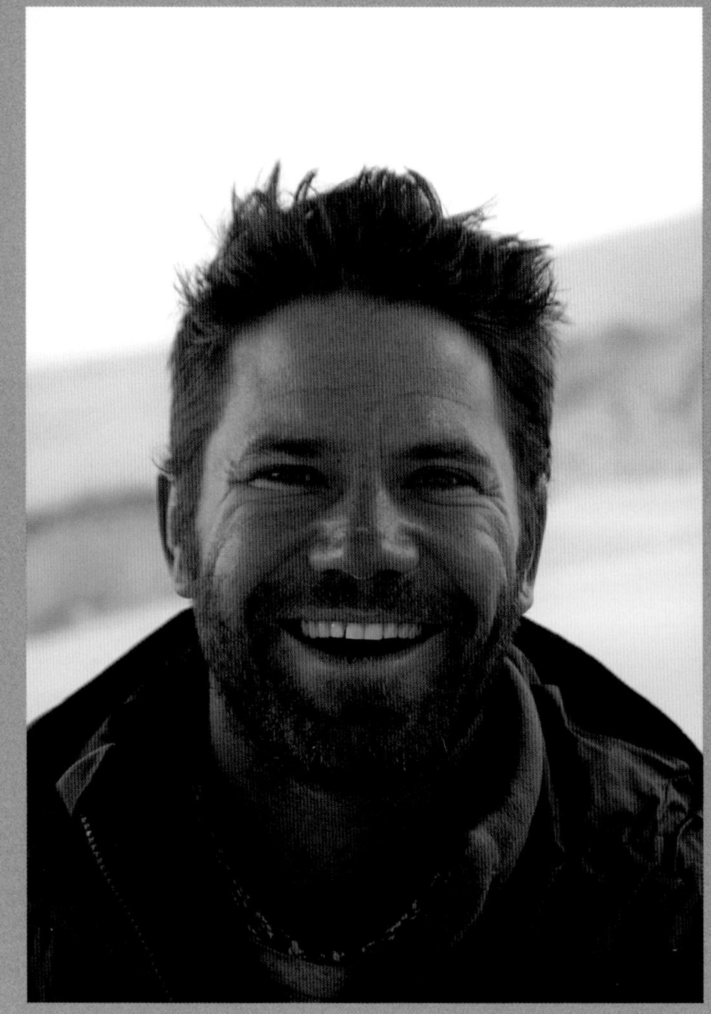

The red squirrel could and should be a poster-child of British conservation. Resplendent in its russet finery, charming, a part of our culture and national mythology, traditionally persecuted from within, and now beleaguered by foreign foes. When I was a youngster, sightings of red squirrel were still commonplace in much of the country. Now you have to make an effort to see one, but it's something I would urge everyone to try and do at least once, because it's an experience you will remember. It is the plucky, pretty underdog who can only survive with our help.

The squirrels are a well-represented group worldwide, with squirrels that burrow and squirrels that glide. However, in the UK we have just the one native Sciurid: Squirrel Nutkin, the busy nut-collecting Sylvanian, with doey eyes, dextrous fingertips, twitching nose and comical ear tufts. They are so precious, and their range is shrinking so dramatically under the manifold attacks of the invasive grey, that anything that rekindles our joy for them is worthy of great credit. Will's work on these pages is to be commended for that reason alone. However, Will should also be recognised for the quality of his images, and for the fact that he has such a genuine passion for the wild world around him. When we met a few years back, he impressed me as a young man with passion, enthusiasm and a mission: one which I am only too happy to support, and be a part of. I wish him much success in what will clearly be a long life in natural history photography and film-making.

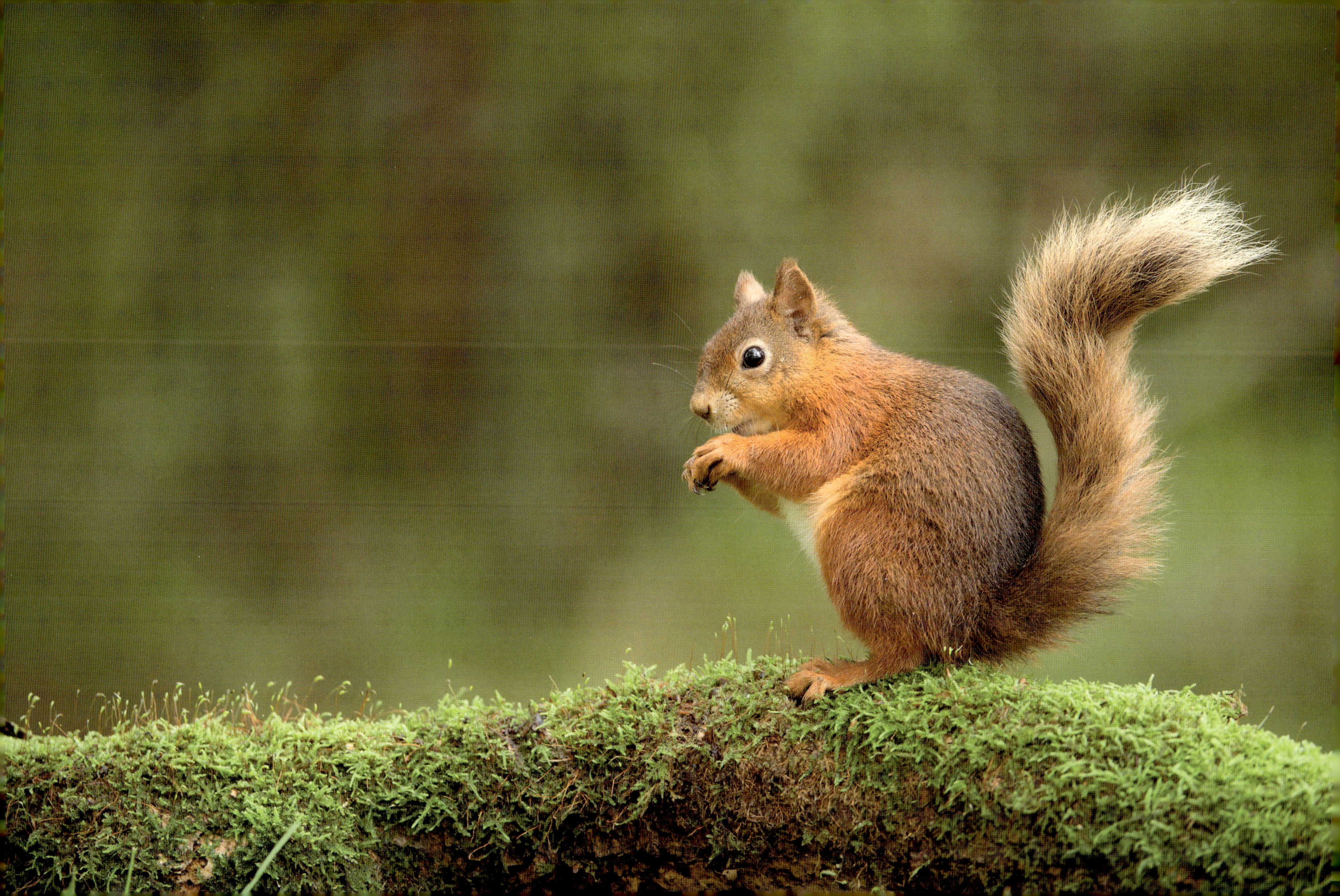

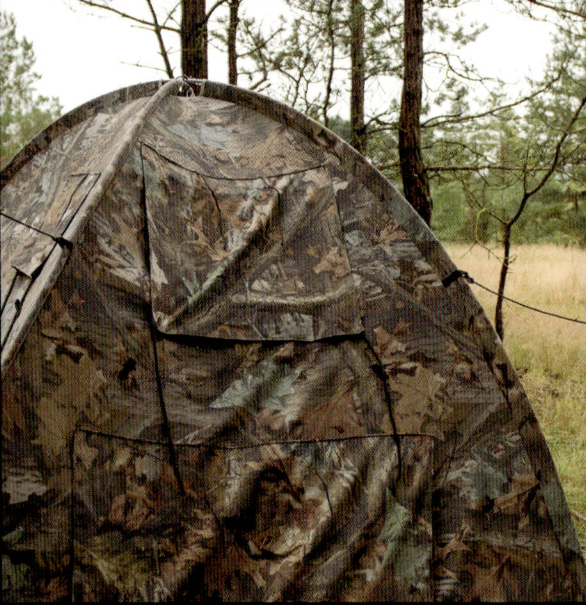

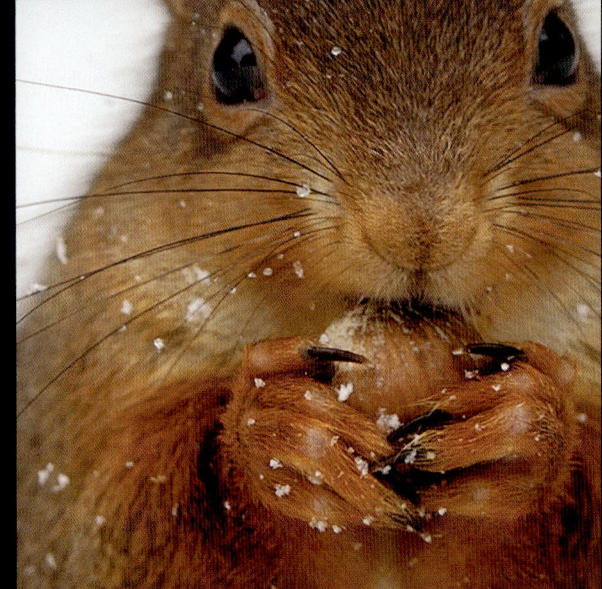

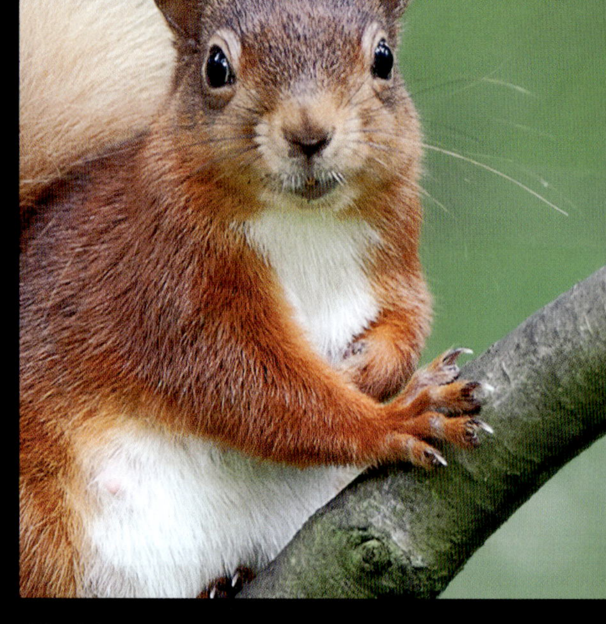

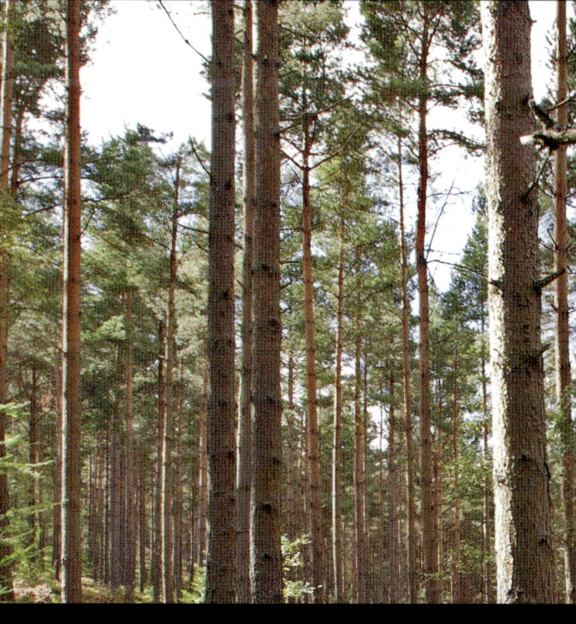

Chapter 3 – Life in the trees

Squirrels have evolved perfectly to live in woodland canopies, with some interesting adaptations.

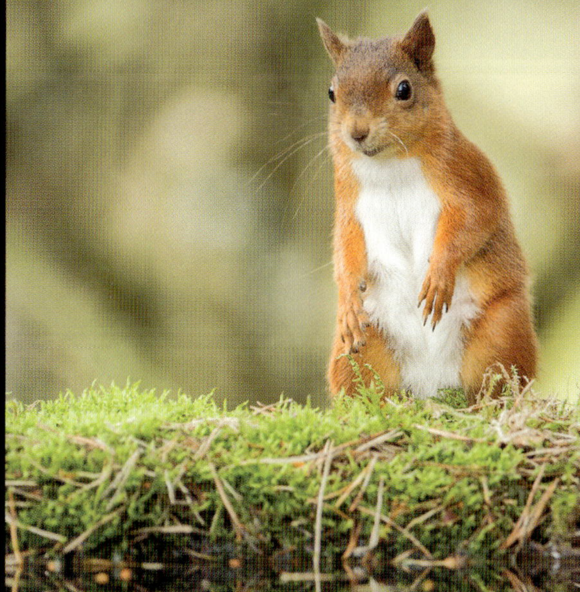

Chapter 4 – Posing for the camera

A 'behind-the-scenes' look at how I capture a variety of my squirrel images.

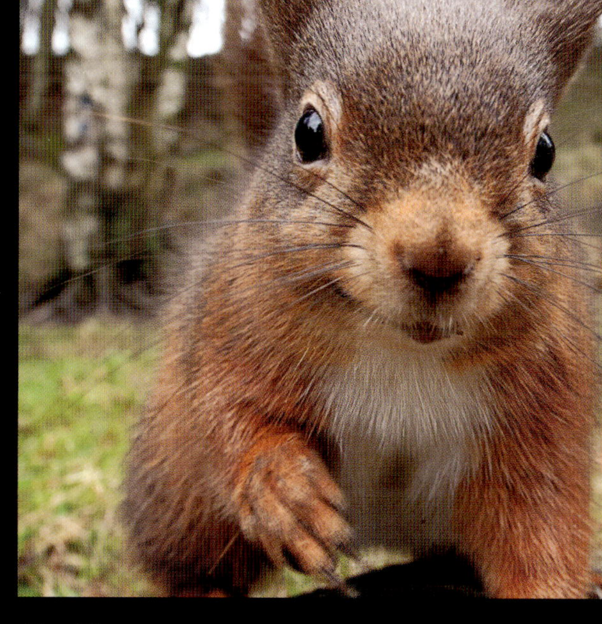

Chapter 5 – Up close and personal

After a while, it is nice to get a new photographic perspective on the squirrels. I take to a shorter lens to document their life.

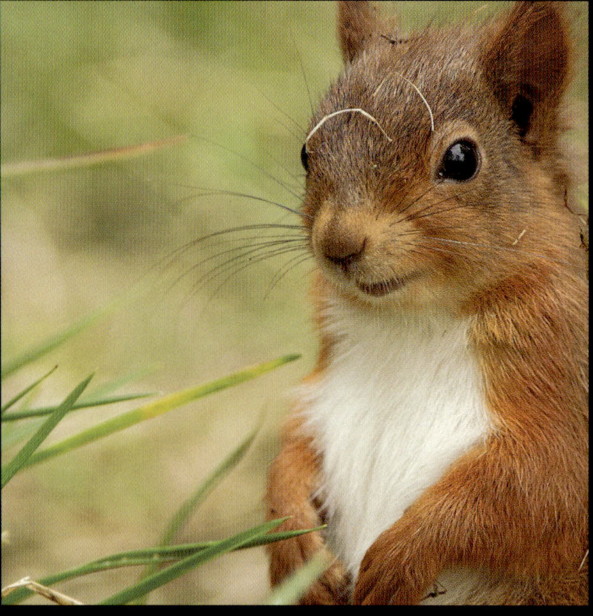

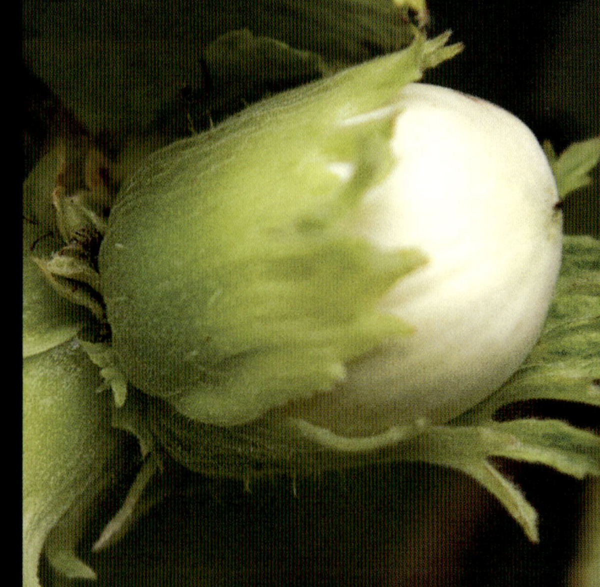

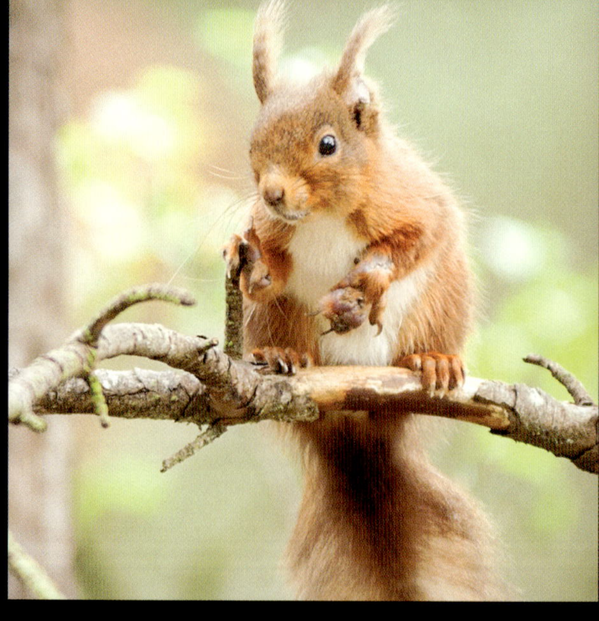

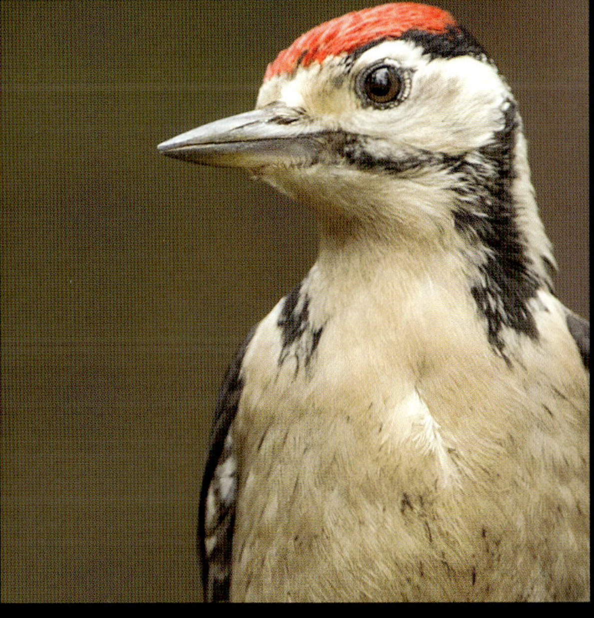

Chapter 9 – Branching out

British woodlands play host to a variety of other birds and mammals. They make for great

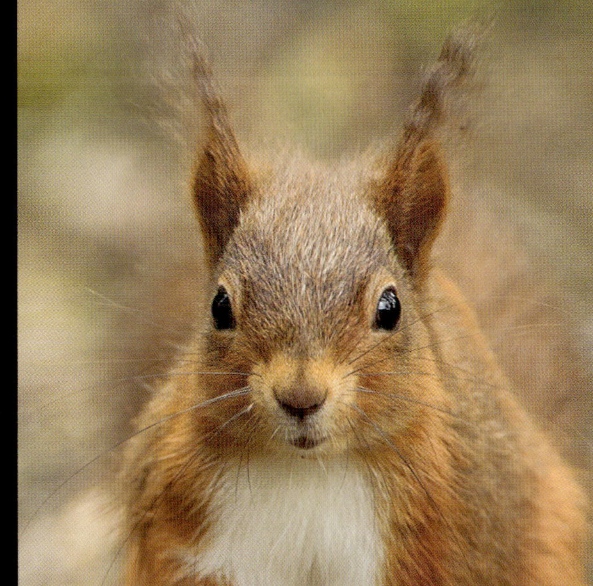

Chapter 10 – How to find squirrels

My top tips on how to view and photograph red squirrels.

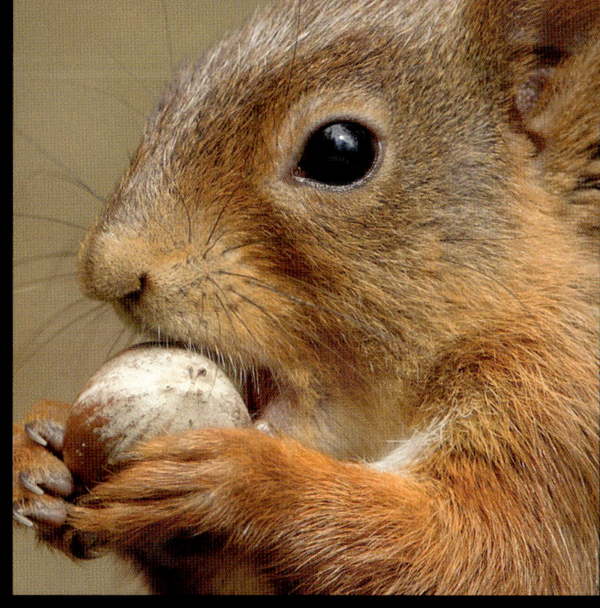

Epilogue – Looking ahead

Discussing the future of red squirrels in Britain.

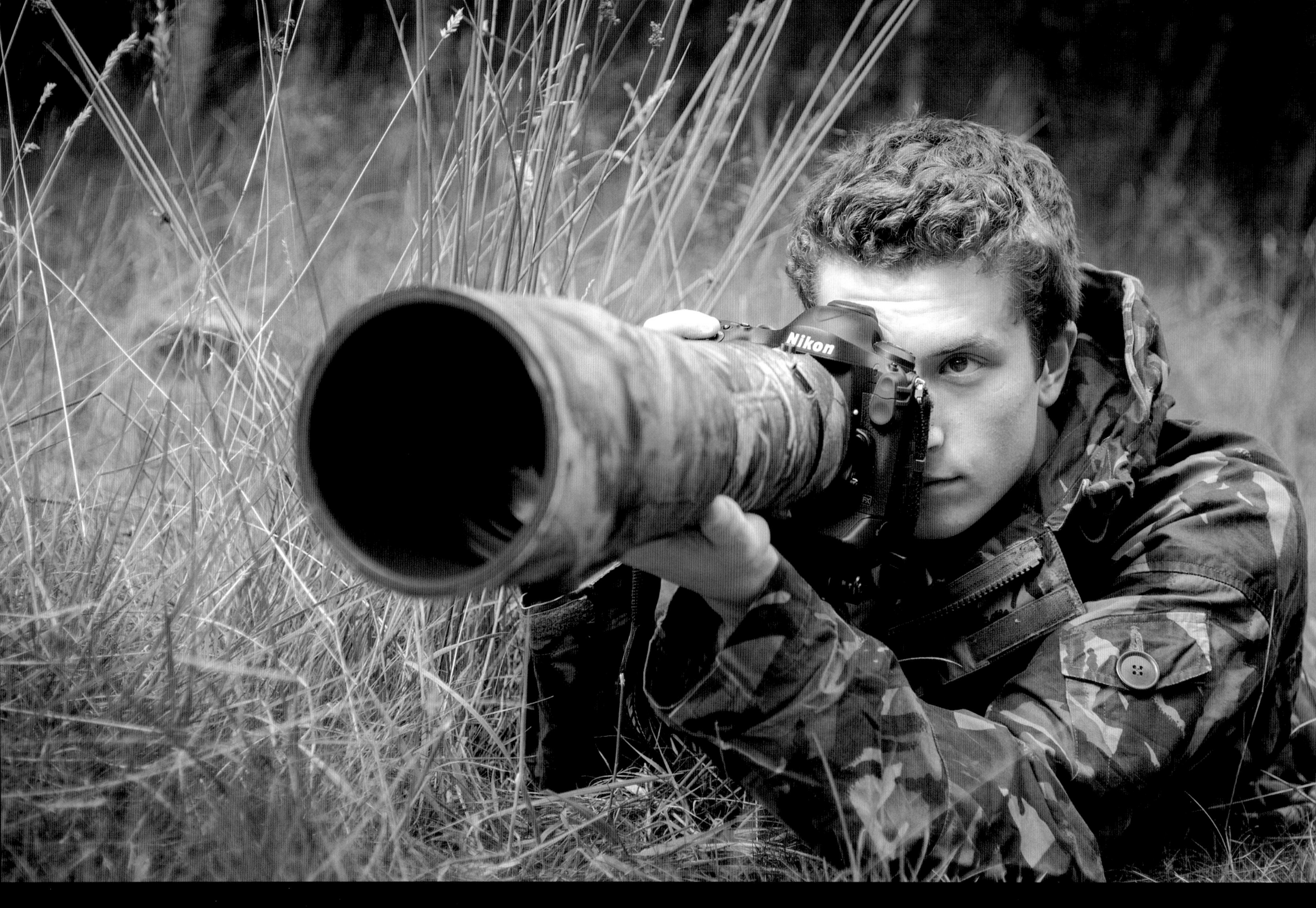

I was twelve years old when my mother and stepfather decided to move to the Northumberland countryside, leaving the city behind. I have always liked wildlife, but living surrounded by pubs and housing estates meant that my access to nature was limited. It was this change of scene that sparked what has continued to be a lifelong interest in wildlife and the natural world.

Soon after moving into our new home, I began to explore the fields outside. I took my parents' simple compact camera with me, and took a few images of the sheep. Naturally I thought they were brilliant at the time, but looking back they were definitely heading for the bin. Even so, I caught the photography bug and quickly saved up and bought my own camera. It was very basic, but it did the job. Ever since then I have continued to take photographs, upgrading my kit as I became more inventive with my photographic style.

I am very lucky where I live, because just a few minutes from the house we have a woodland that plays host to a population of red squirrels. At first I didn't know this, and instead journeyed to Kielder Forest to sit waiting in their public hide. But after a few months, we spotted what we thought was a red squirrel running into the trees back at home. I soon set up a hide, and was treated to close views of our own reds. By then I had fallen in love with these delightful creatures. Their playful natures and individual characters are what I strive to capture in my images. Many people have never seen a red squirrel, and so I feel privileged to be able to spend so much time with them.

It was photographing these squirrels that showed me photography and natural history was something I would be involved in for a long time. Whilst red squirrels are excellent subjects, I do point my lens elsewhere and enjoy photographing as many different species as possible. But it isn't just capturing the image that interests me: sometimes I like just to watch and observe the wildlife instead of staring down the viewfinder. It is easy to get lost in the determination

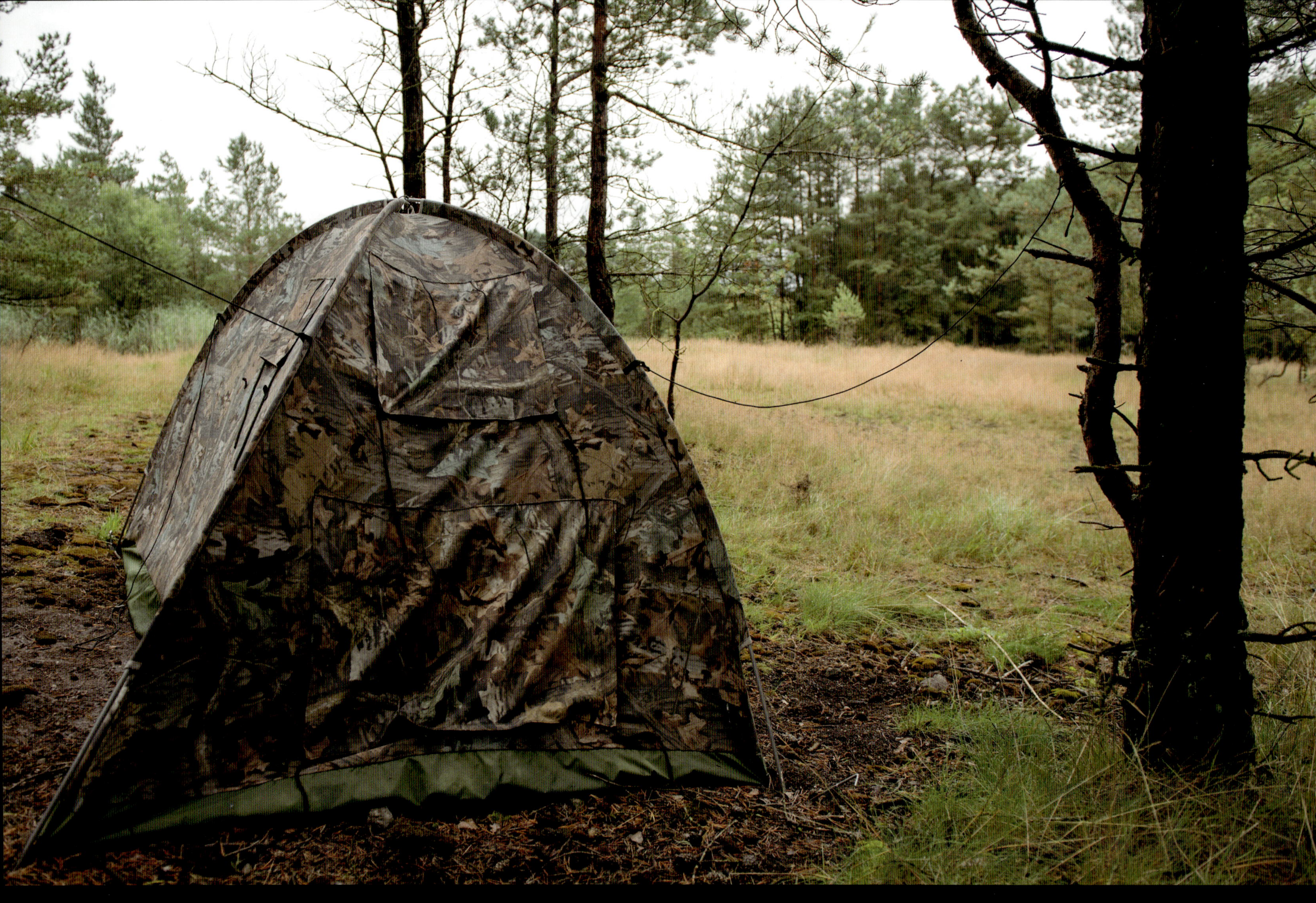

to capture the perfect photograph, and as a result miss out on really enjoying and taking in a special moment.

I have decided to study zoology at university, as I wish to develop my scientific knowledge of wildlife. I can learn only so much through observation in the field, so a degree in something that I love to do would be ideal. As an aspiring natural history documentary presenter and film-maker, I hope this will allow me to develop some of the skills required to work in such a competitive industry.

For a long time now I have wanted to produce a book about red squirrels, as they are such popular animals that play a big part in my life. I hope that once you have finished reading, you will have gained an insight into the life of our elusive friend. All the squirrel images in this book are from the UK, most of which were taken in Northumberland near my home. For that reason, you may even begin to spot certain individual squirrels in different images.

If you are in an area where you think there could be red squirrels, it may help to keep your eyes on the ground as well as looking into the trees. Squirrels will leave signs of their presence, the most obvious of which will be shredded pinecones scattered all over an area underneath their favoured tree. They will tear off the plates of the pinecone with their teeth to get at the seeds inside. You may also find half of a hazelnut shell; the evidence of a squirrel having enjoyed one of its favourite delicacies. If you are lucky, you may even hear the chatter of a red squirrel nearby.

Right: One of my favourite squirrels, "Patch", climbs down a tree.
Opposite: My office!

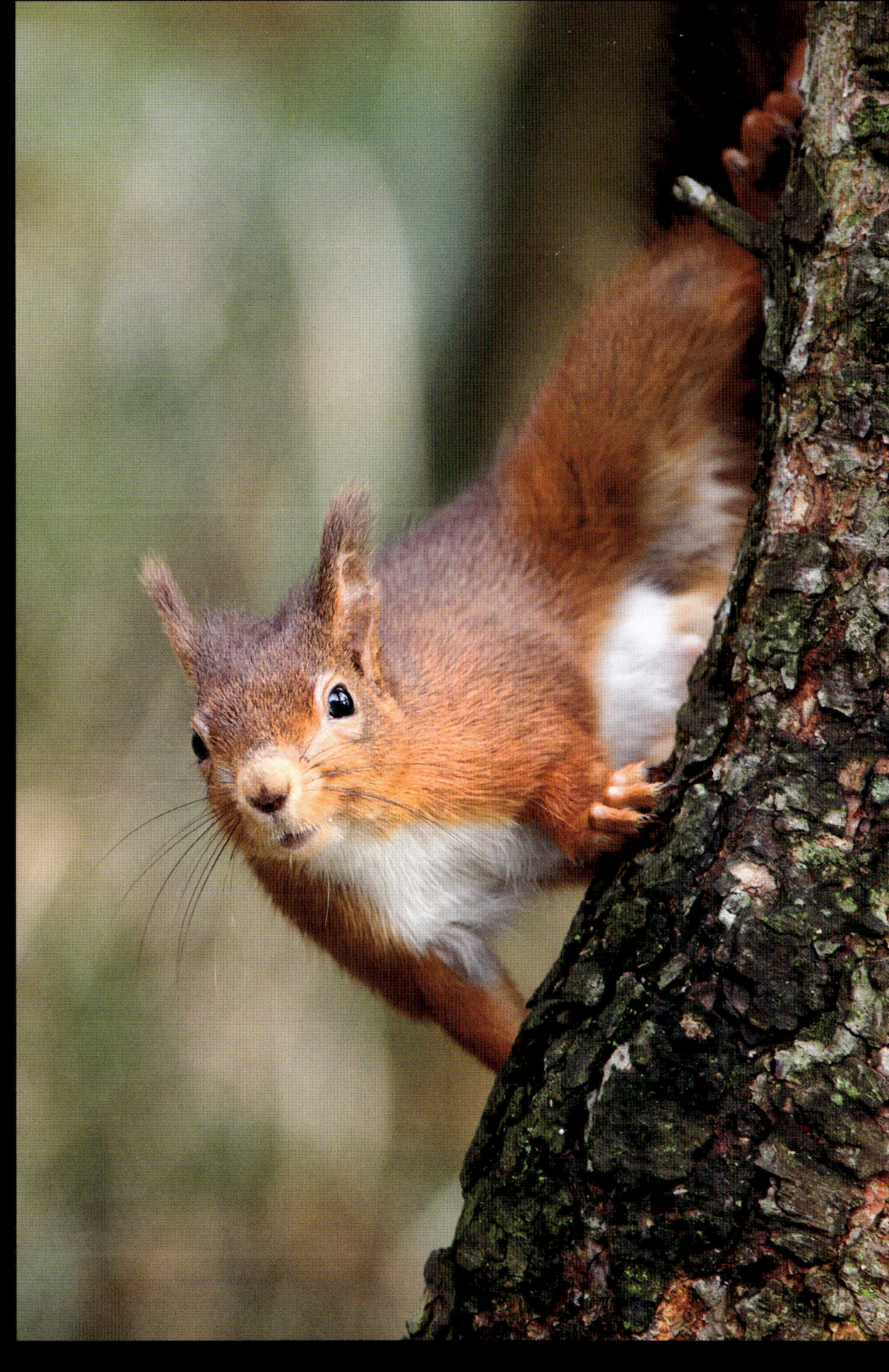

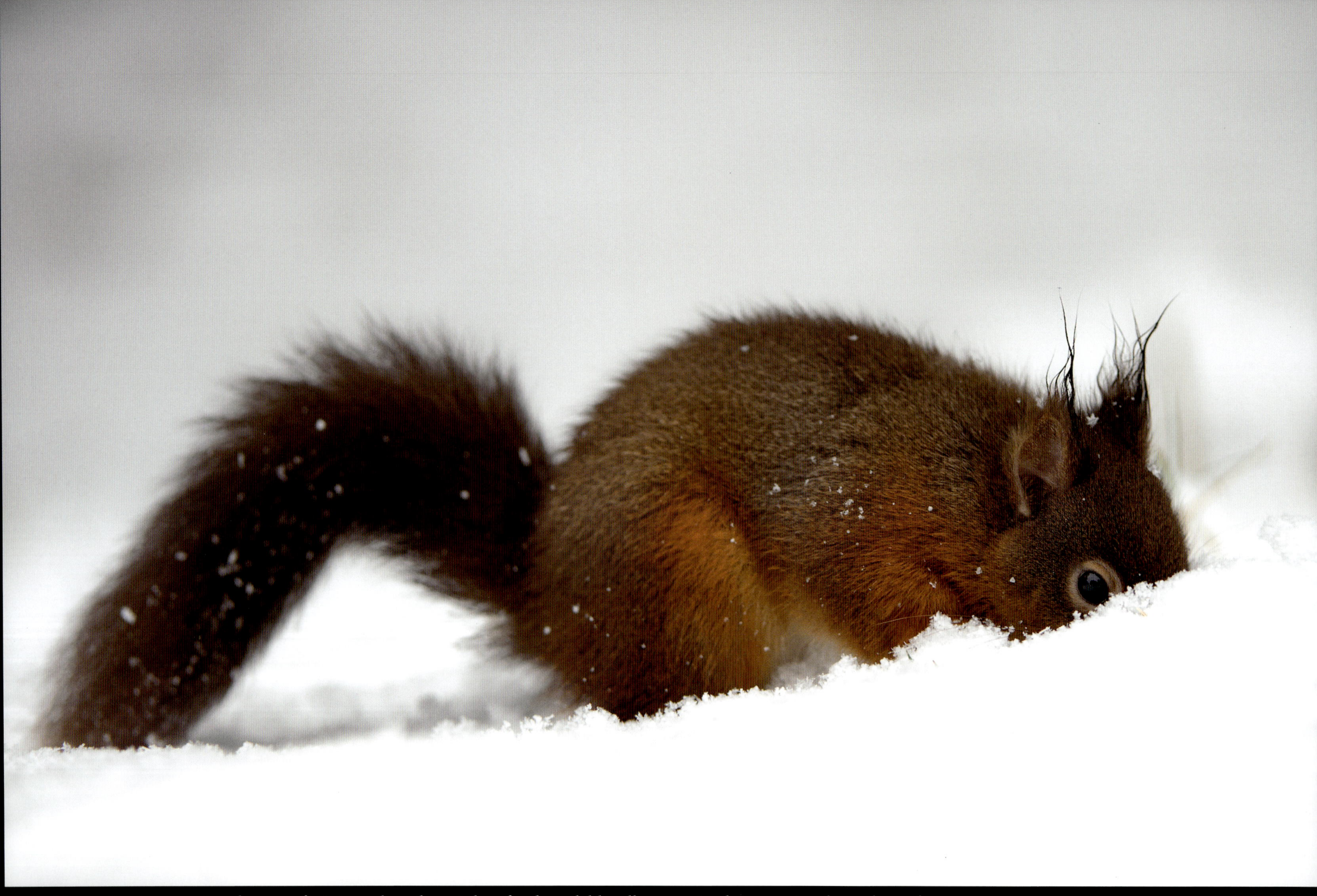

Above: Storing nuts in advance of winter, when there is less food available, allows squirrels to survive throughout the year.

Getting ready for winter

If you ask any young child to picture a squirrel, they will describe one running around and burying nuts. It is strange, if you think about it, that squirrels are known so well for their appetite for all things nutty, when in fact they eat a variety of other things too. In the past, red squirrels were persecuted because of their occasional habit of stripping the bark on trees to get to the juicy sap. They would bite a ring around the tree, killing everything upwards of it. It comes as no surprise then, that the foresters of the time were often not their biggest fans.

Autumn is a time of plenty for red squirrels. There are lots of tasty treats to get their paws on, as well as a variety of edible fungi scattered across the woodland floor. However, they must resist temptation to gobble it all up and instead ensure they have cached enough food for the winter time. It is important that they have the cupboards stocked for when most of the trees are bare. In a woodland containing coniferous trees, pinecones are available for almost all of the year. This provides a lifeline for squirrels, meaning there is at least some food always available to supplement their diet during the harshest season of the year.

Squirrels don't hibernate and are active throughout the year, although they will move around less during the cold winter months and spend longer in their dreys. Winter brings with it a thicker coat for red squirrels, making them even better subjects for photography. Furthermore, their characterful ear tufts become much thicker and longer than they are during the spring and summer. It is for this reason that my favourite time to photograph the red squirrels is during winter.

Every season of the year has its own problems when trying to get the squirrels to pose for the perfect photograph. With their decreased activity, capturing them in the snow can mean sitting freezing for hours in a small hide (having forgotten the flask of hot chocolate) whilst they are tucked up in bed. For me, the challenge makes the moment when I capture the image I'm waiting for that little bit more

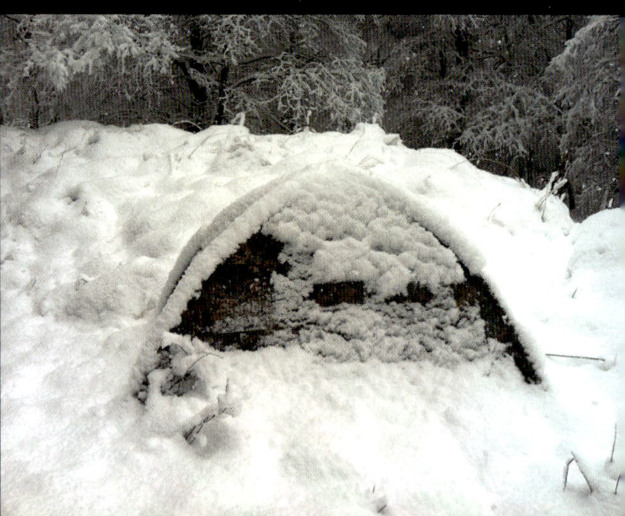

rewarding. I remember in January 2013, I was walking back home from my hide through the many inches of snow that had fallen. I had forgotten to bring any gloves; a mistake which I soon regretted. Never have my hands gotten so cold, and when I walked into my heated house I was in a lot of pain as my fingers began to warm up.

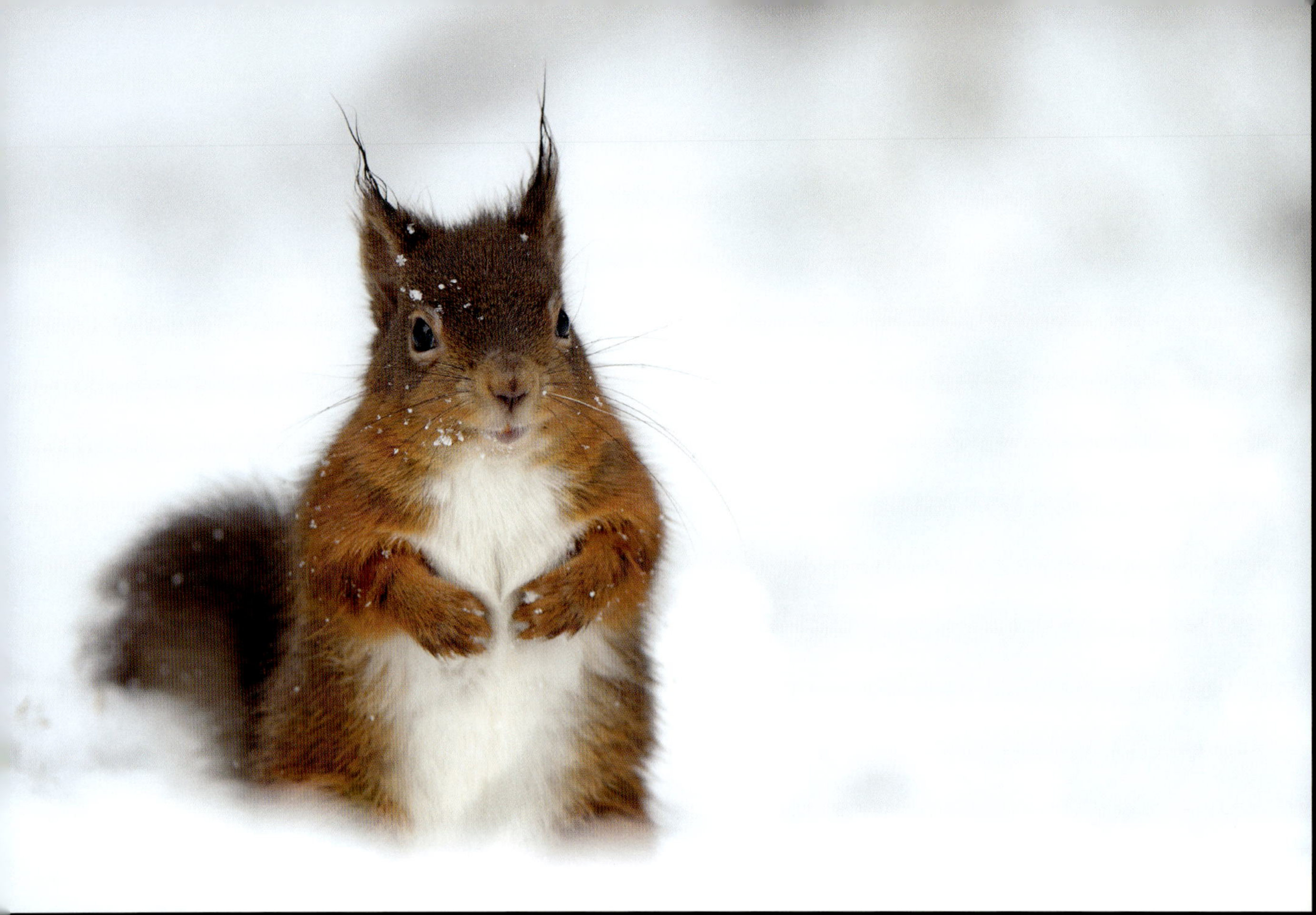

The results of that mistake were worth it though. I had spent five hours laying on my chest in the snow, so I was delighted when the squirrels turned up. They were busy foraging; their heavy red coats contrasting beautifully with the pure white surroundings. As the snow gently drifted down from the clouds above, flakes would rest on their fur before gradually melting due to the squirrel's body heat.

I will always, like many, find winter to be the most magical time of year. The pine trees have thin branches, causing the snow to settle in delicate lines all over them. This results in the entire woodland being transformed into what can only be described as a scene from the world of Narnia. The spectacle is breathtaking and every year it fills me with joy. Going to sleep one night with green fields outside, then to awake to such a scene never becomes tiresome.

Back in April 2012 we had around five inches of unexpected snowfall overnight. This must shake things up a little for the squirrels, especially if it is for a longer duration than a couple of days. Luckily the snow shower passed as quickly as it had come, but it did allow me to capture more snow-filled images.

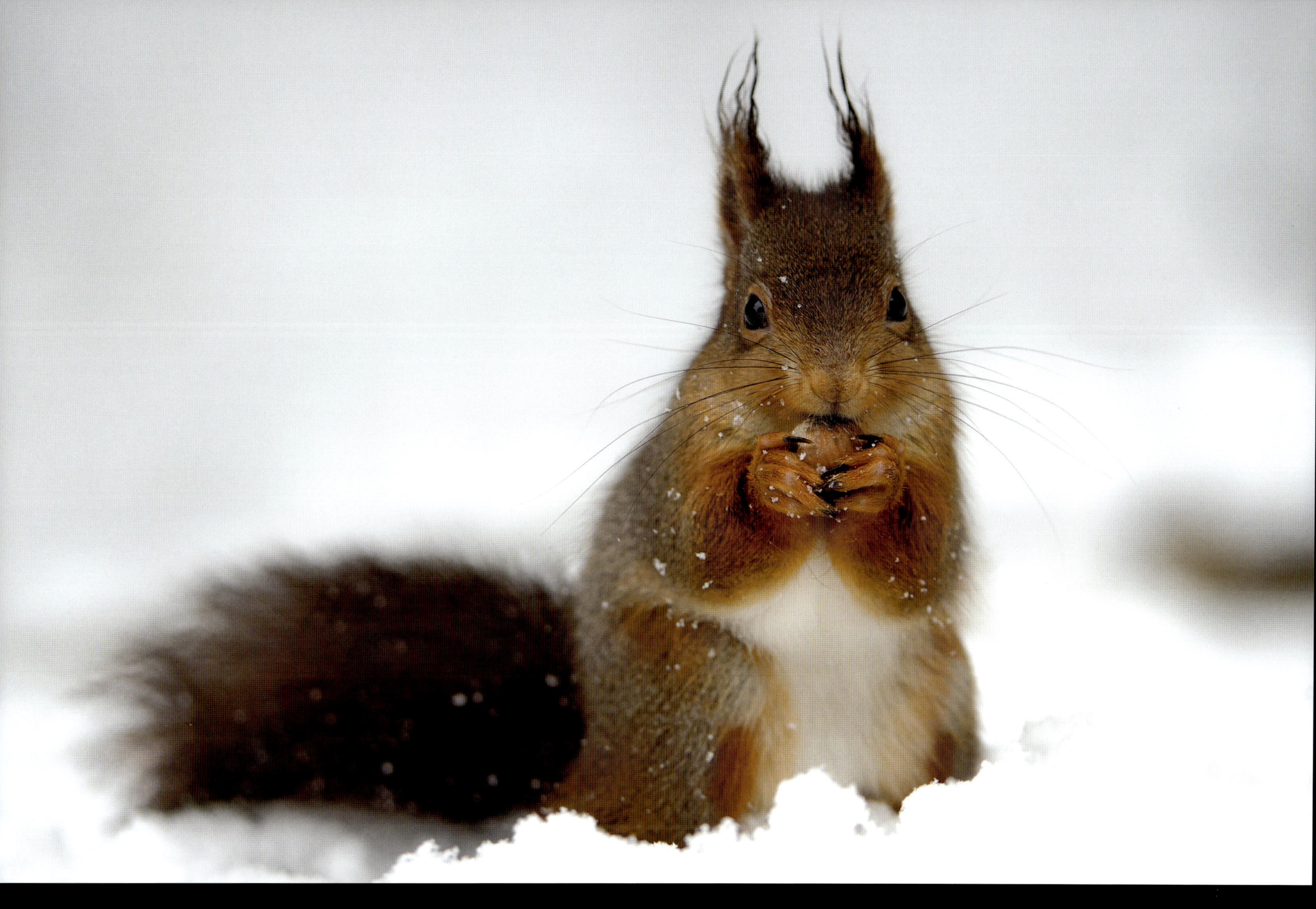

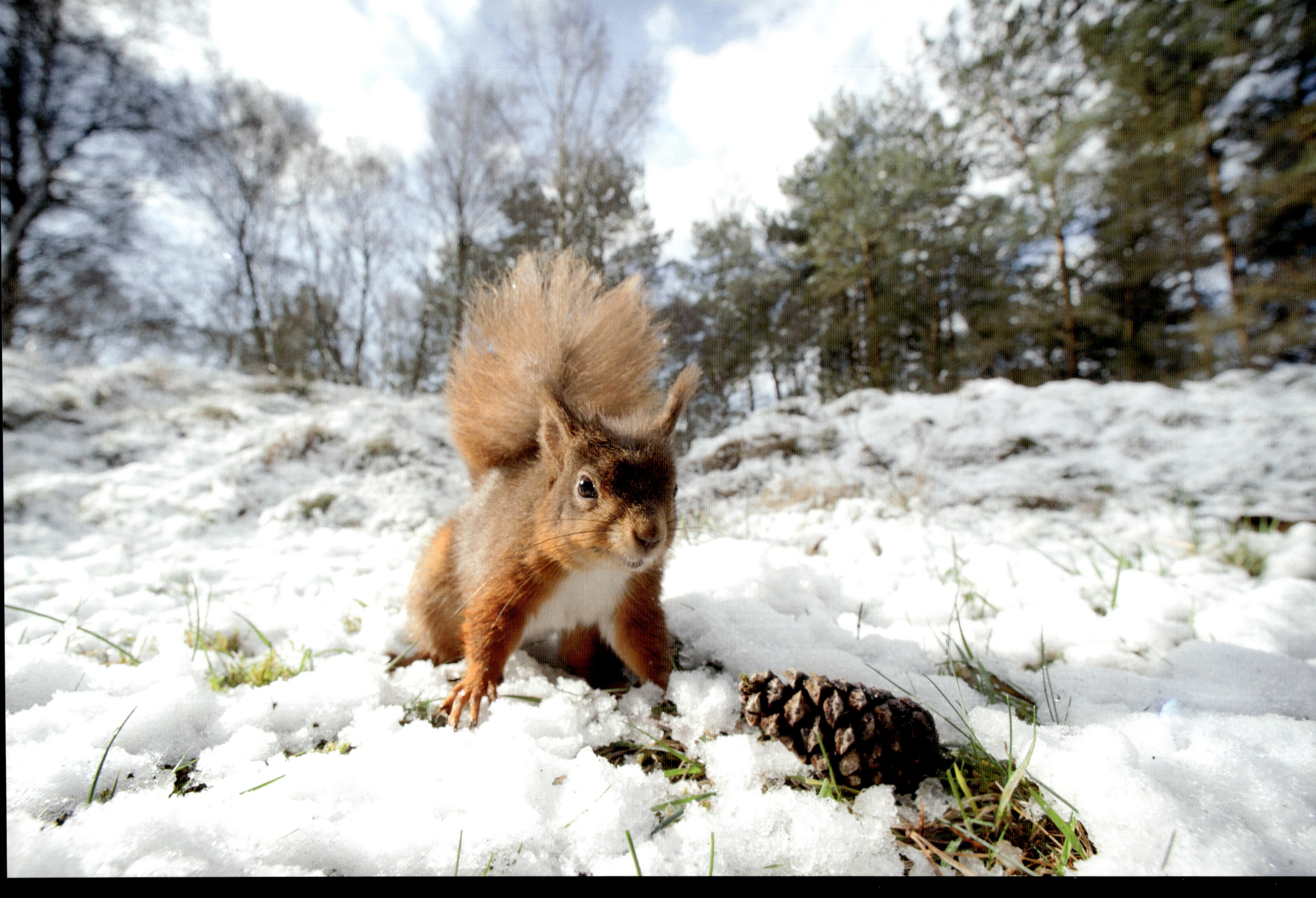

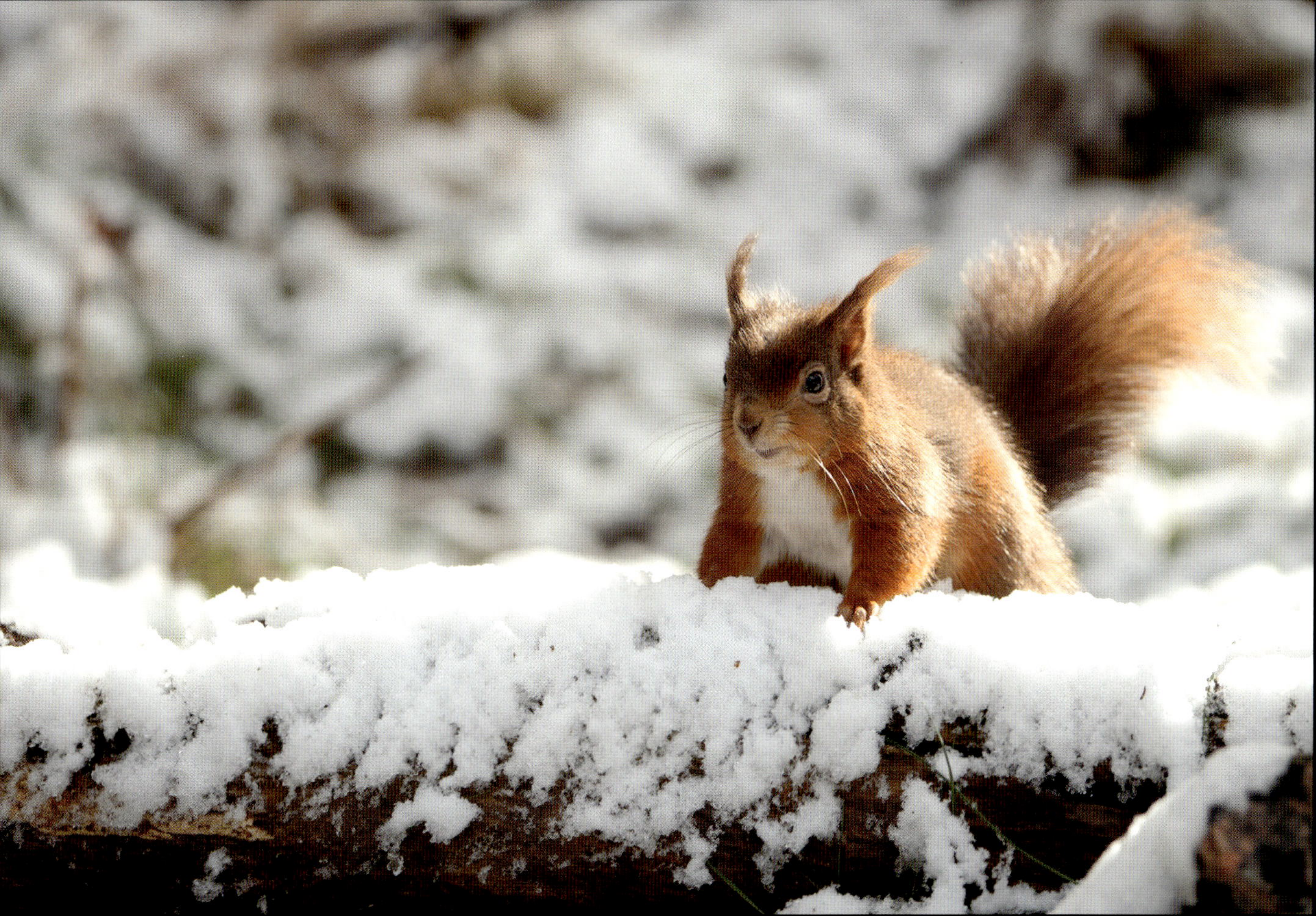

Usually I would find myself stuck in a classroom when the snow was falling, which was infuriating as that was the last place I wanted to be. I welcomed the snow in April, as it was during the school holidays, allowing me to finally get some of my first "winter" images.

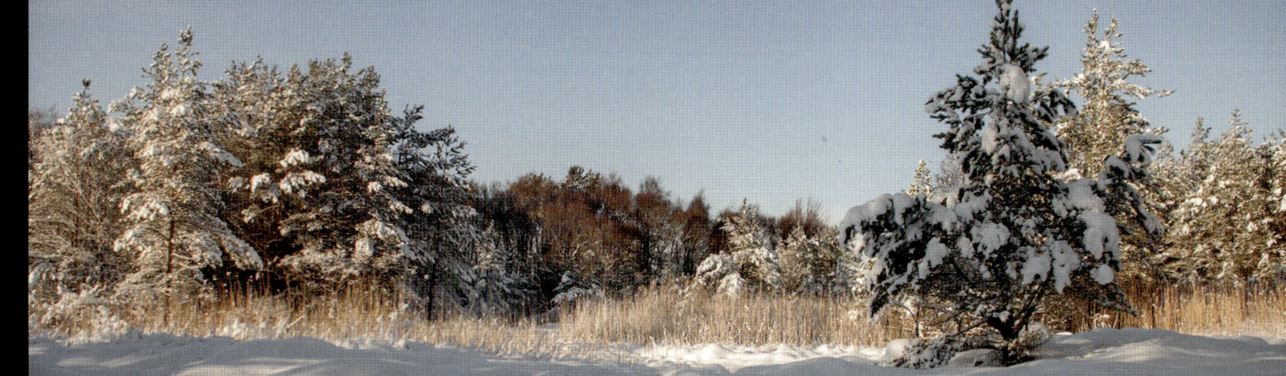

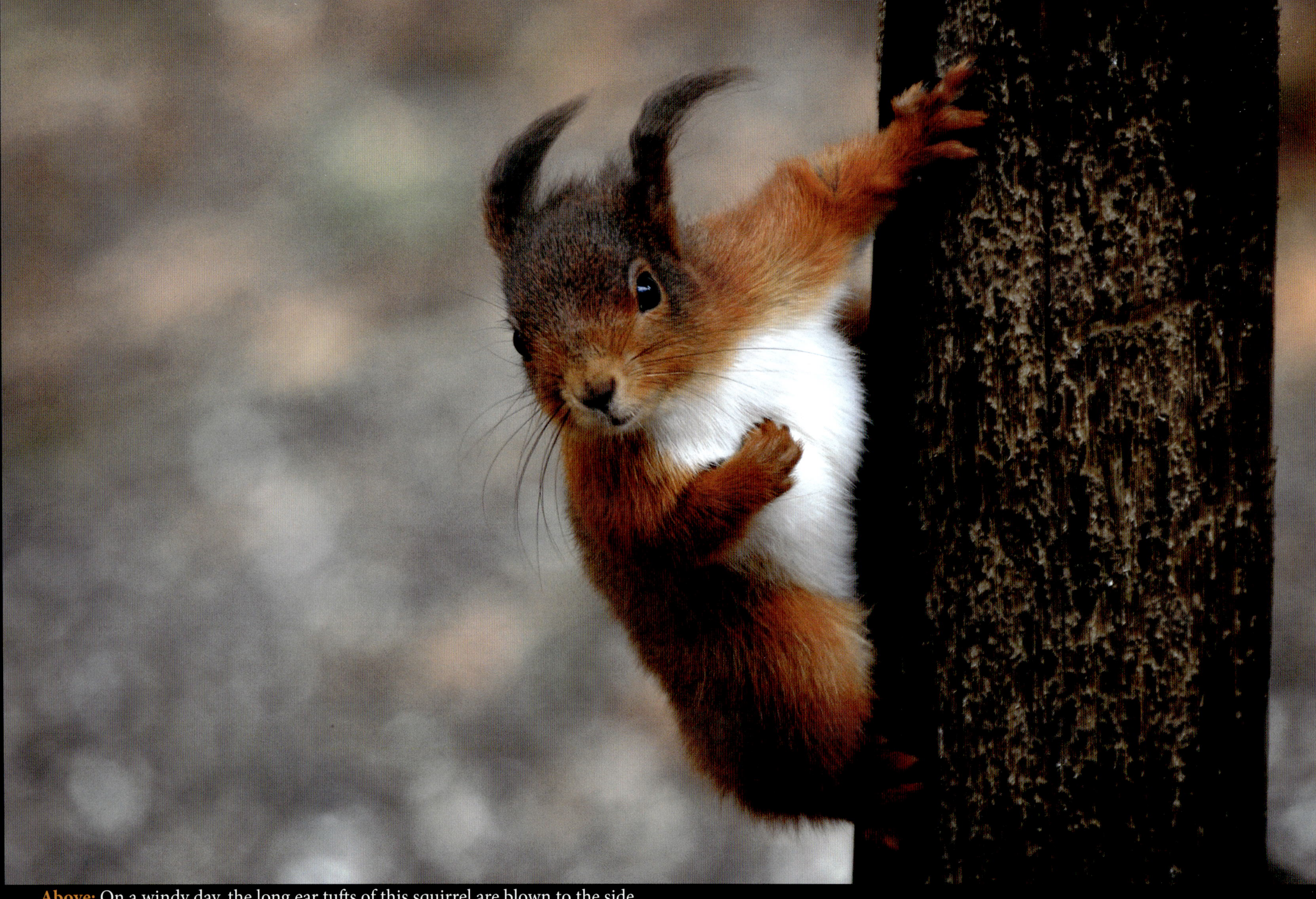

Above: On a windy day, the long ear tufts of this squirrel are blown to the side.

My favourite characteristic of red squirrels is, of course, their beautiful red coats. Although their long ear tufts, which are just one way they differentiate from the invasive grey squirrel, come in at a close second. There are many changes and differences in a squirrel's appearance throughout the year, and it is fascinating seeing how separate individuals differ from each other.

A red squirrel's ear tufts are prominent in the winter months, as they are an ideal asset for keeping the thin membranes that are their ears warm. With blood vessels so close to the surface of the skin, these tufts act as insulation from freezing conditions. During the summer months the tufts will become thinner, sometimes even becoming absent completely.

One way to identify a red squirrel kitten is that it will often, but not always, have only wisps of hair on its ears. Although with there also being some tuftless adults, other factors must be taken into account to age the animal. When eating a hazelnut, a young squirrel will sit in a tree for a long time trying to crack it open. An adult will quickly split the nut in half with its teeth, but a kitten will shred the hazelnut and break it into pieces.

The inexperienced young reds will also bury hazelnuts near to where they find them, a habit that brings misfortune their way. I once spent an amusing day in the hide where one of the kittens was working hard for a couple of hours to bury hazelnuts all around the hide area. Once she had finished building up her stores, another of the kittens came along and dug them all up again. This is one of the reasons that they quickly learn to travel further afield with their quarry.

Red squirrels moult their coats twice a year, but their ear tufts and tail are only moulted once a year. These two moults occur during spring and autumn time. From August and onwards their thicker winter coats begin to develop, beginning at their rump and progressing towards the head.

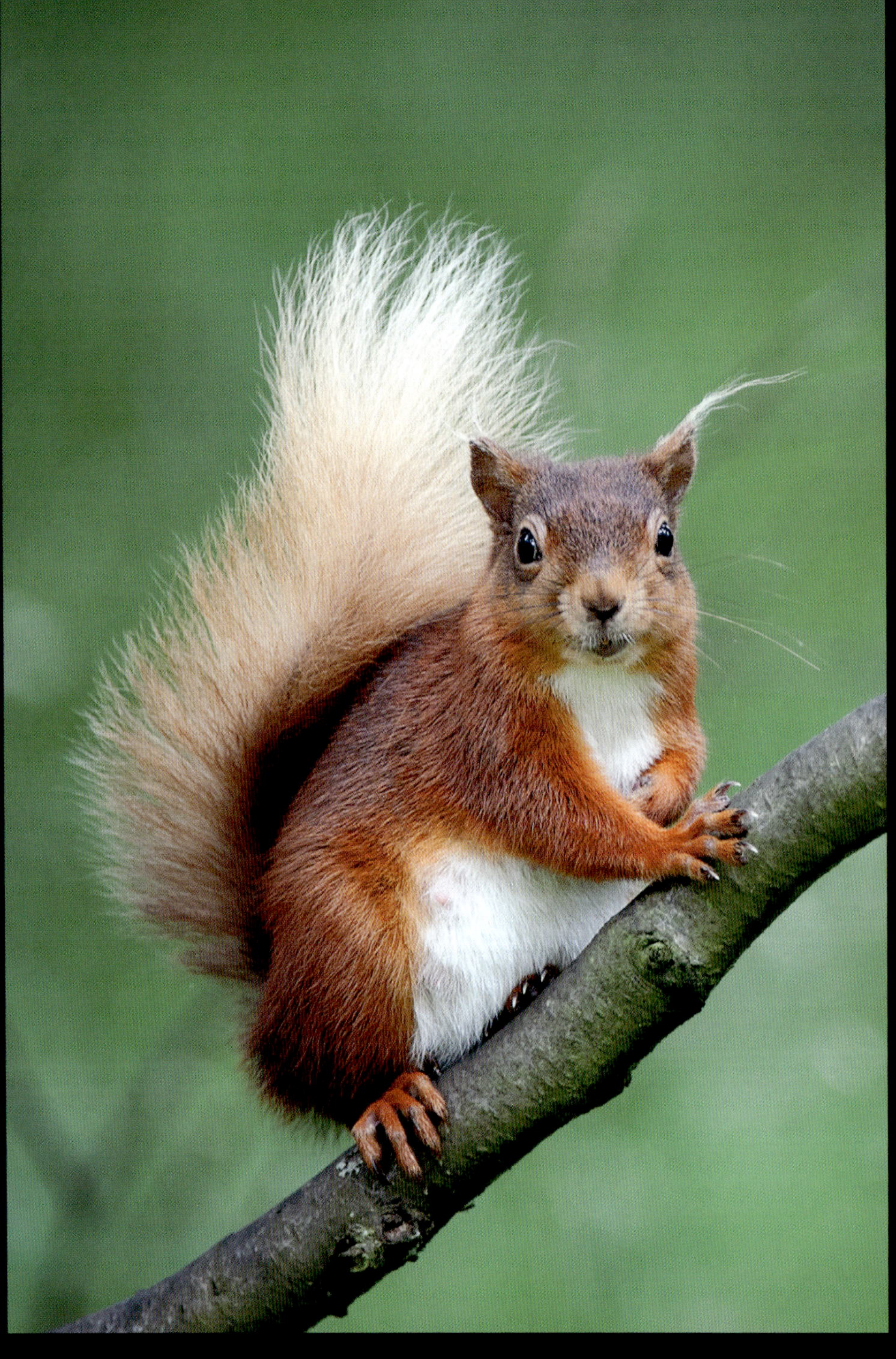

The coat of a red squirrel can vary greatly. Whilst some appear very ginger, others can appear much more grey in colour. One of my favourite squirrels that visited my hide one year had a very silvery tone on its back, making it stand out from the others. In fact, this variation can be so great that in some other European countries you can find red squirrels that are entirely dark grey. I spent a week in Hungary one winter to photograph white-tailed eagles, but spotted one of these extremely dark individuals. It was fascinating, for someone who spends so much time around the much redder variant of the same species.

These differences in their coats can mean that some people mistake one species for the other. Luckily, it isn't just the coat that enables us to tell them apart. Grey squirrels do not have any ear tufts, and are physically much bigger than red squirrels. Grey squirrels will also appear to have a light, white "halo" of hairs fringing their tails, whereas red squirrels will not. If you do manage to spend a little time with reds, it will quickly become second nature to identify them and grey squirrels will look extremely different, however ginger they may appear to be.

For centuries red squirrels were hunted for their pelts. It was called "vair" and was reserved only for the aristocracy. As well as being used for luxurious trimmings on various garments, noble ladies would also wear slippers made of vair.

Left: This squirrel has a striking, blonde tail.
Opposite: A red squirrel with a silver colouring to its coat.

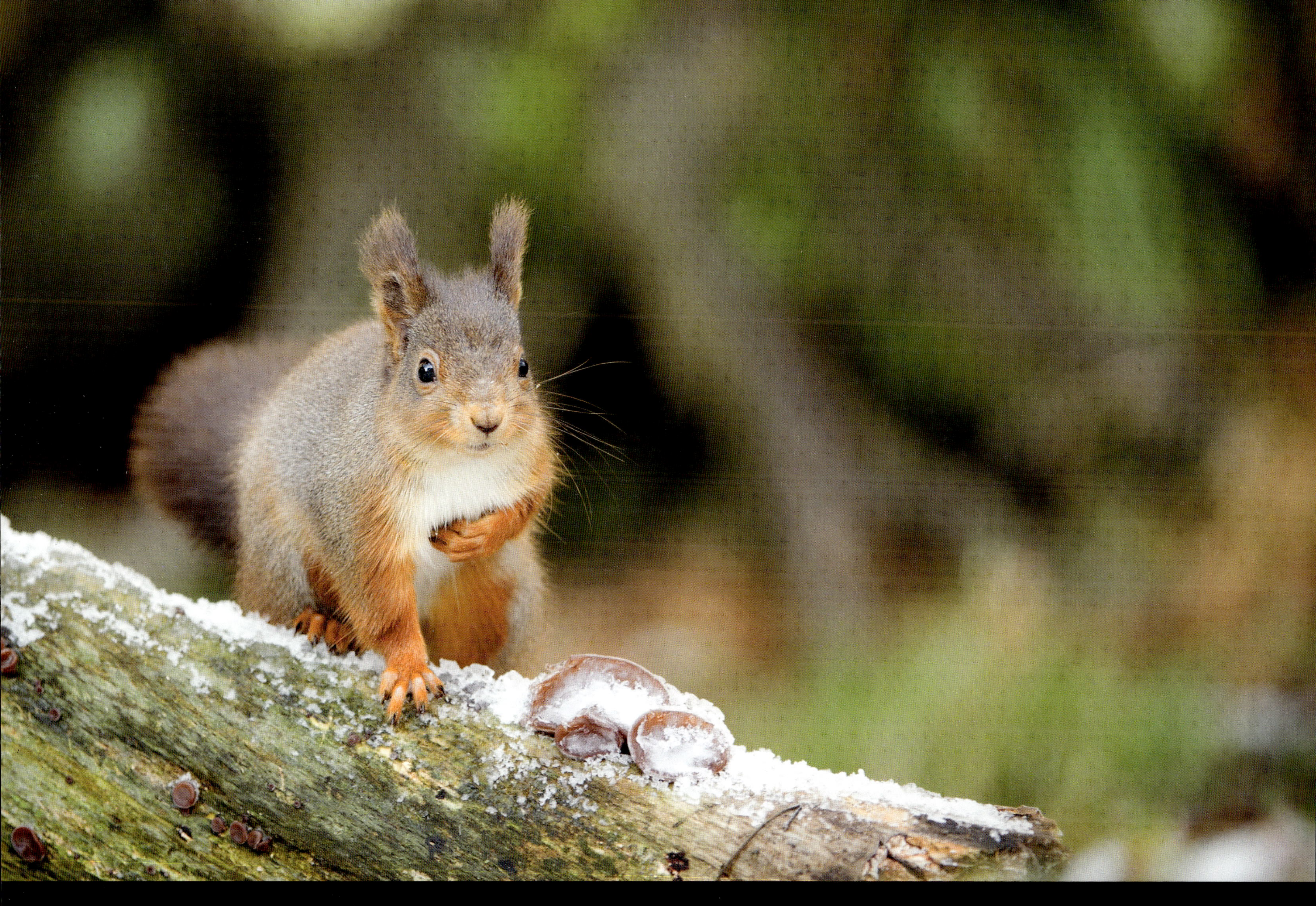

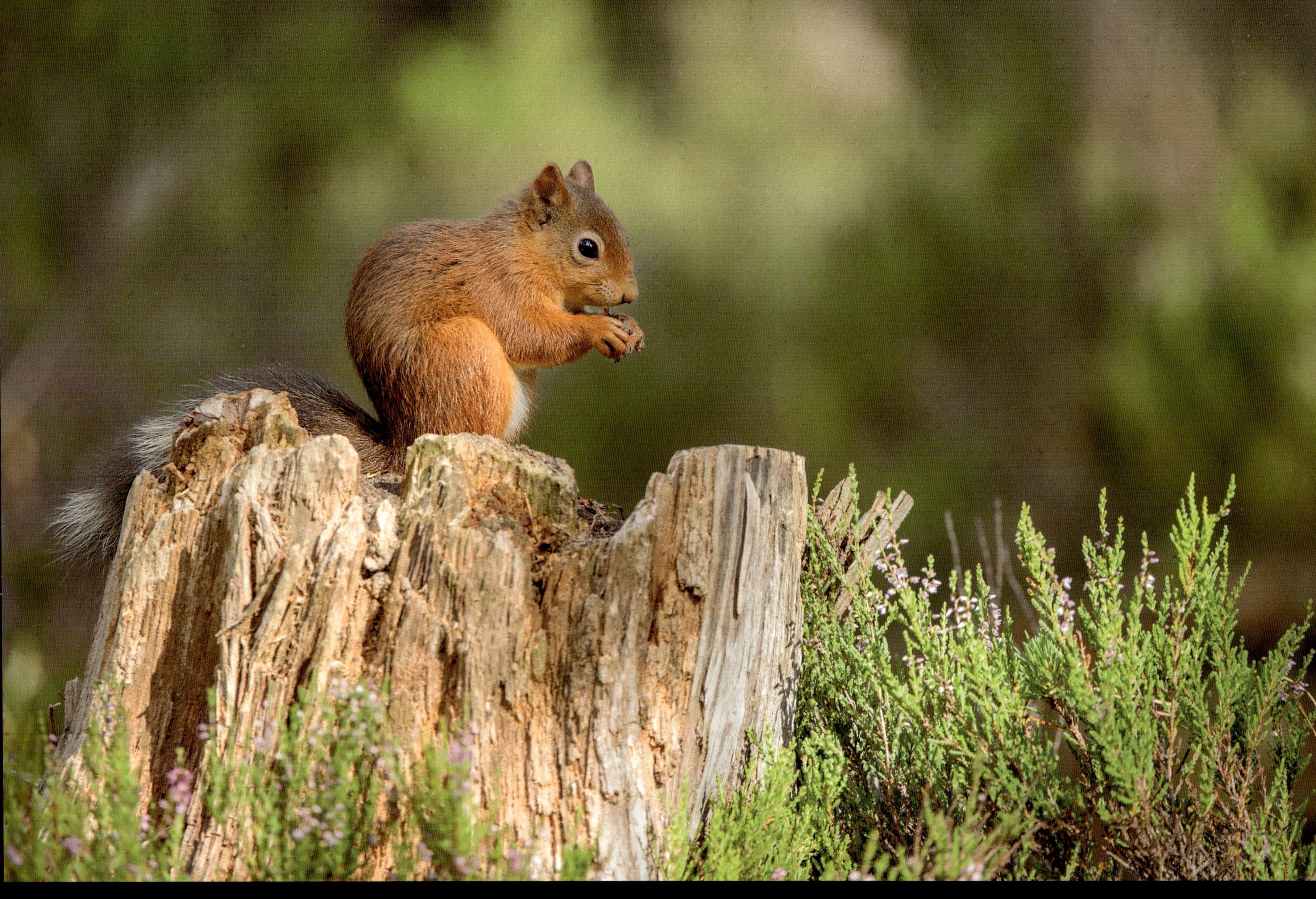

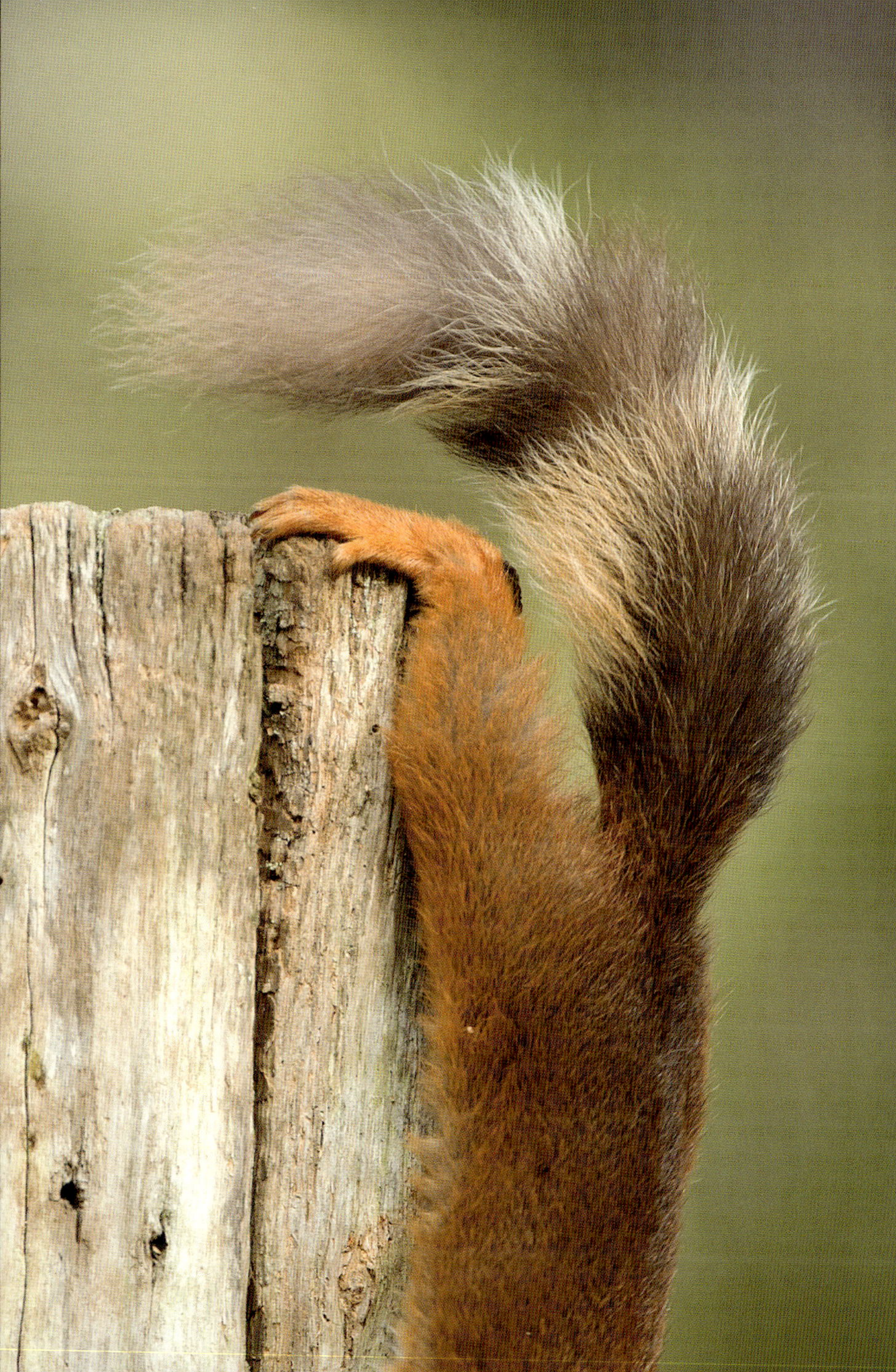

There are many variations in how a red squirrel looks. As a zoologist, I am fascinated by what differences in animals can emerge from the chance mixing of different genes. The most beautiful red squirrel I have seen surprised me with the most amazing tail. It had blonde rings around its otherwise dark tail, giving it a raccoon-like appearance. Unfortunately for me this particular squirrel was photographed in Scotland, and so she isn't a resident in my own local woodland.

It is differences like this which help me to identify certain squirrels. If you don't spend a lot of time with red squirrels they will often look just about the same as each other. However, with observation, it is possible to notice very slight physical differences. Whether it be a mark on the side of its nose, or a different shade of colour in its fur, it gradually becomes easier to see them as individuals.

There have been times when I haven't been able to spot any real differences between them. It is then that I have had to look for the different behavioural traits of each squirrel, using their actions to see who is who.

Left: The most beautiful red squirrel tail I have ever seen.
Opposite: The striped squirrel poses amongst some heather.

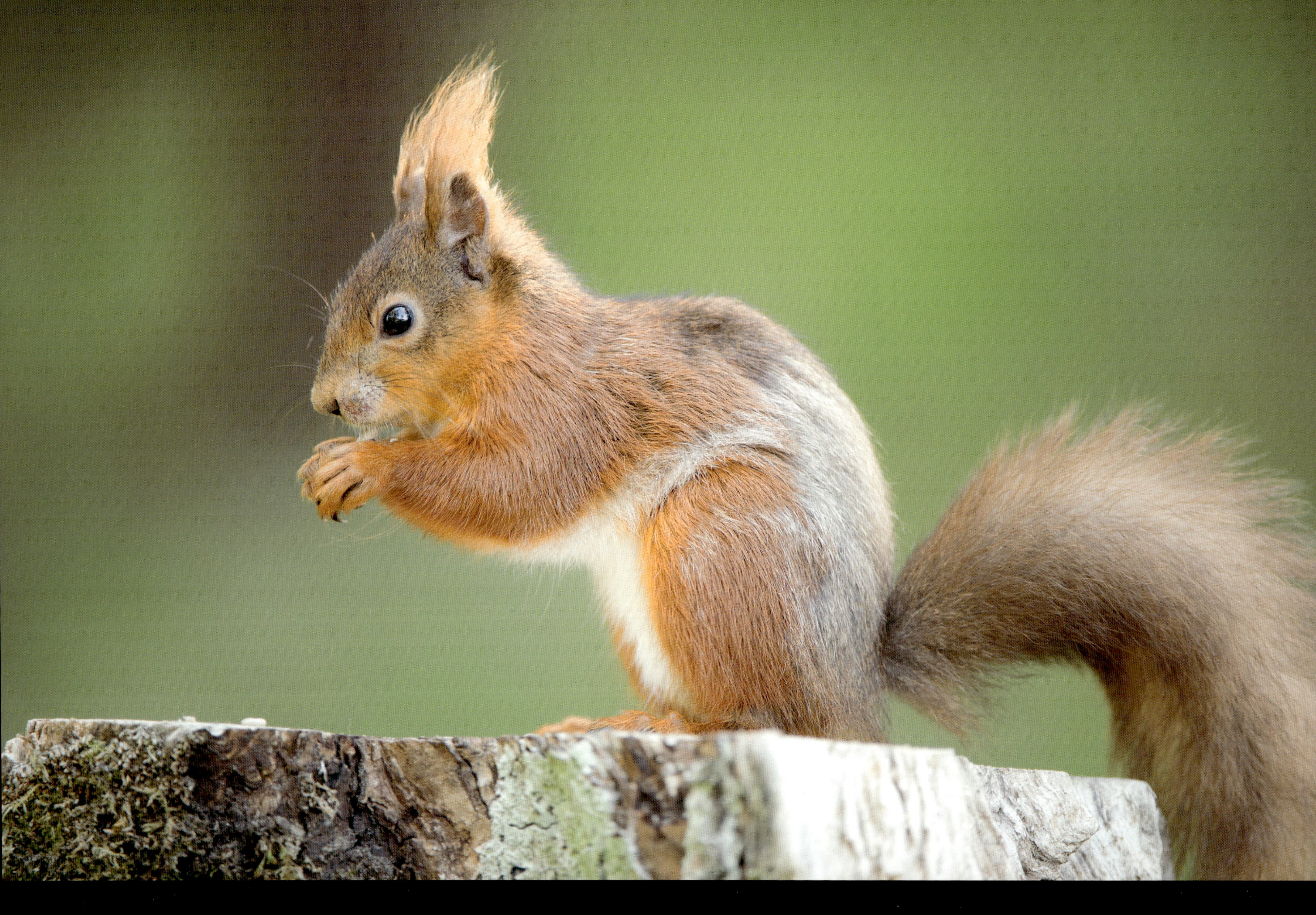

Changes in a squirrel's coat aren't always due to genetics. One spring I went to watch the squirrels at my hide, and was concerned to see that one individual had a patch of fur missing on its back. Obviously with the continuous threat to red squirrels any problem instantly becomes a worry, but it was soon established that it wasn't anything life-threatening. Still, a squirrel with missing fur is much less photogenic. Soon more patches developed, and it was not long until the condition spread to the other two squirrels in the wood. The most likely cause of this was an infestation of lice, causing the squirrels to bite and scratch at their fur to bring about the patches.

The interesting part of this occurrence was when the lice disappeared and their fur grew back. Sometimes, and certainly in this case, the fur can actually return grey due to damage to the skin cells.

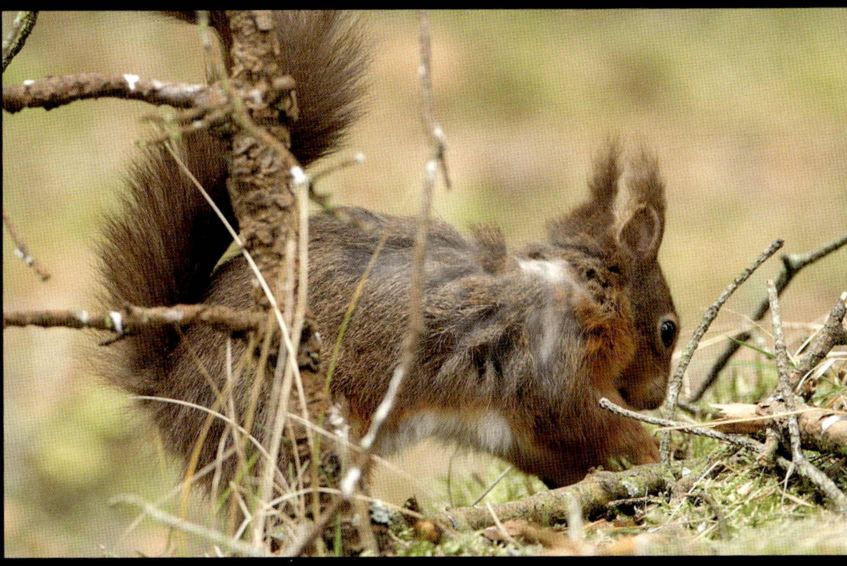

Above: The patchy fur caused by constant biting and scratching.
Right: A young squirrel.
Opposite: After an infestation of lice or similar, the fur sometimes grows back grey in colour.

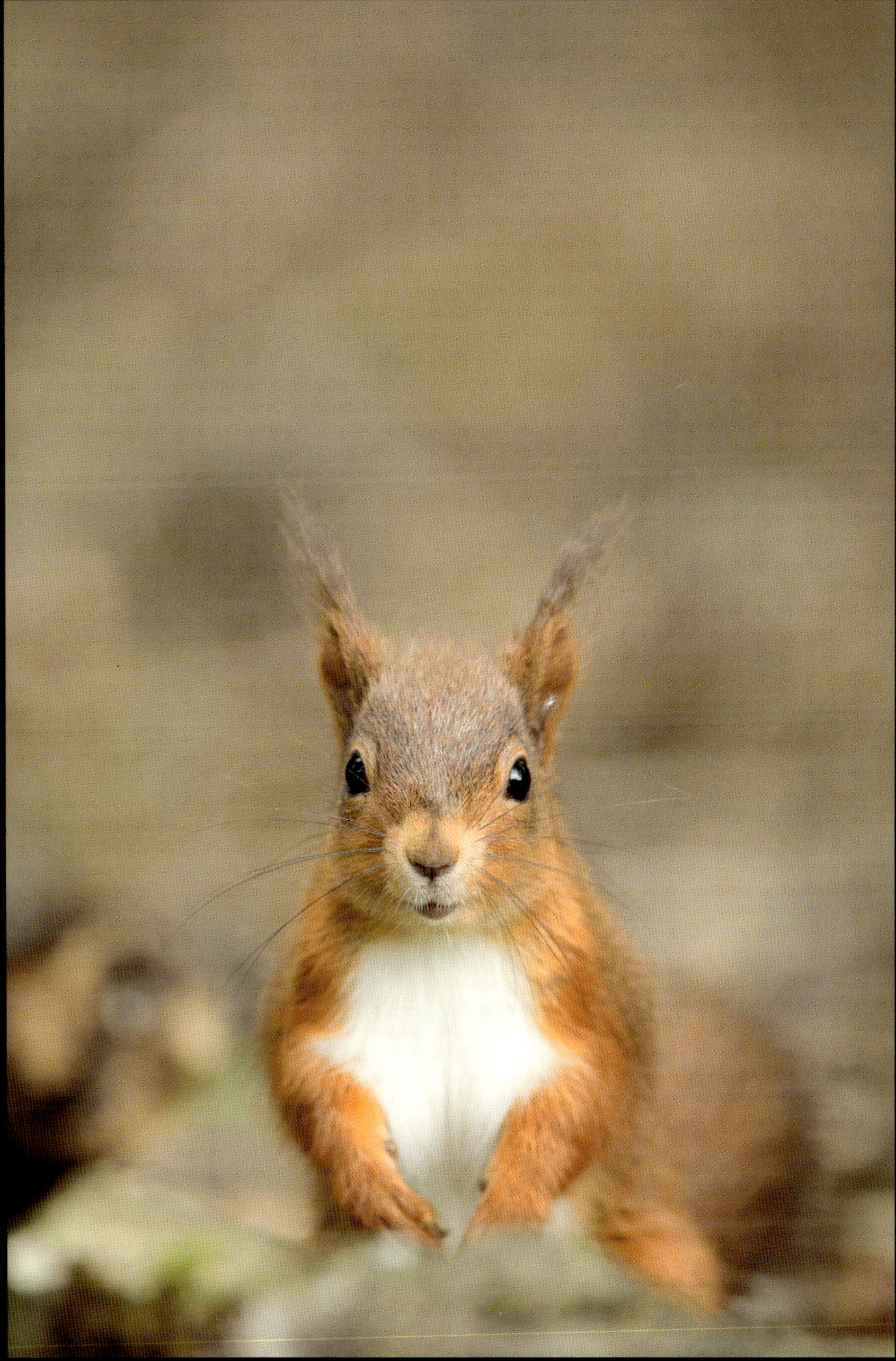

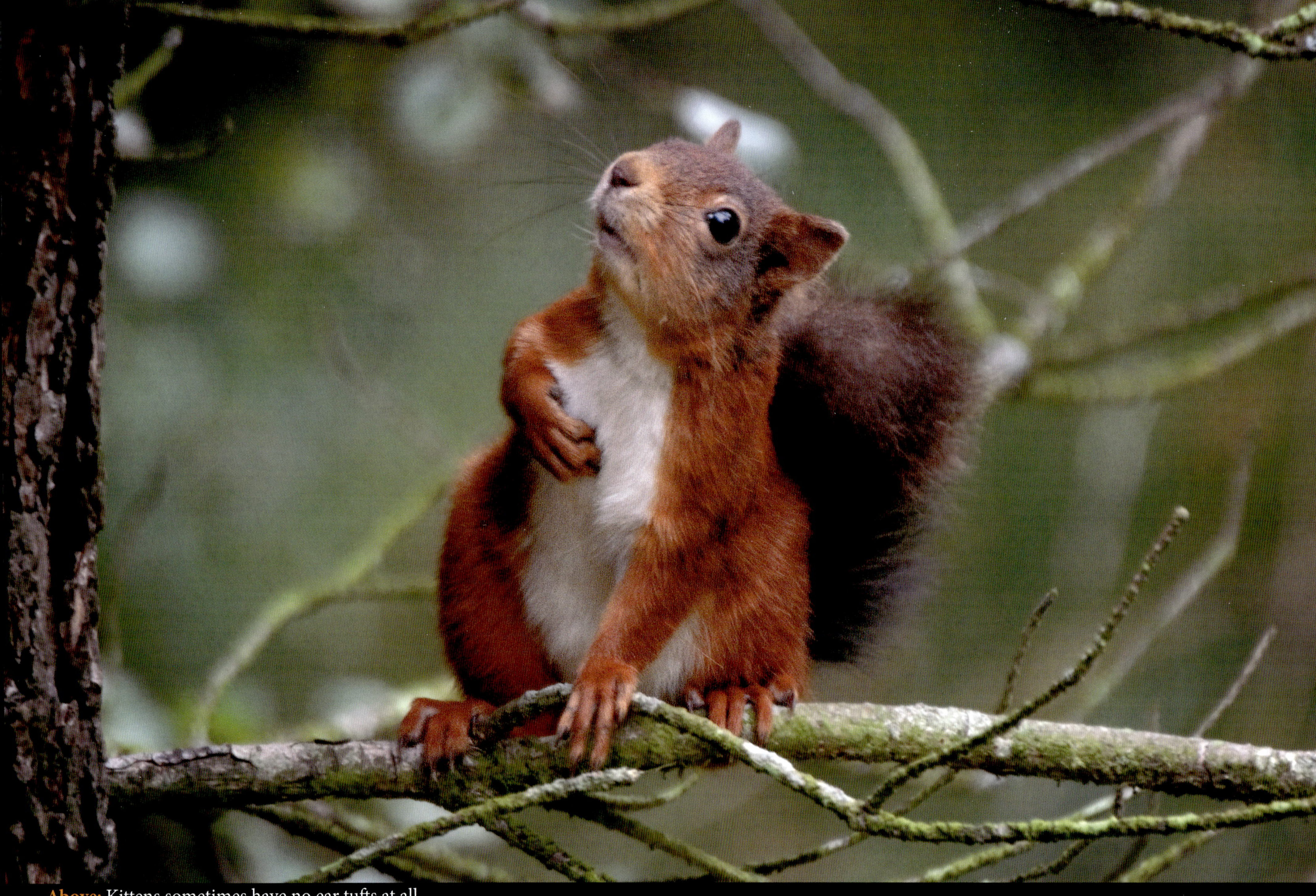

Above: Kittens sometimes have no ear tufts at all.

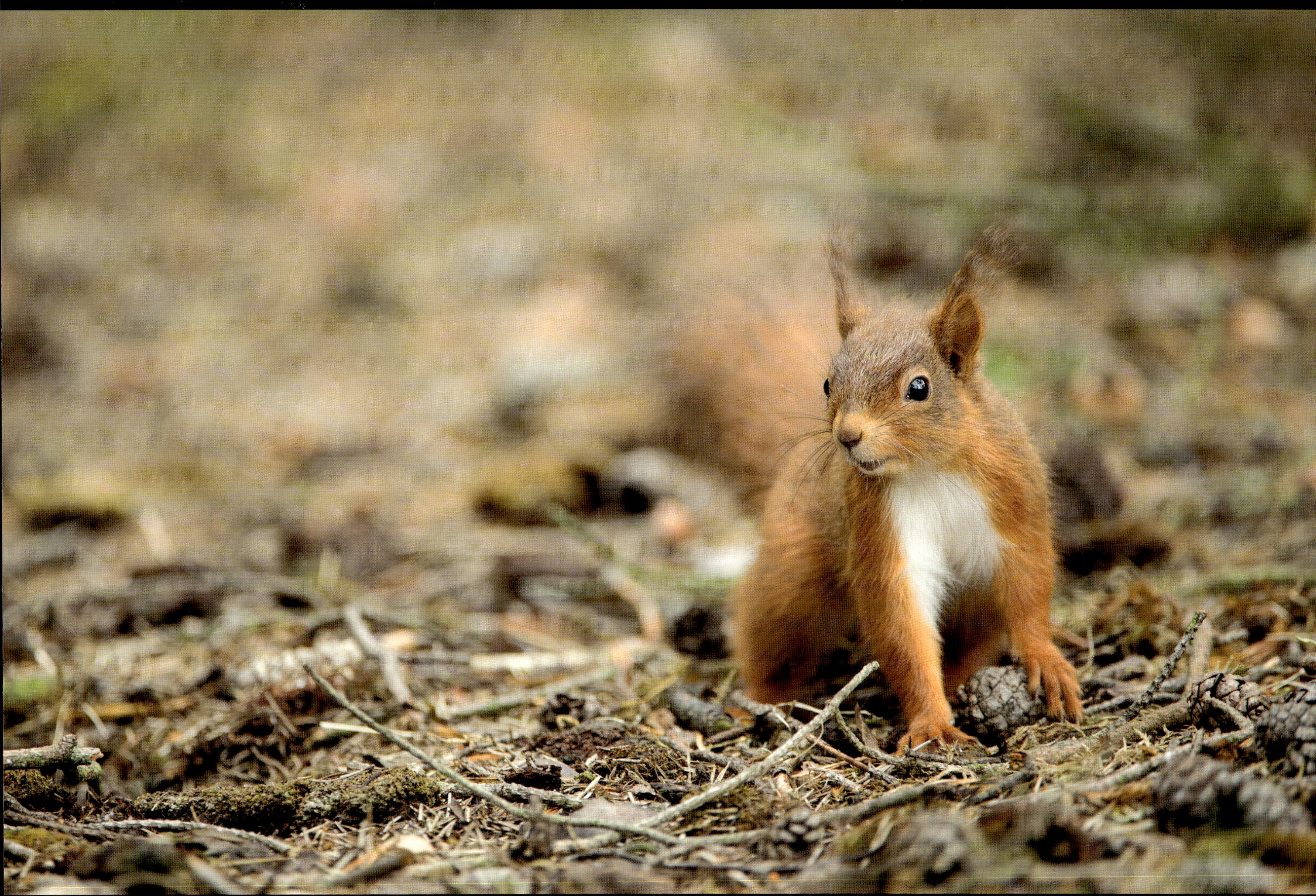

Above: Blonde hairs on this squirrel's forehead allowed me to identify it amongst the others.

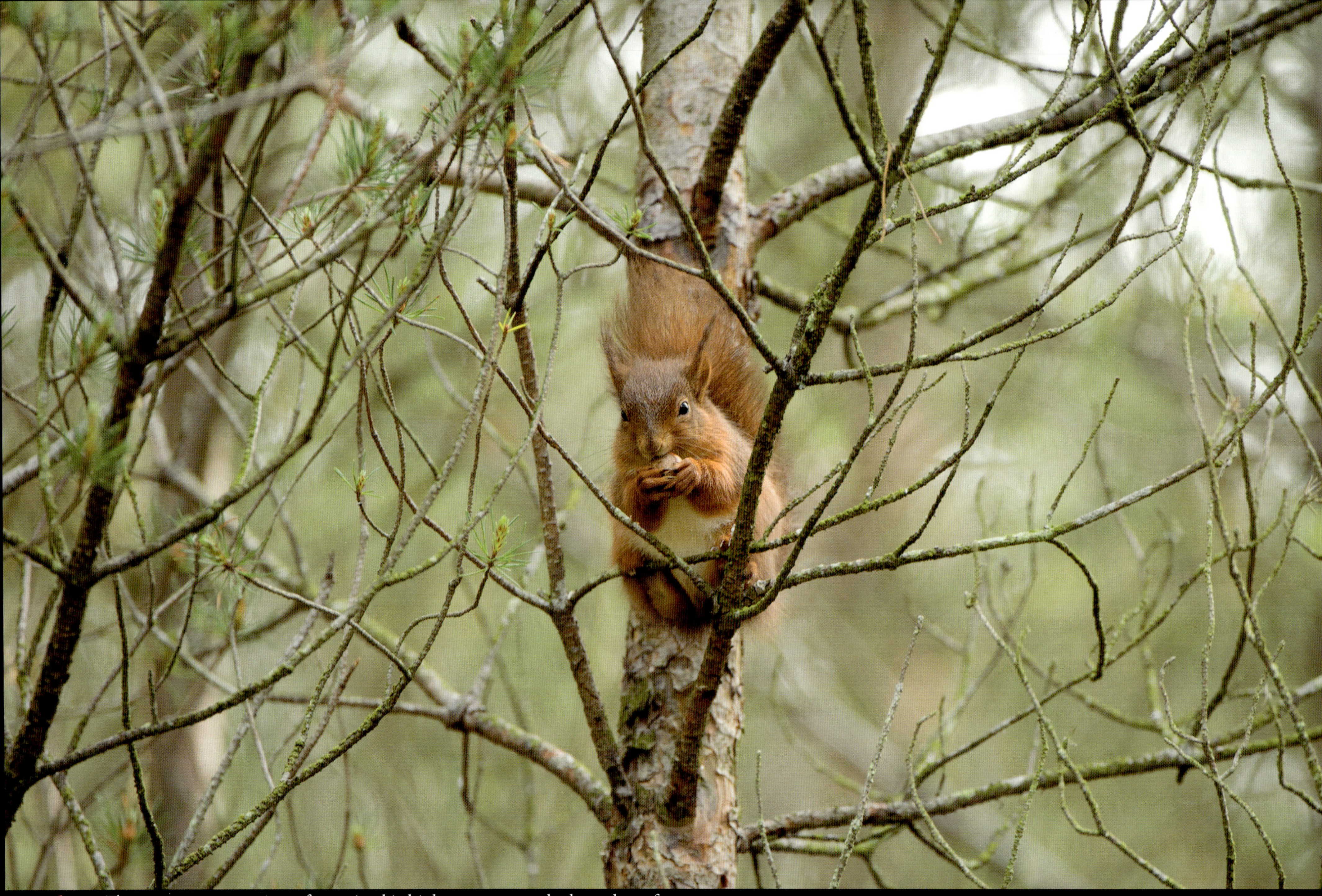

Above: The most common view of a squirrel is high up amongst the branches of a tree.

Life in the trees

Red squirrels live an arboreal life (they live in trees) and are well adapted for it. They have long, powerful limbs which are perfect for climbing and jumping. Using their forefeet, they will hook their claws into the bark and anchor themselves against the tree. Their hind legs then push them upwards, and the process continues.

Their forefeet have four toes, whilst their hind feet have five longer toes. The extra toe allows for increased stability, particularly when sitting. Their especially suited limbs even enable them to move down a tree head first, something only a handful of other mammals can do.

I have heard many people say that the bushy tails of squirrels act as some sort of parachute when jumping, but this is not true. However, they can be used like a rudder, helping to guide squirrels onto their target branches. They can jump distances of two metres or more (but with less confidence at greater distances), which is a reasonably long way in relation to their own size. Jumping is an excellent way to evade predators and move quickly through the trees.

Red squirrels weigh between 270 and 360 grams (around a third lighter than the grey squirrel), meaning that they are very light. The obvious advantage of this is that they can move along very thin branches in pine trees without breaking them and falling to the ground. This allows them to reach pinecones and other foods located near the ends of these branches. It has also been suggested that this allows them to evade predators such as the pine marten, which is too heavy for the thinner branches.

Squirrels also have a very wide field of view. If we look at an object, but want to look at another object somewhere to the left, we have to look directly at it. For a squirrel, it can observe its surroundings without moving its eyes. This is because the cones within their retinas are not just focussed on one particular point.

The benefits of this attribute mean they are able to easily navigate the chaotic mess of hundreds of branches and twigs. Watching them racing through the trees so often, I wonder how they don't occasionally damage their eyes on sharp twigs. Their excellent eyesight is clearly the answer to this problem.

Red squirrels will live in both deciduous and coniferous woodlands, both of which offer them a different range of foods. Unfortunately, grey squirrels are more competitive in deciduous woodlands due to the nature of nuts and seeds available.

Right: "Patch" balancing on some very thin branches.
Opposite: Coniferous woodland is perfect for red squirrels.

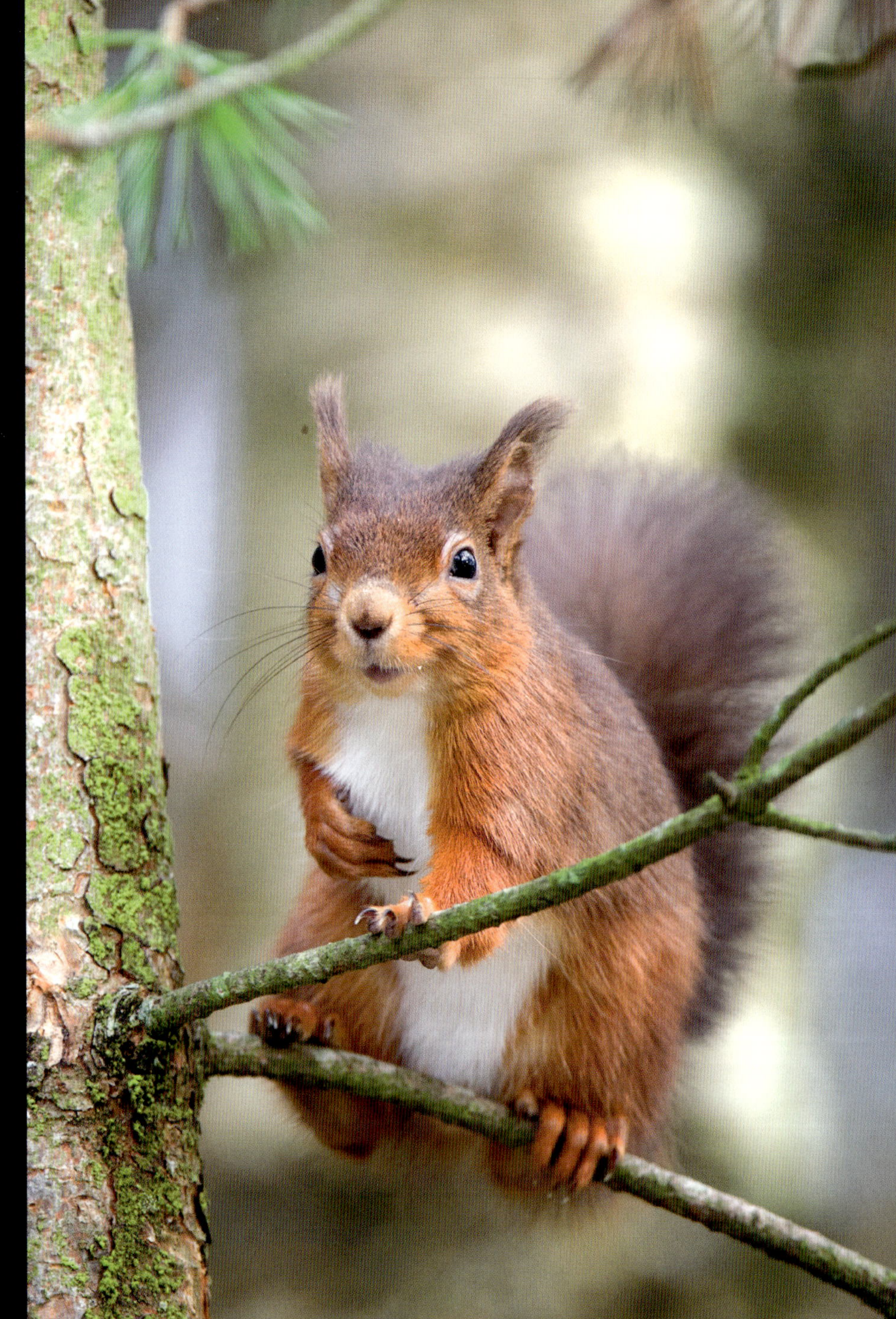

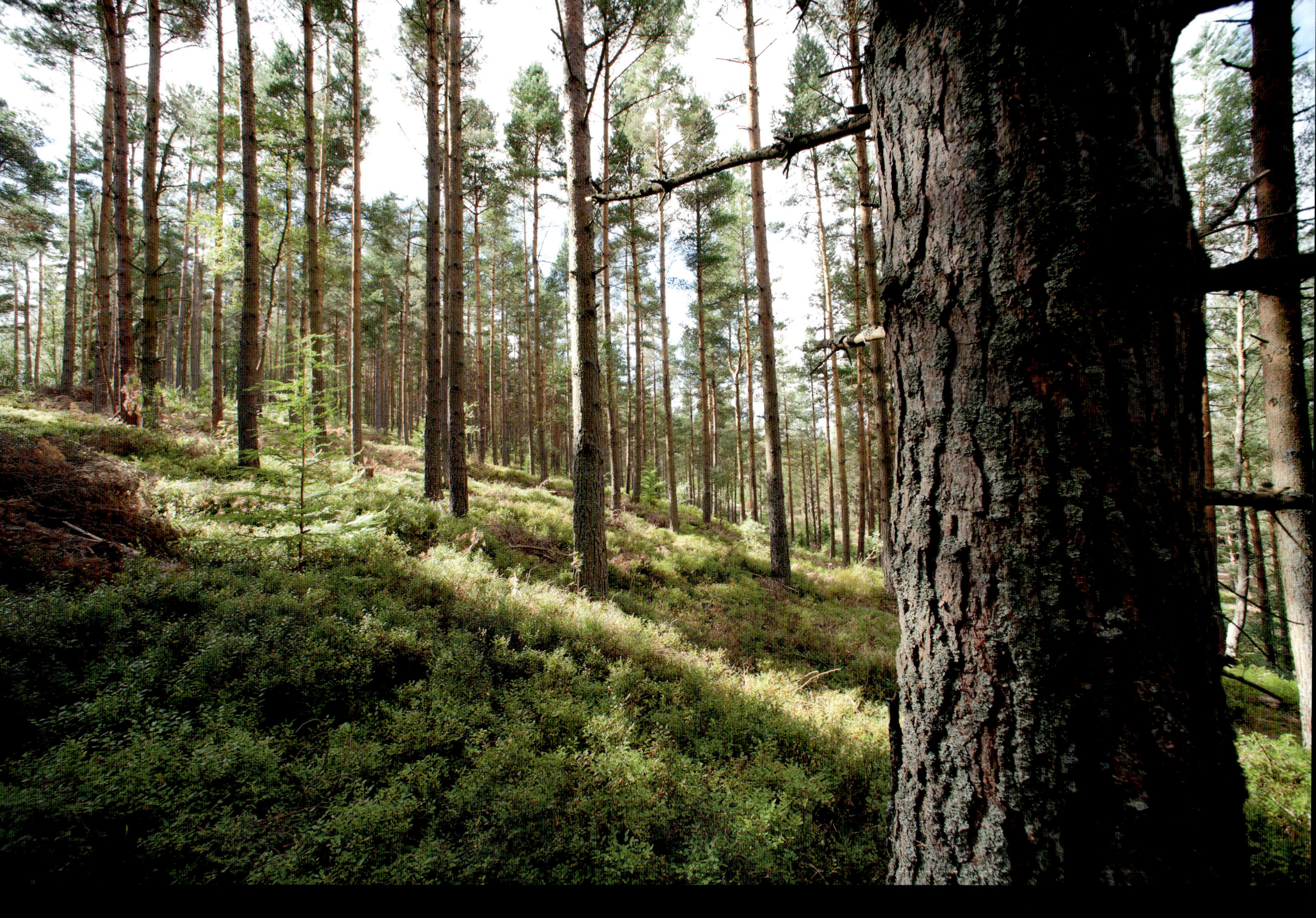

Red squirrels act as nature's gardeners. Their habit of caching nuts and seeds acts as a natural planting mechanism. They are a valuable method of seed dispersal, helping the cogs of the ecosystem to keep on turning. A squirrel never manages to dig up all of its caches, so some of them germinate and produce new trees. They also disperse the spores of many different fungi. By eating them, they ingest the spores and deposit them in their faeces.

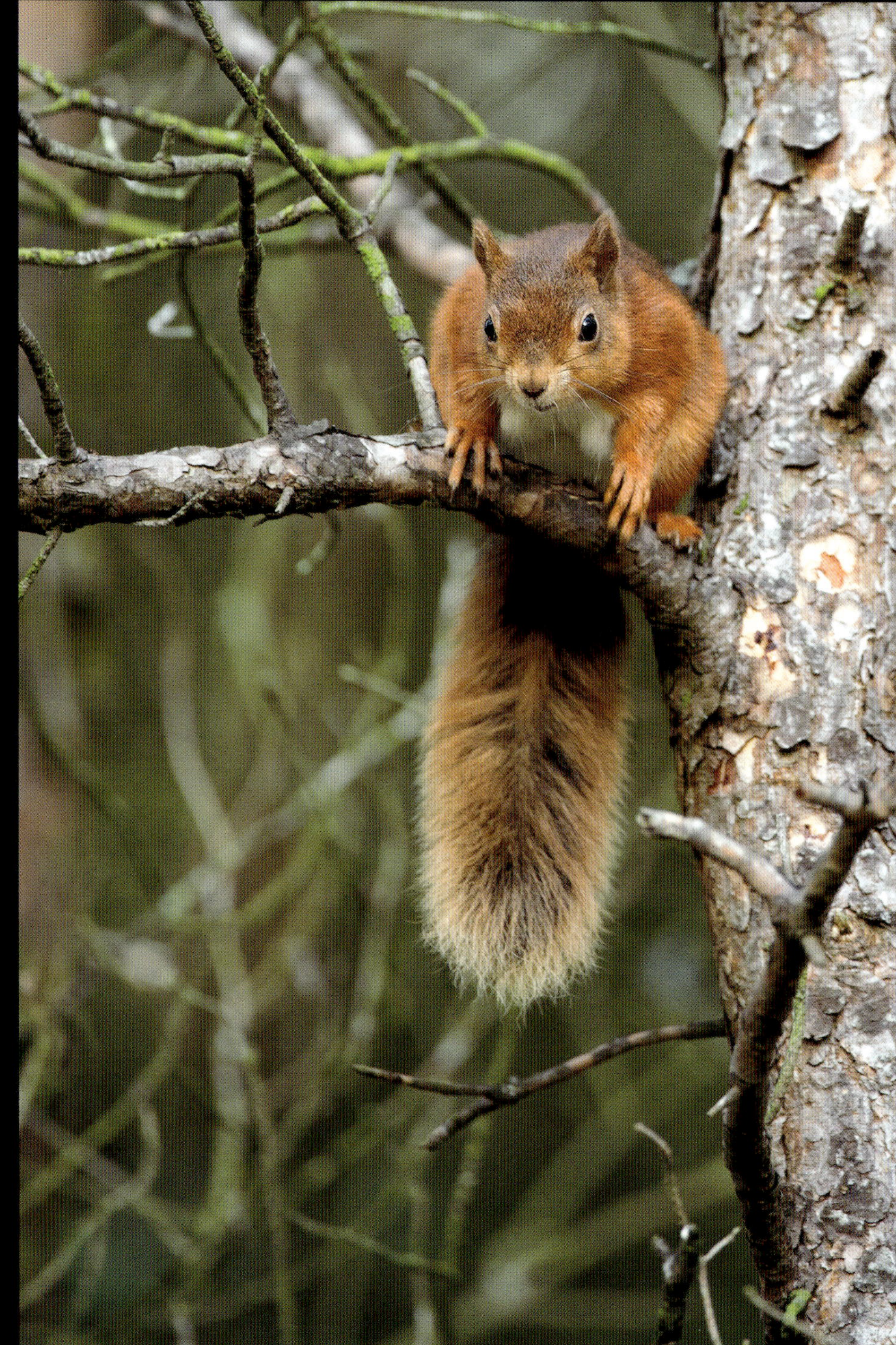

Right: At home in the trees.
Opposite: Squirrels will search for the best places to bury their nuts.

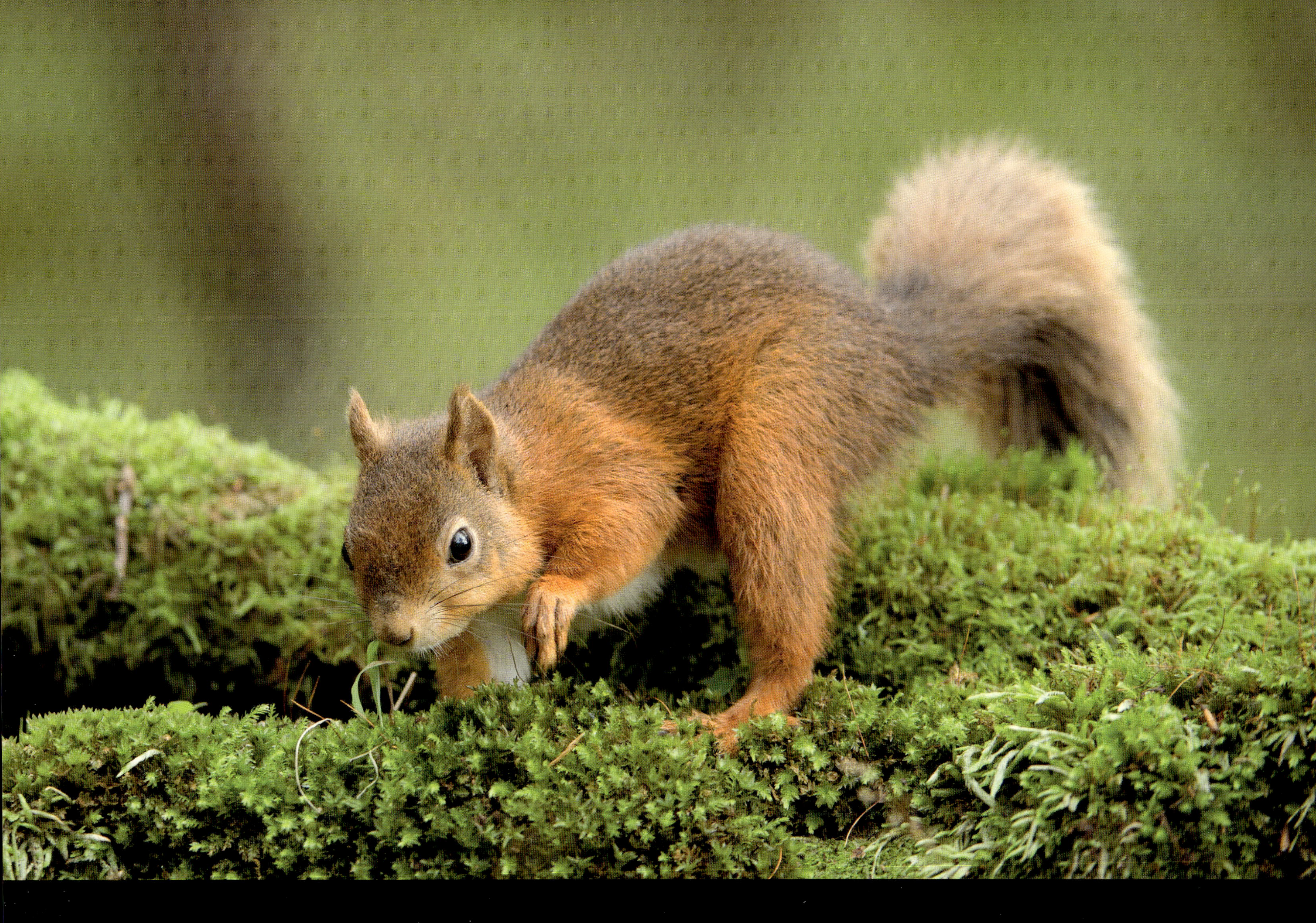

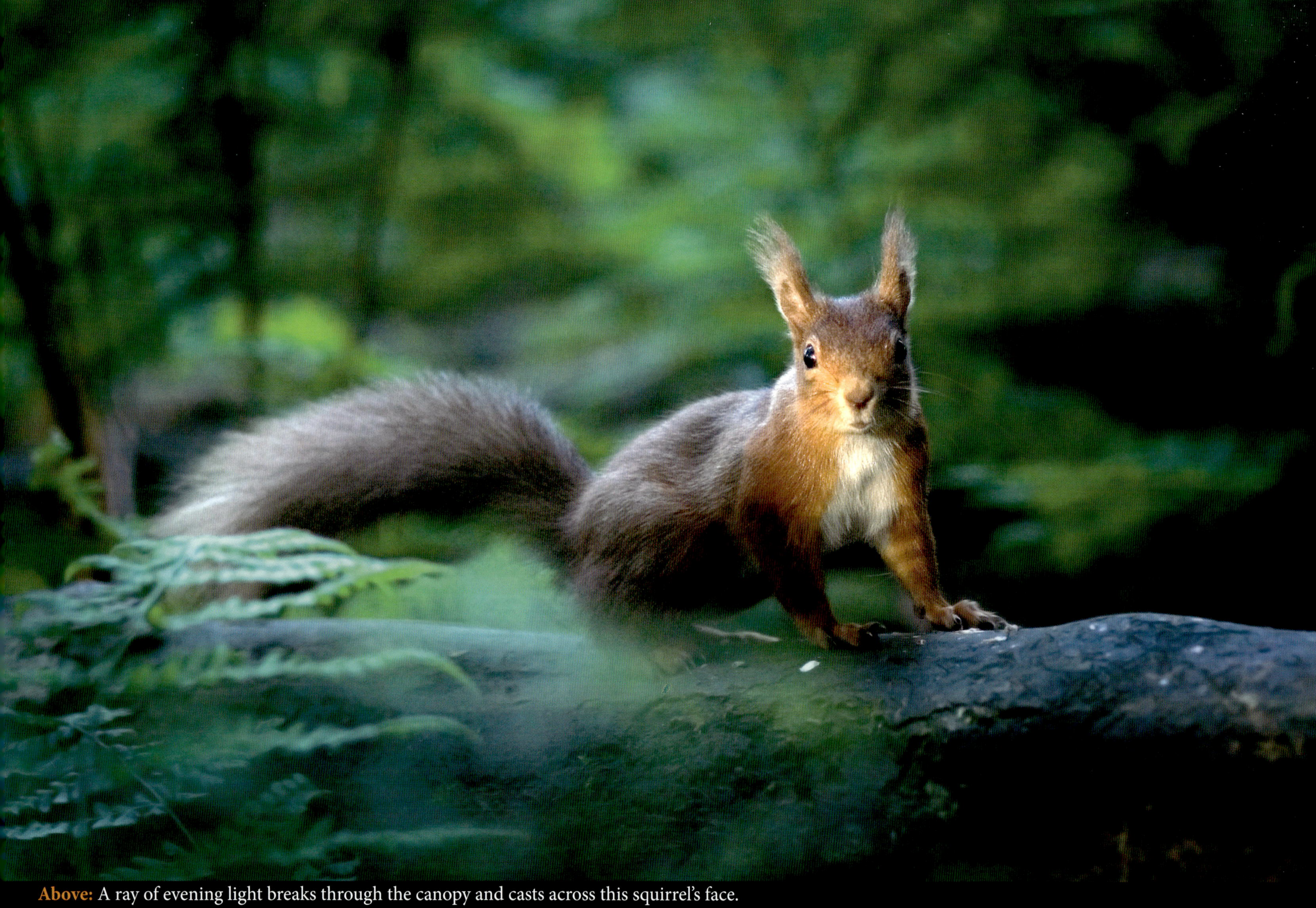

Above: A ray of evening light breaks through the canopy and casts across this squirrel's face.

Posing for the camera

I like to try and capture something a little different than just a pretty portrait of a red squirrel. Don't get me wrong, they have their place and I love it when I manage to snap something that shows off their beauty, but it is also fun to set up little "projects" with the squirrels.

Back in 2009, when I was fourteen, I had an image in my mind of a squirrel backlit by the sun. I imagined that its fur would light up with a golden halo, but alas the sun was in the wrong position. At this point I was still photographing squirrels in Kielder Forest, and the canopy is very thick there. Unfortunately for me, the whole area was cast in shadow. At the time I was shooting with a very slow telephoto lens, as it was all I could afford, and the light was causing many problems. All I could do was switch to a macro lens which had a much wider aperture, but meant I had very little reach with the zoom.

I sat waiting, half hidden amongst the bracken. It wasn't long before a red squirrel ran along the log in front of me, and stopped to stare at the strange boy hiding in the undergrowth. As luck would have it, it stopped with its head positioned perfectly where a ray of sunlight had broken through the canopy and was shining on the log. I quickly snapped the image, but to my surprise it then hopped off the log and ran right up to me. They must be reasonably used to people in Kielder Forest, as it is such a popular area for walkers, but their inquisitive natures mean they just have to take a closer look.

One of my more recent projects with the squirrels was to capture them at the edge of a pool of water, ideally with a reflection. The only way to do this was to build a pool, but the first problem I faced with this was the lack of space around the hide. Almost anywhere that I positioned a pool would be obstructing the view for other photographs. The only possible area left was on very uneven ground, which would cause a problem keeping the pool level. Even so, I had no choice and decided to try and work with the challenging terrain.

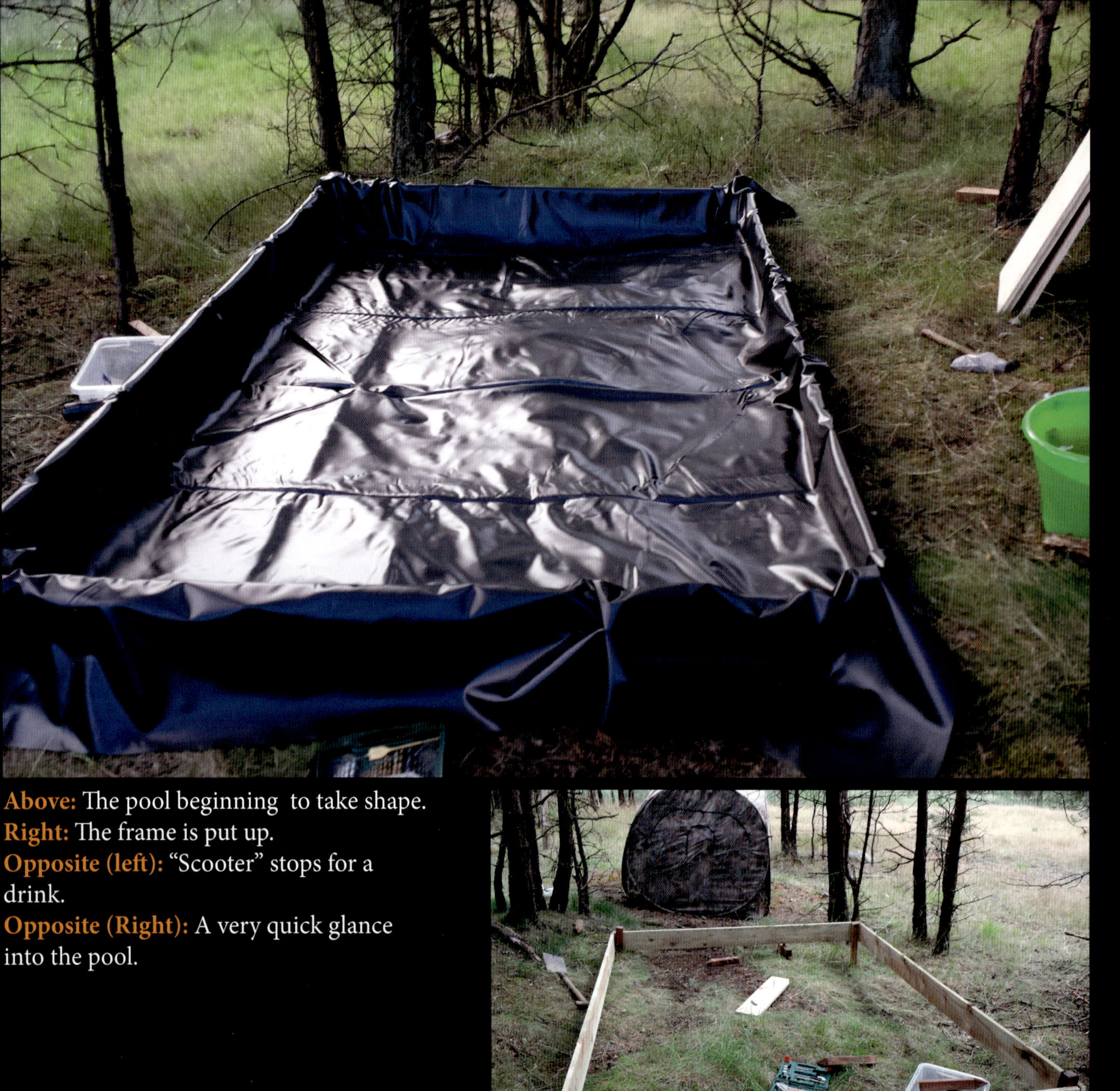

Above: The pool beginning to take shape.
Right: The frame is put up.
Opposite (left): "Scooter" stops for a drink.
Opposite (Right): A very quick glance into the pool.

I must admit that DIY is not my strongest point. A previous attempt at building a hide a couple of years earlier resulted in it spending more time on the ground than stood upright.

The wooden frame was put up first, ensuring that it was entirely level. I then undertook the challenge of trying to even out the ground as much as possible, which was largely successful. A big sheet of pond liner was the next addition, finally giving it the appearance of a pond.

Naturally, the woodland is not close to any taps and a hose pipe was out of the question. Fortunately there is a stream not far from the hide, and so I began the task of filling the pool bucket by bucket. There were well over one thousand litres to be added, and it took two solid days' work to fill it to the top. The labour was worth it though because the more water that was added, the greater the reflection looked.

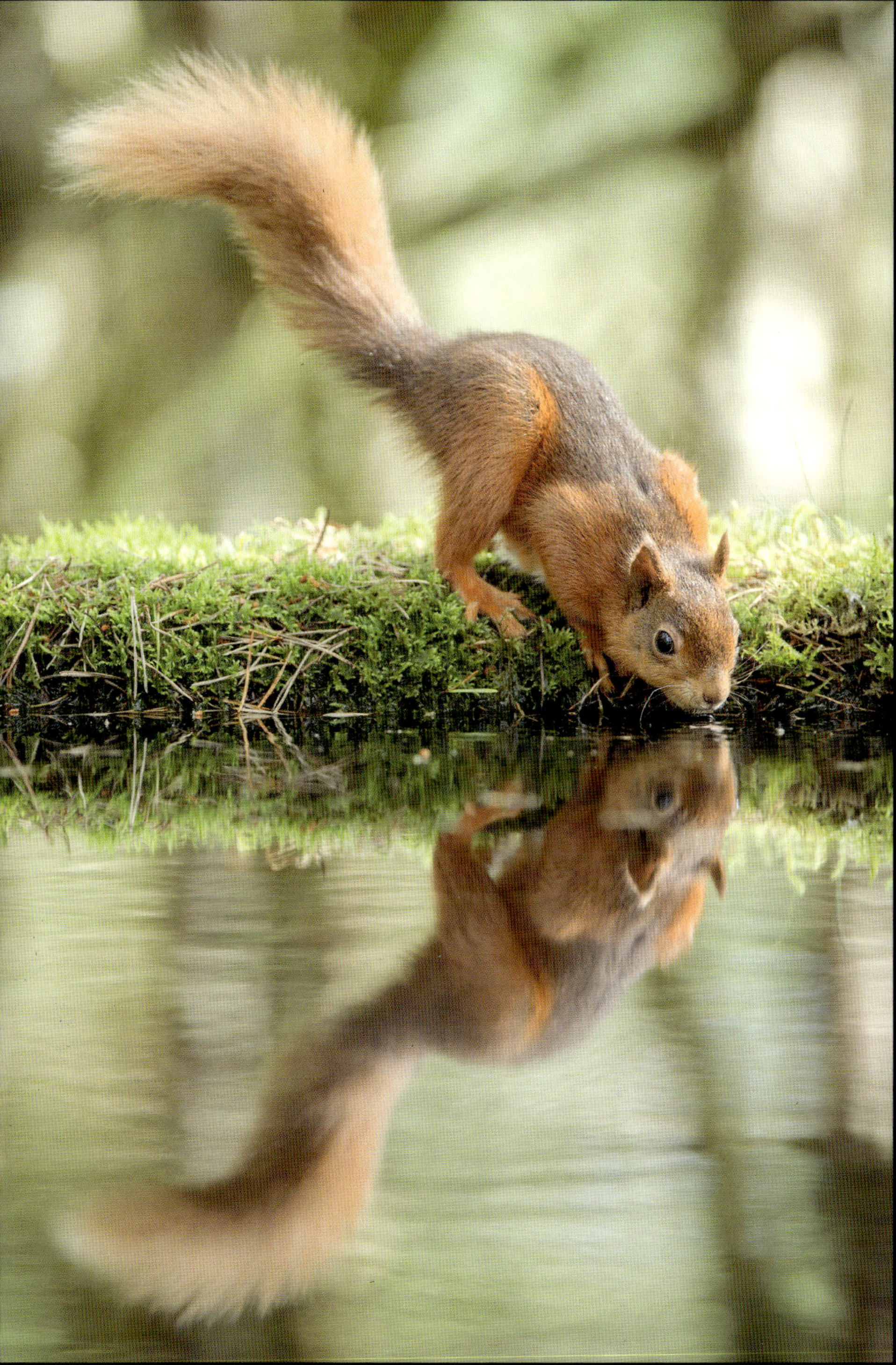

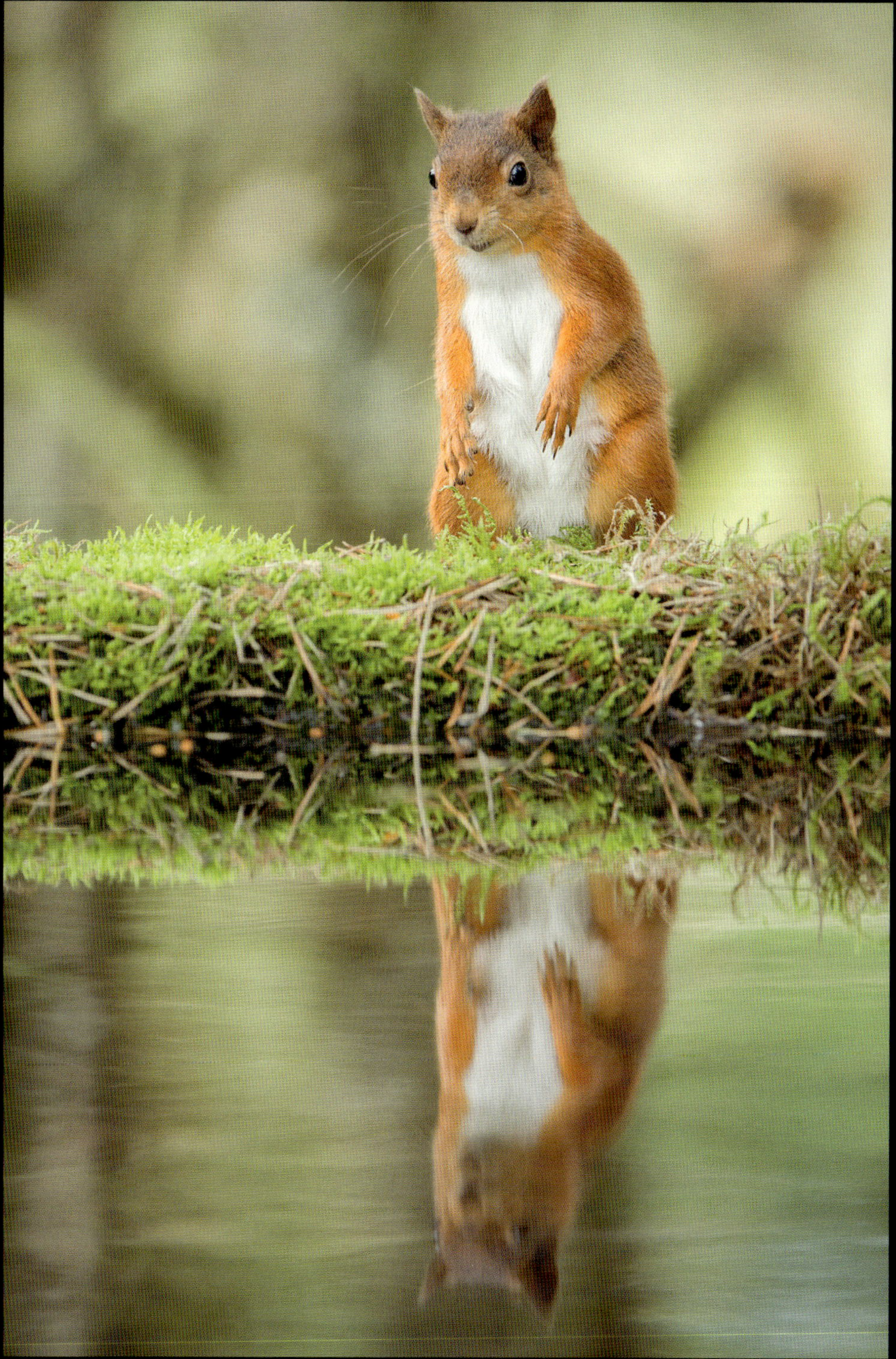

After a few sessions waiting beside the pool with no luck, one of the squirrels decided to venture towards the new structure and check it out. She hopped onto the side and, to my great surprise, began drinking from the pool. This behaviour is not often seen, as they get most of their fluids from their diet. I was dealing with some very harsh lighting that day, but the pool was doing its job and giving a new slant to my images.

I also wanted to capture red squirrels jumping in the air. They are very athletic and the speed at which they jump is quite fast. This presented a problem straight away, as I could only photograph them in bright sunshine if I wanted to freeze the movement. There was also the difficulty of getting the focus correct on the image, since the "flight path" was never the same.

Having placed some hazelnuts on a carefully positioned platform, the squirrels would leap through the air to reach the nuts. It took many frustrating, but enjoyable, attempts to capture them mid-jump.

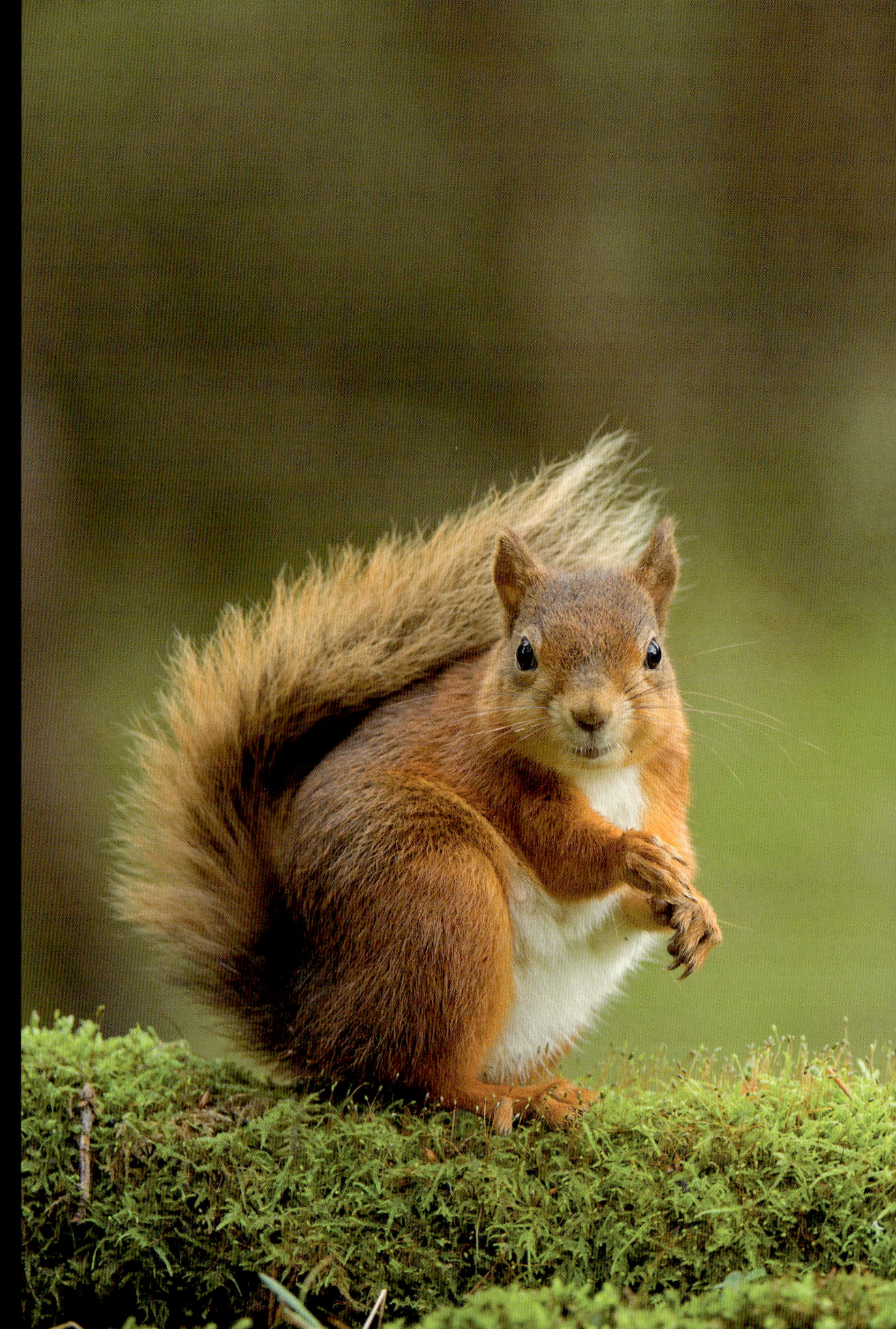

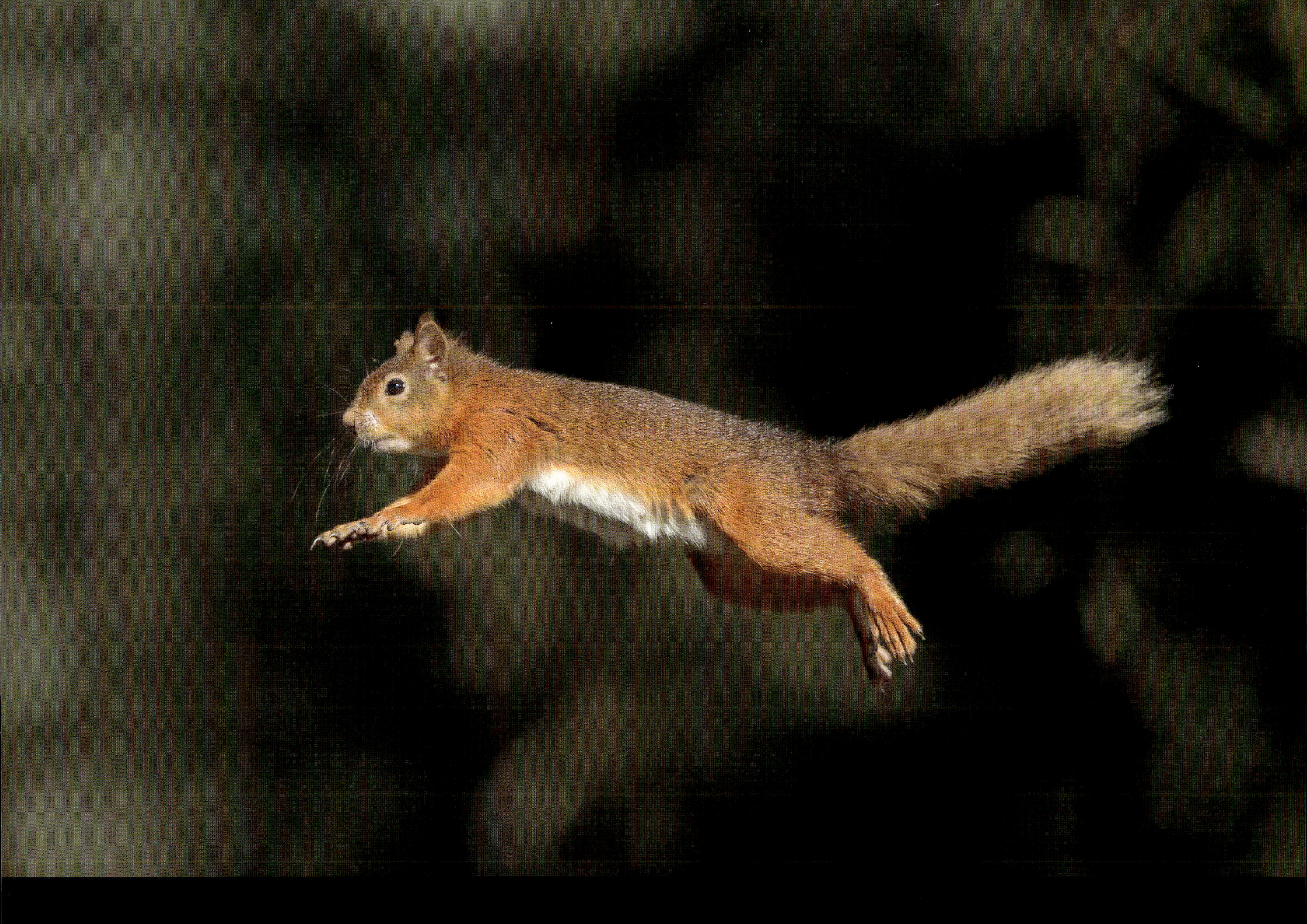

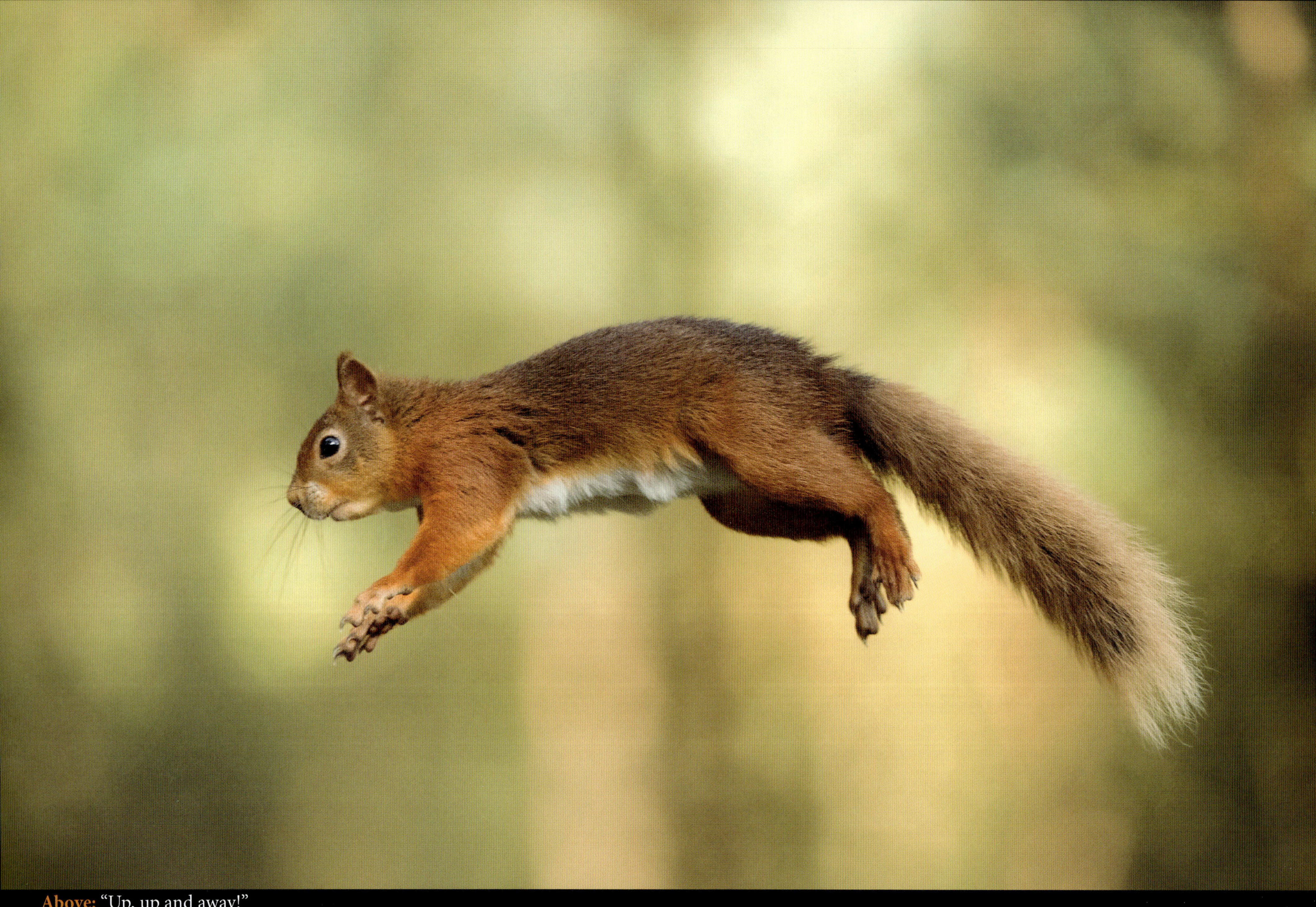

Above: "Up, up and away!"

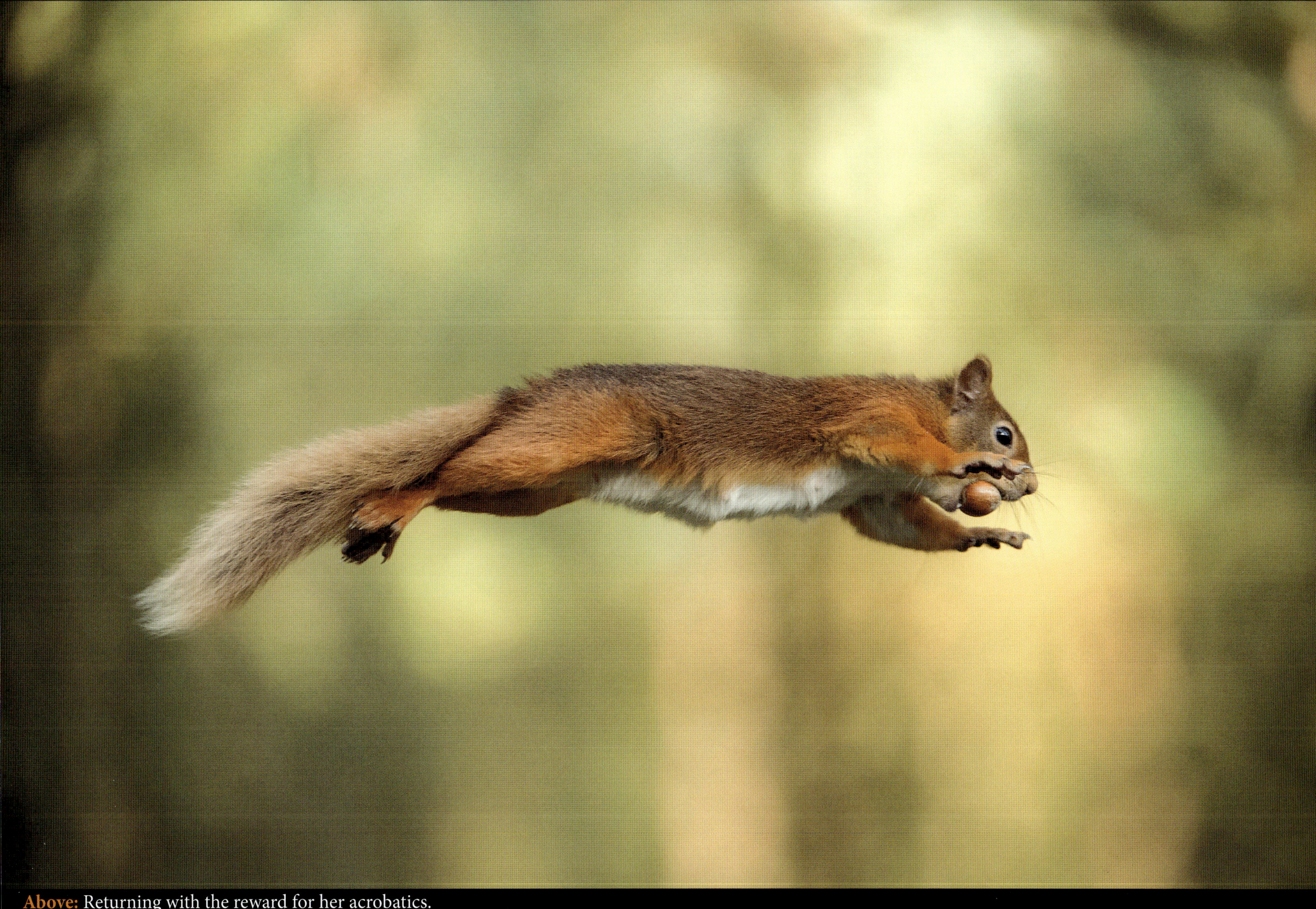

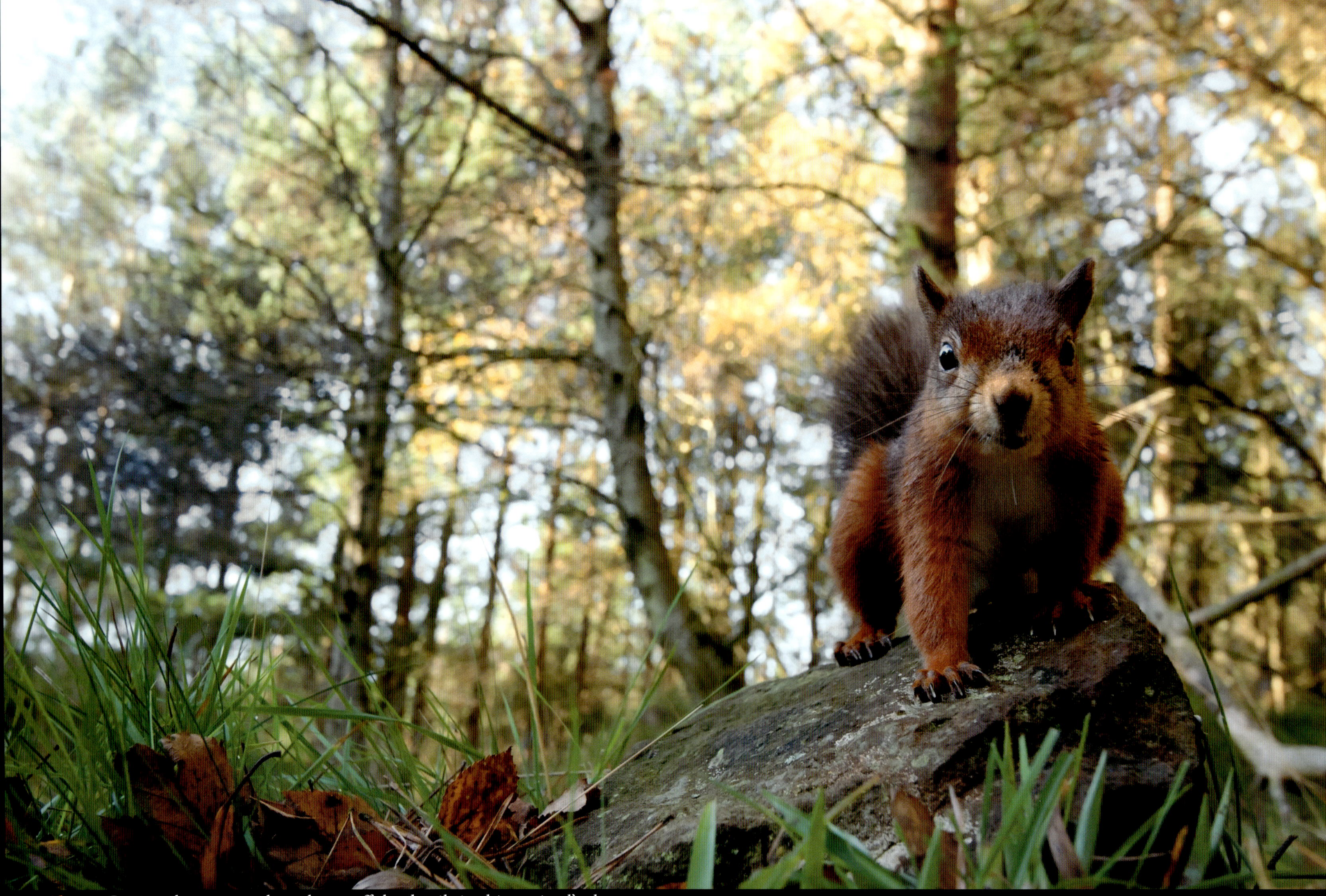

Above: Getting the camera close shows off the details in this squirrel's claws.

Up close and personal Chapter 5

Photographing squirrels is great fun, but after many thousands of hours of looking through a telephoto lens there came a time when I felt I needed a change. The problem I find with being zoomed in all the time is that it is nearly impossible to have the whole environment of your subject in the frame. I wanted a change to my style of red squirrel photography, for the time being anyway.

Usually you would shoot a landscape scene with a wide angle lens. So why not incorporate that into my wildlife photography? I got hold of a remote release, and before I knew it I was propping my camera up with all manner of twigs and stones I could find. The camera sat in position outside the hide, whilst I waited inside with a trigger. The main difficulty was that, because the focus was set manually, I had to hope the squirrel ventured into the right area of the depth of field.

The first time the squirrel spotted the camera sitting idly on the woodland floor was a moment I will always remember. Through observing and studying red squirrels for such a long time, you begin to see their different personalities. One may be bold and mischievous, whilst another may be more cautious and shy. But every squirrel does the same thing when presented with a new, alien object. As soon as the first squirrel came into the clearing, it shot up into the branches of the nearest tree and began to make its signatory "chuck, chuck, chuck" noise. They combine this with a period of ferocious tail wagging and hopping up and down on the branch.

Once it had been established that the camera was not actually an oddly-shaped predator, the squirrel in question cautiously made its way down the side of the tree. It bounded forward and circled the camera, intrigued by this new visitor (or possibly by the little pile of hazelnuts positioned underneath the lens). It wasn't long before temptation overcame its nervousness, and our curious friend hopped forwards to the camera. "Click, click" went the shutter, and with a flash the

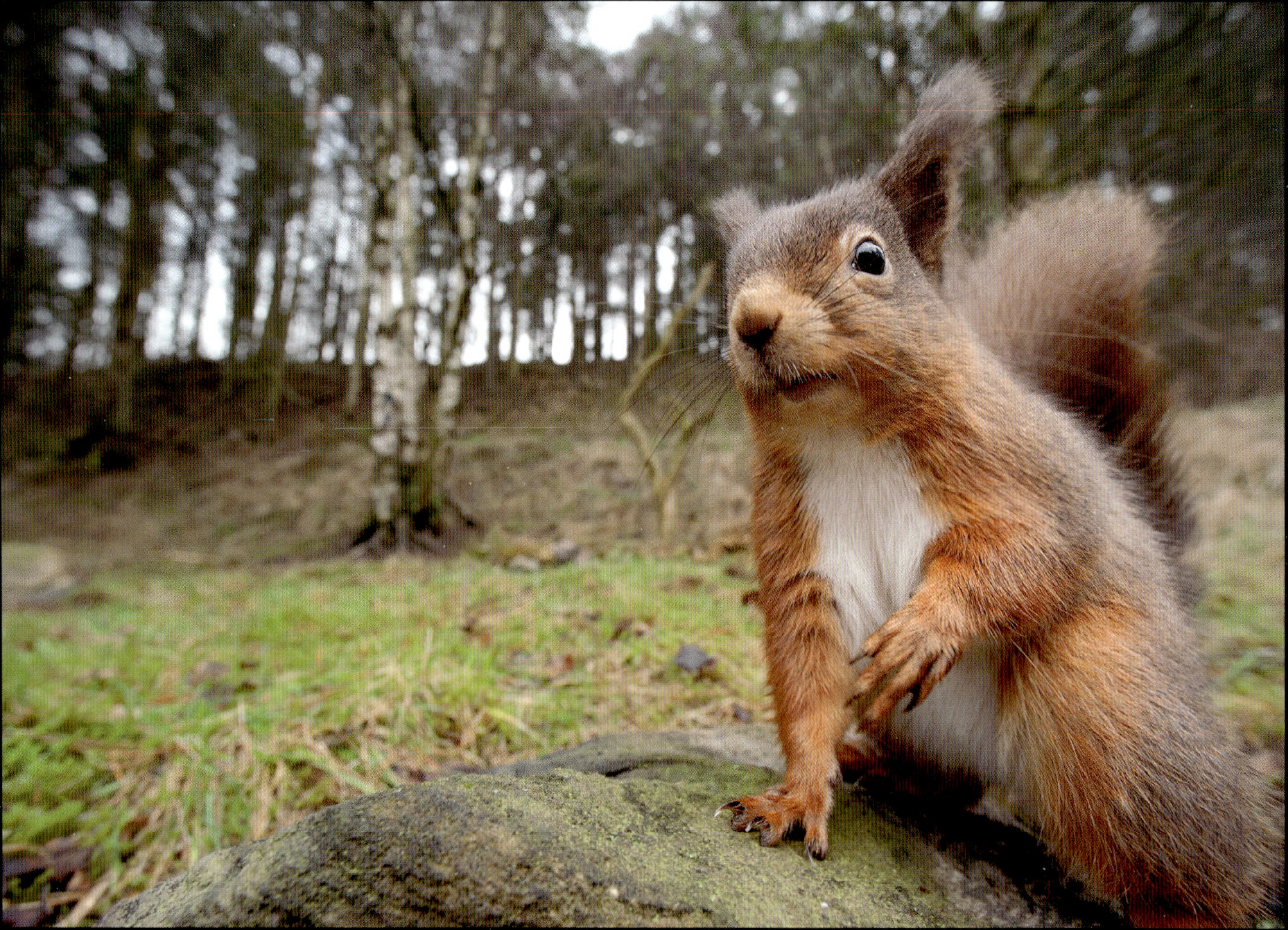

Above: A squirrel checks out his reflection in the lens.
Right: Shooting on a 14mm lens means that the squirrel is only a few inches from the camera when I take the shot.
Opposite: My favourite image from the wide angle series; a red squirrel reaching out to the camera.

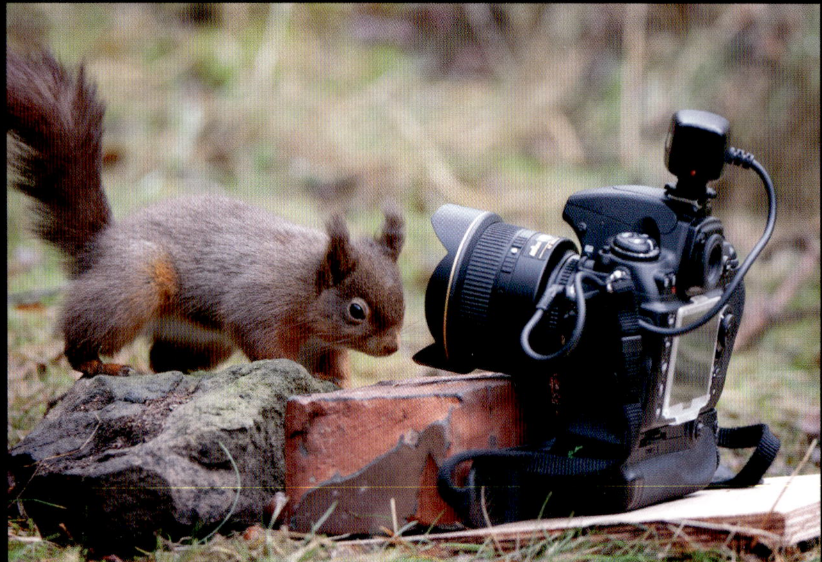

squirrel zipped up the tree. At first I did wonder if the noise would keep them at bay, but after some more intense tail wagging, it came back down and was soon posing in front of the camera. I was very surprised at how quickly they got used to the camera, and after a few hazelnuts had been eaten they would happily sit still whilst I clicked away.

Squirrels make for great subjects, and it is possible to make every image different to the last. I find using a wide angle lens is great for this, as they appear to be reacting to their reflection at times.

Since they had become so used to the camera, I decided it was time to get some more interesting interactions with it. This was purely for fun and to produce a humorous photograph. Whilst one of the squirrels was away burying a hazelnut, I jumped out of the hide and positioned my telephoto lens on a tripod with a few nuts nearby.

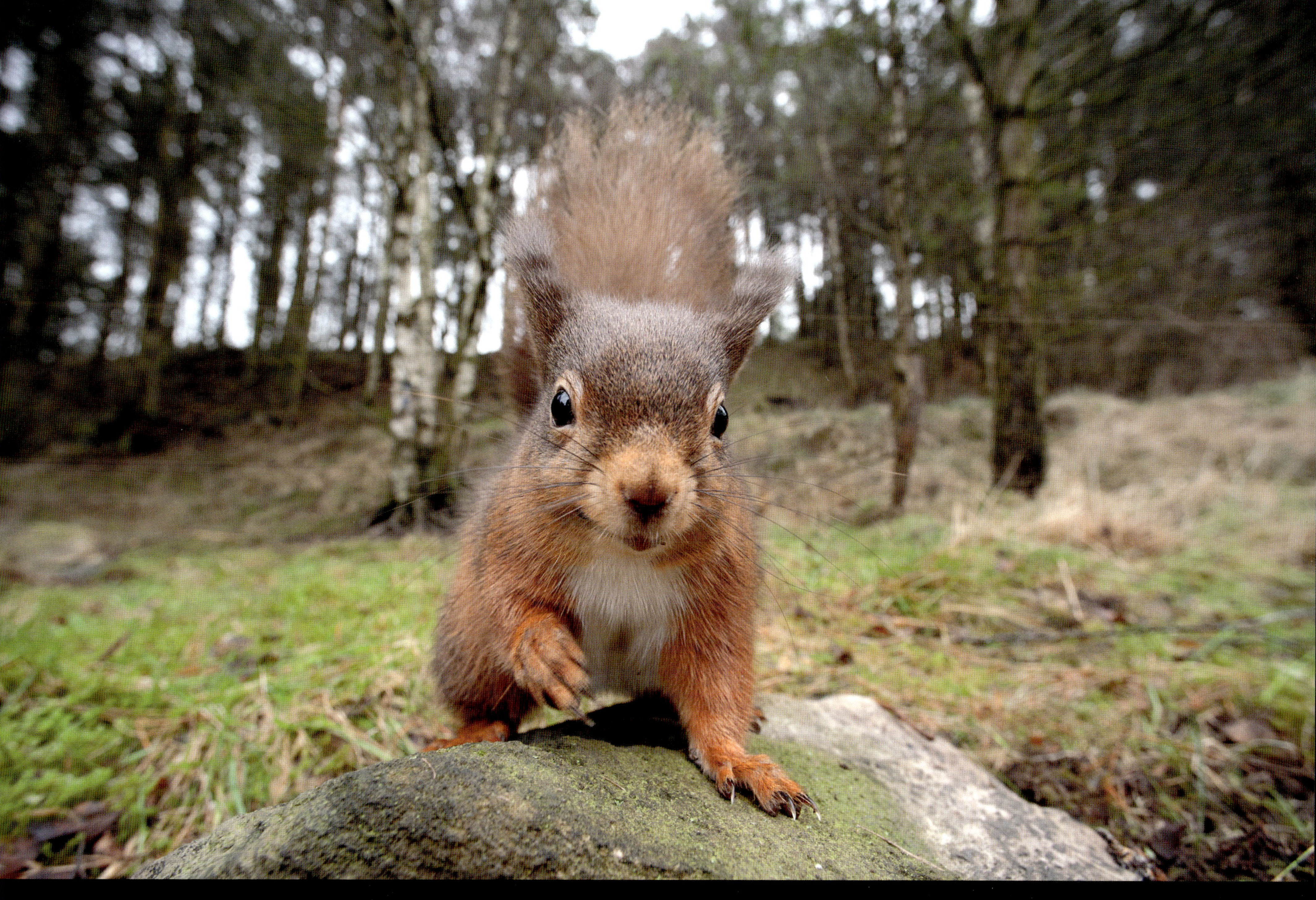

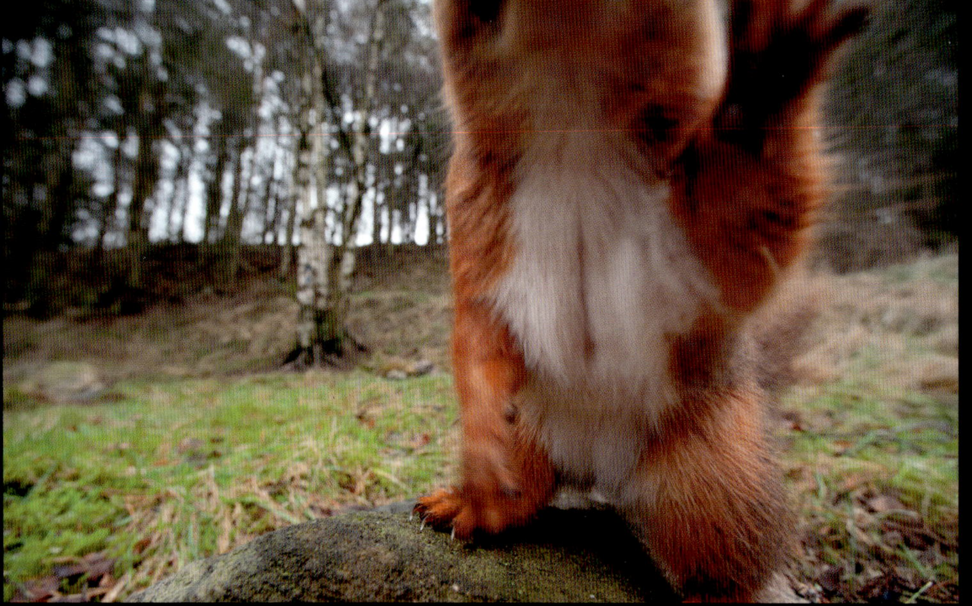

Straight away the squirrel began to sniff at the camera, before quickly grabbing a hazelnut and running off to eat it. The first few times it came to investigate I didn't quite get the shot I was looking for. This was down to the squirrel carelessly placing its head behind the camera or not looking interested enough! You just can't get the staff.

Finally, he placed one paw up against the camera body and, as luck would have it, posed as if to be taking a photograph. This image became very popular relatively quickly, but not because of any photographic skill of course.

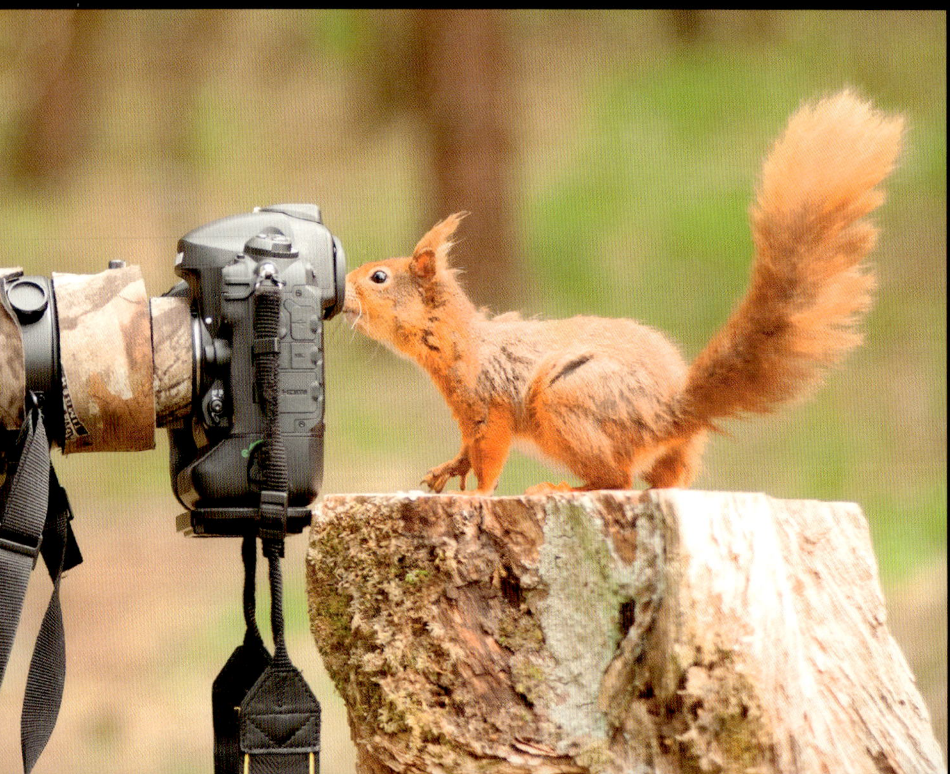

Top Left: Sometimes they get *really* close.
Left: The curious squirrels will happily check out any new additions.
Opposite: Posing in front of the camera.

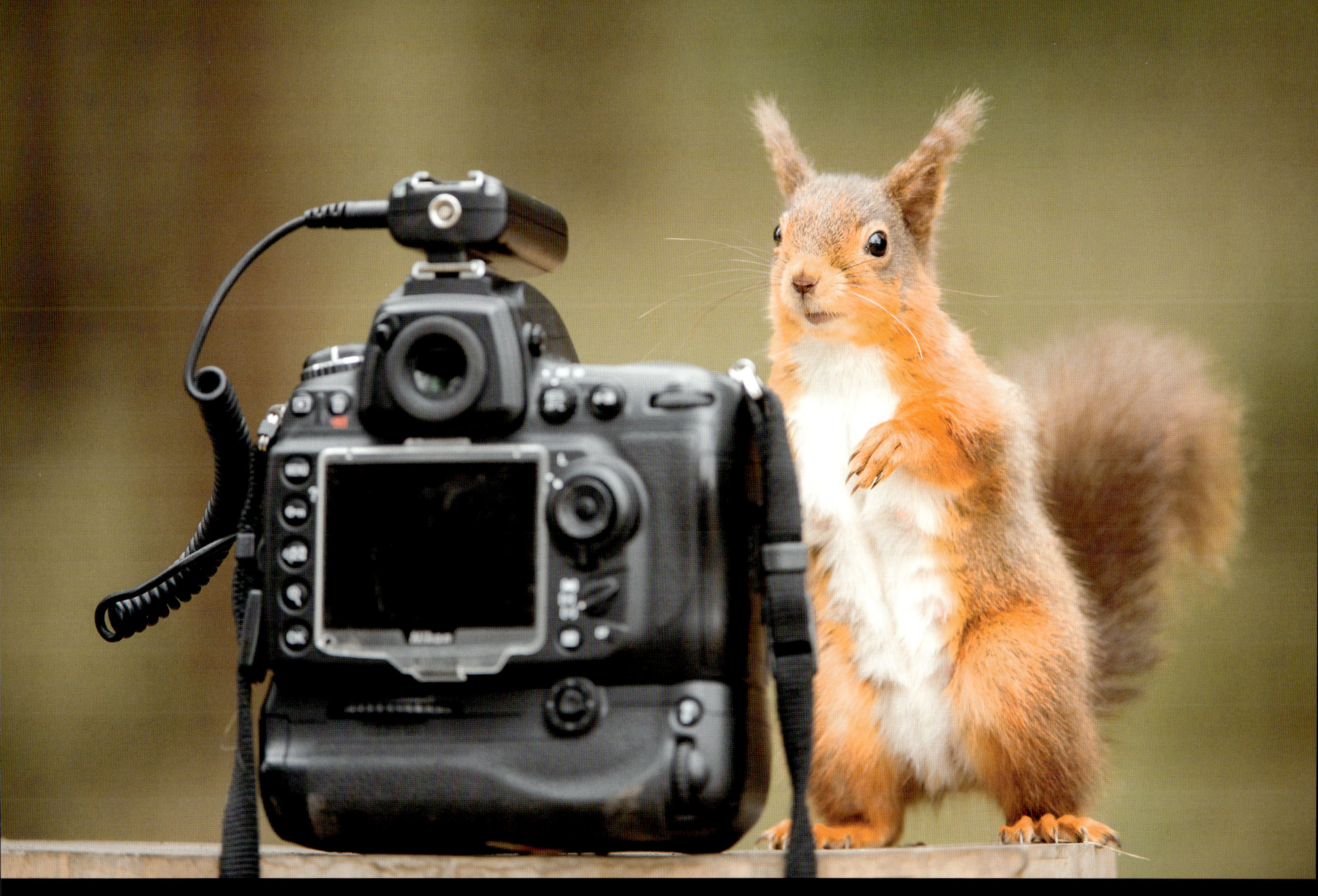

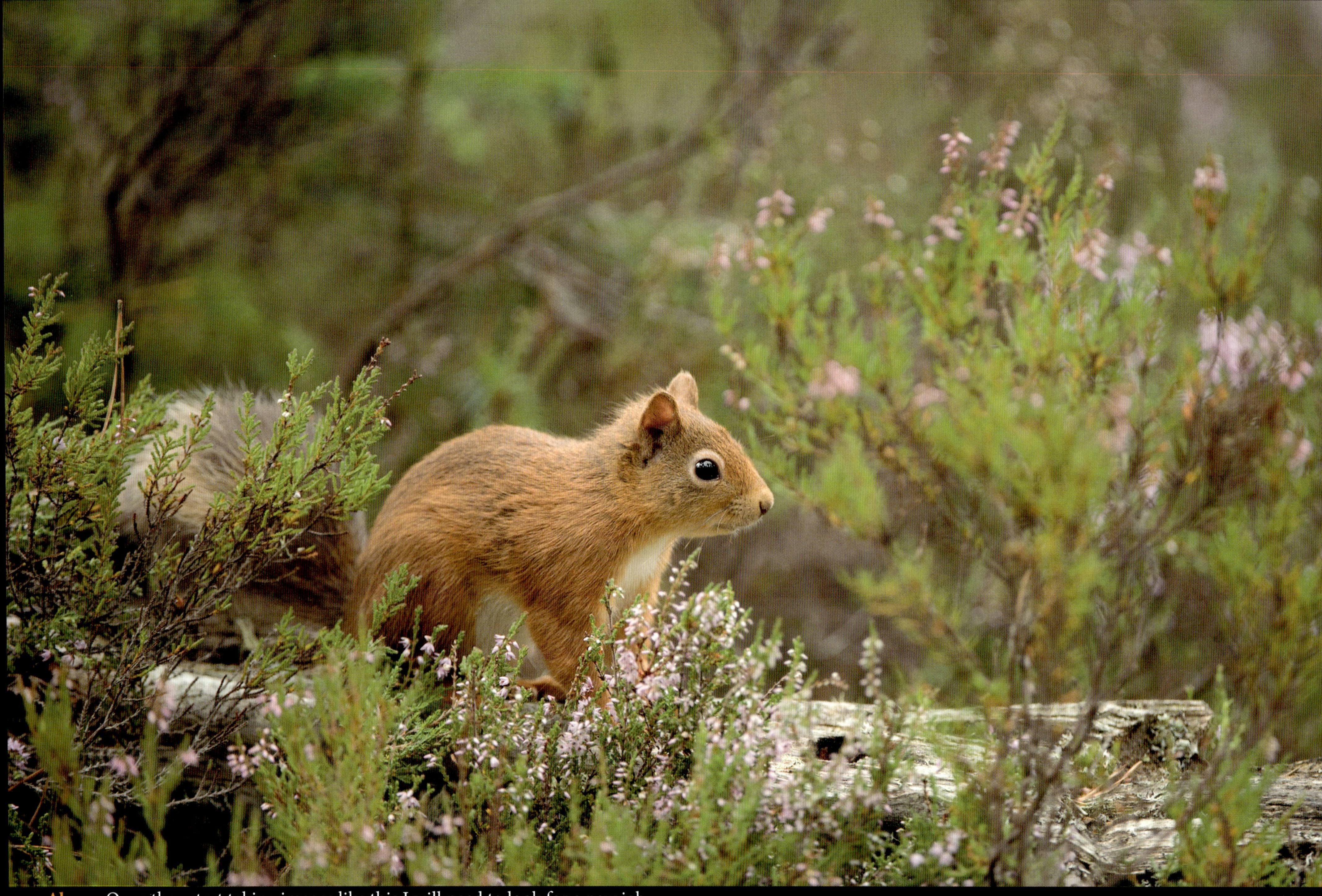

Above: Once they start taking images like this I will need to look for a new job.

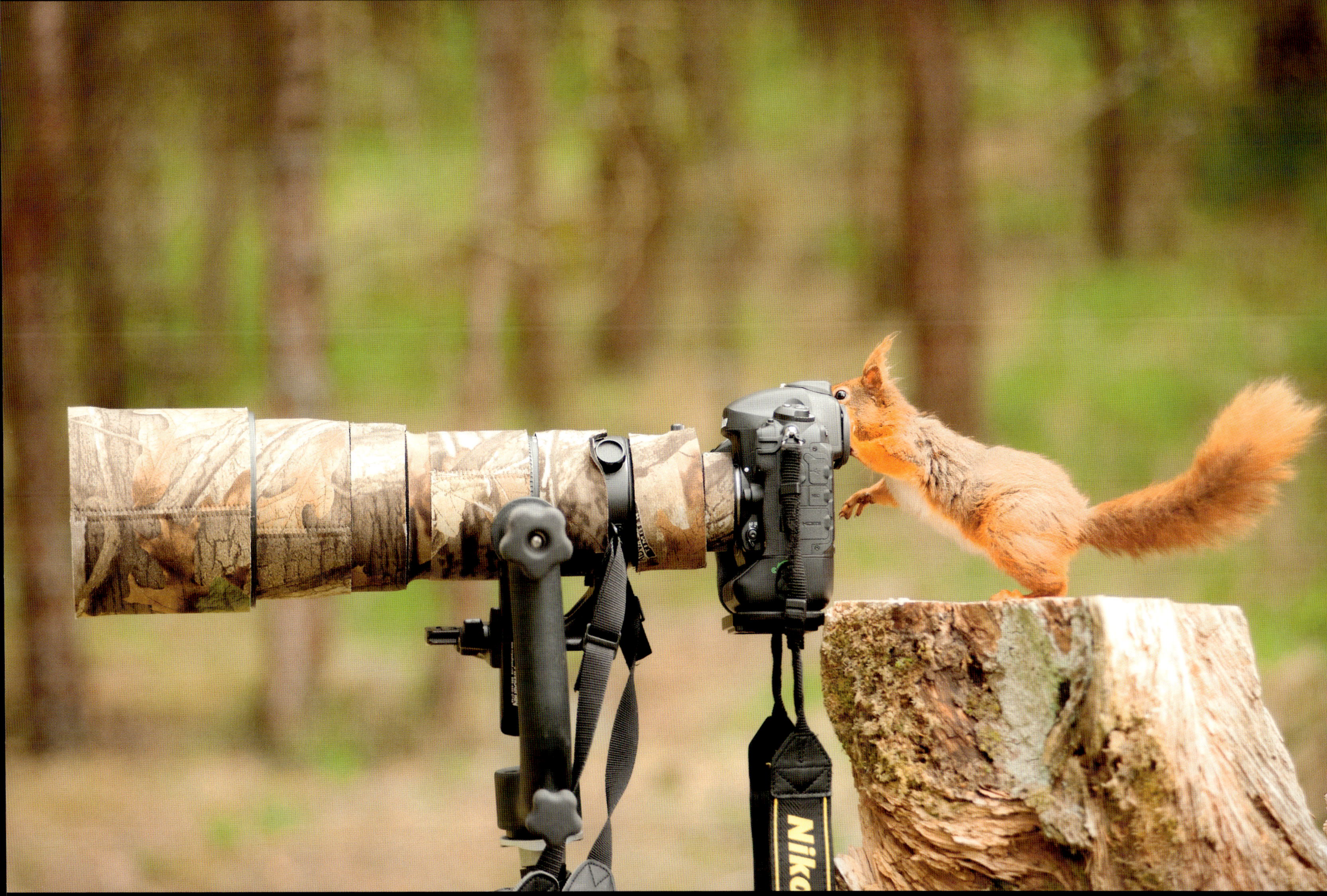

Above: "Now everyone line up and say NUTS!"

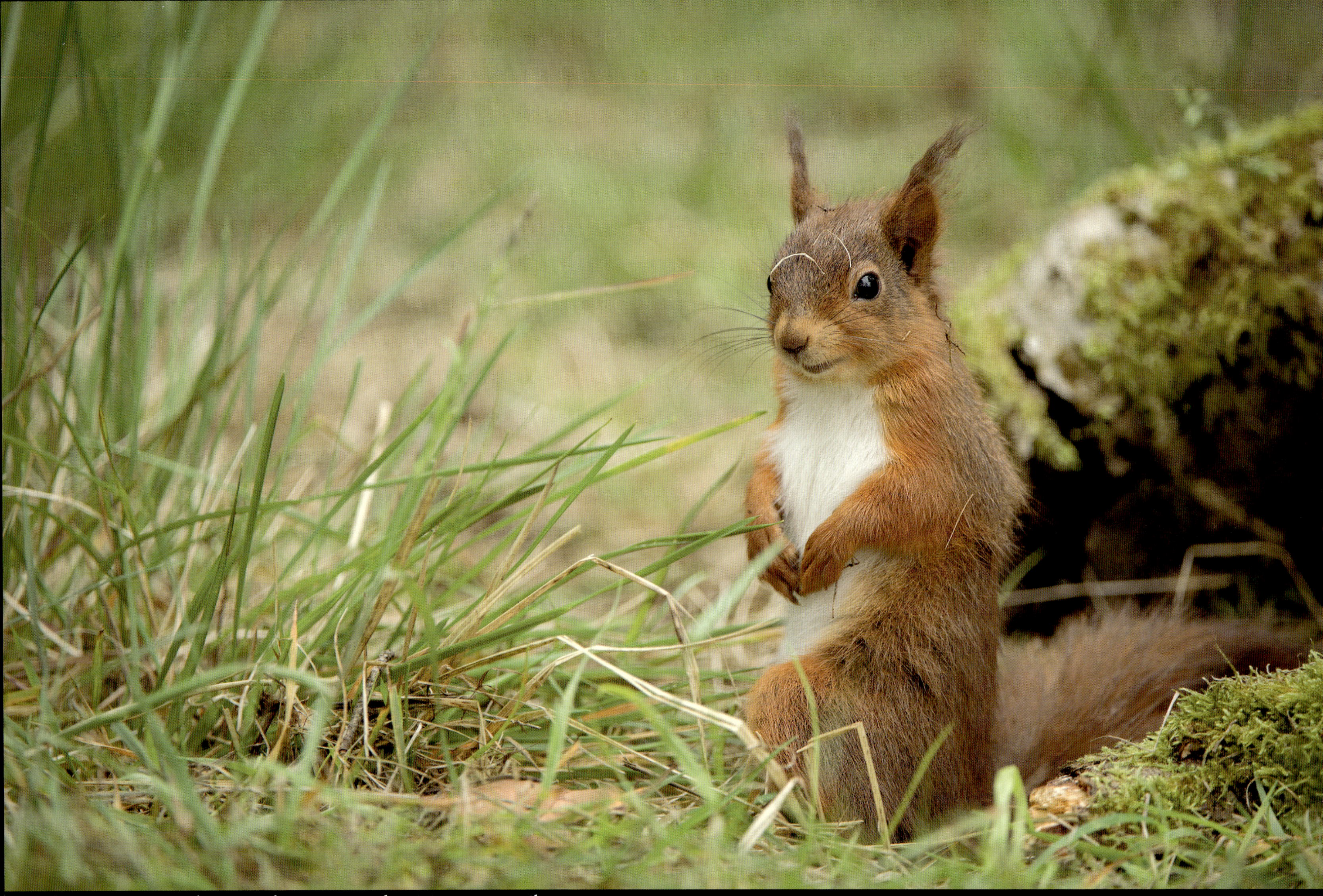

Above: Sometimes the squirrels can seem to be giving a wry smile.

Every year the population of red squirrels in my woodland changes. This means that some squirrels leave, roaming around in the search for new territories, whilst others will move into the wood. It is sad to see some of my favourite characters leave the area, but this mixing is healthy as it ensures there is no interbreeding.

But it is also an exciting time of year when the population shift occurs. It is almost like meeting new people, as I have to start again in learning their behavioural patterns. I love to see what characters arrive once they settle down again, and so far I have not been disappointed with the new visitors.

However, whilst the red squirrels are breeding and moving around, so are the grey squirrels. This means that we have to be extra vigilant and active with our conservation efforts to control the grey squirrels. Without our work, the reds would soon be pushed out by the influx of greys.

The most common place a red squirrel chooses to make its home is called a drey. This is a domed nest, enclosed all the way around apart from an entrance hole at the front. They are lined with soft moss and other materials, ensuring that the nests are as comfortable as possible. This means they are an ideal place to keep warm in the winter and to relax in the shade during hot summer days.

A large ball of sticks in a tree would seem like it should be easy to spot, but I have spent a lot of time with my neck craned upwards looking into the canopy for them with no success. Eventually I will find them, but it is interesting how your imagination can mould branches into a ball shape and trick your eyes. Dreys are positioned within the forks of branches or close against the tree's trunk. Wherever they choose, it must be stable and minimise the risk of the drey blowing out in high winds. An unstable drey in a storm would not end well for the occupants, especially one with young kittens in, since they are usually placed at quite a height.

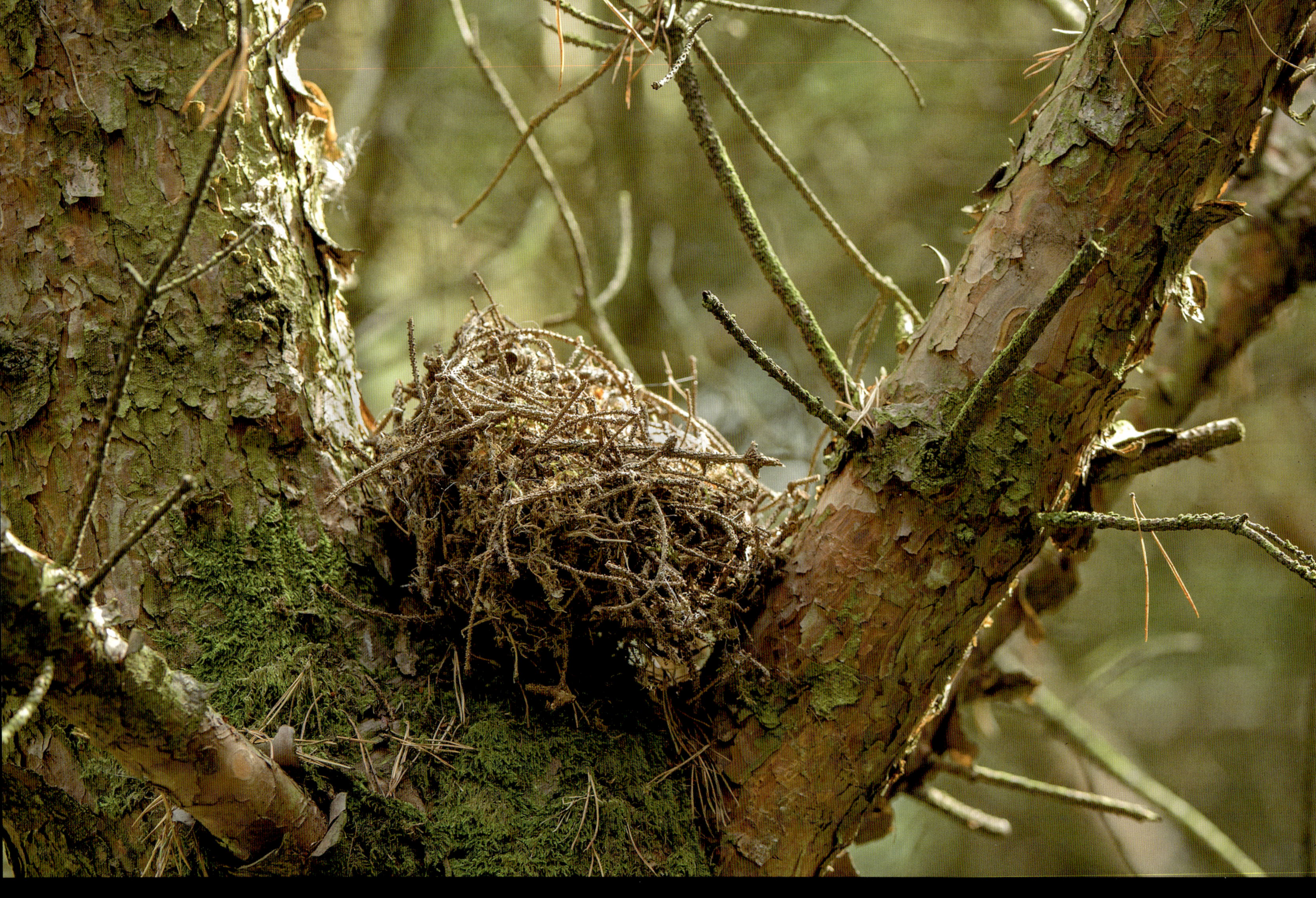

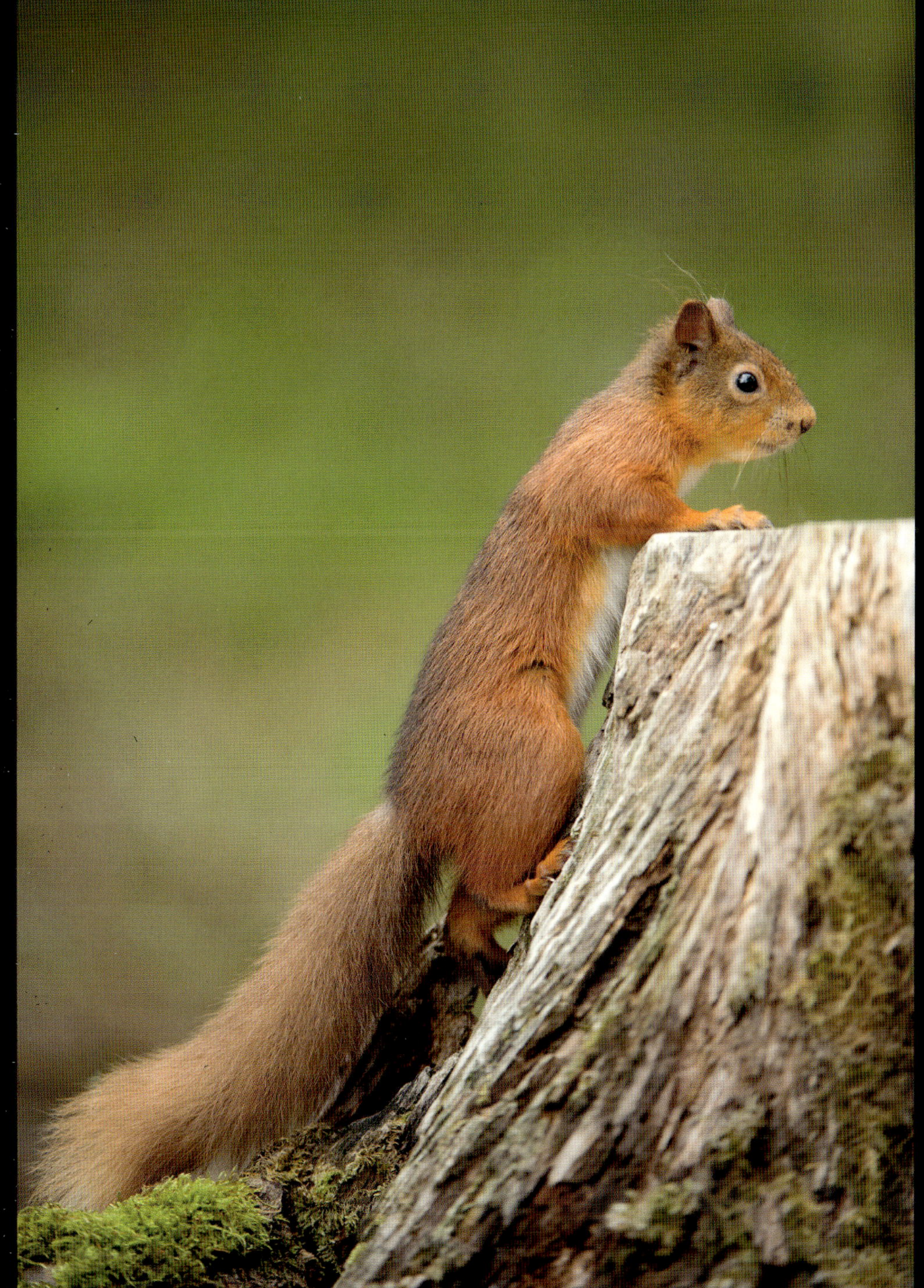

It is normal for a squirrel to have multiple dreys, allowing it to change where it sleeps every few days. This is beneficial as it helps to prevent the spread of disease and build-up of lice and fleas. Red squirrels will share dreys, especially in colder weather, which means that the transfer of fleas is highly likely. The fleas will mostly live in a drey's soft lining, so moving around stops their numbers increasing too much.

It is rare to see two squirrels sitting happily next to each other. Whenever two come into close proximity of one another it ends up causing a frantic chase around the trees and a lot of noisy chattering. I find it very sweet to think that whilst they will race around after each other during the day, they will snooze happily together by night. Sometimes there can even be more than two squirrels sleeping in one nest, although I think it must get quite crowded eventually.

Courtship chases occur most frequently from the months of January to March, although this behaviour will occur throughout the year. If you see a flash of red through the trees followed by another, it is likely that you have caught a fleeting glimpse of their chase. Whenever there are two squirrels chasing around my hide, I usually hear it before I see it. The giveaway signs are the rapid scratching of claws against bark, followed by a frantic chattering noise from both parties.

Left: "Stripe" was one of the kittens of 2013.
Opposite: A red squirrel drey in the fork of a tree.

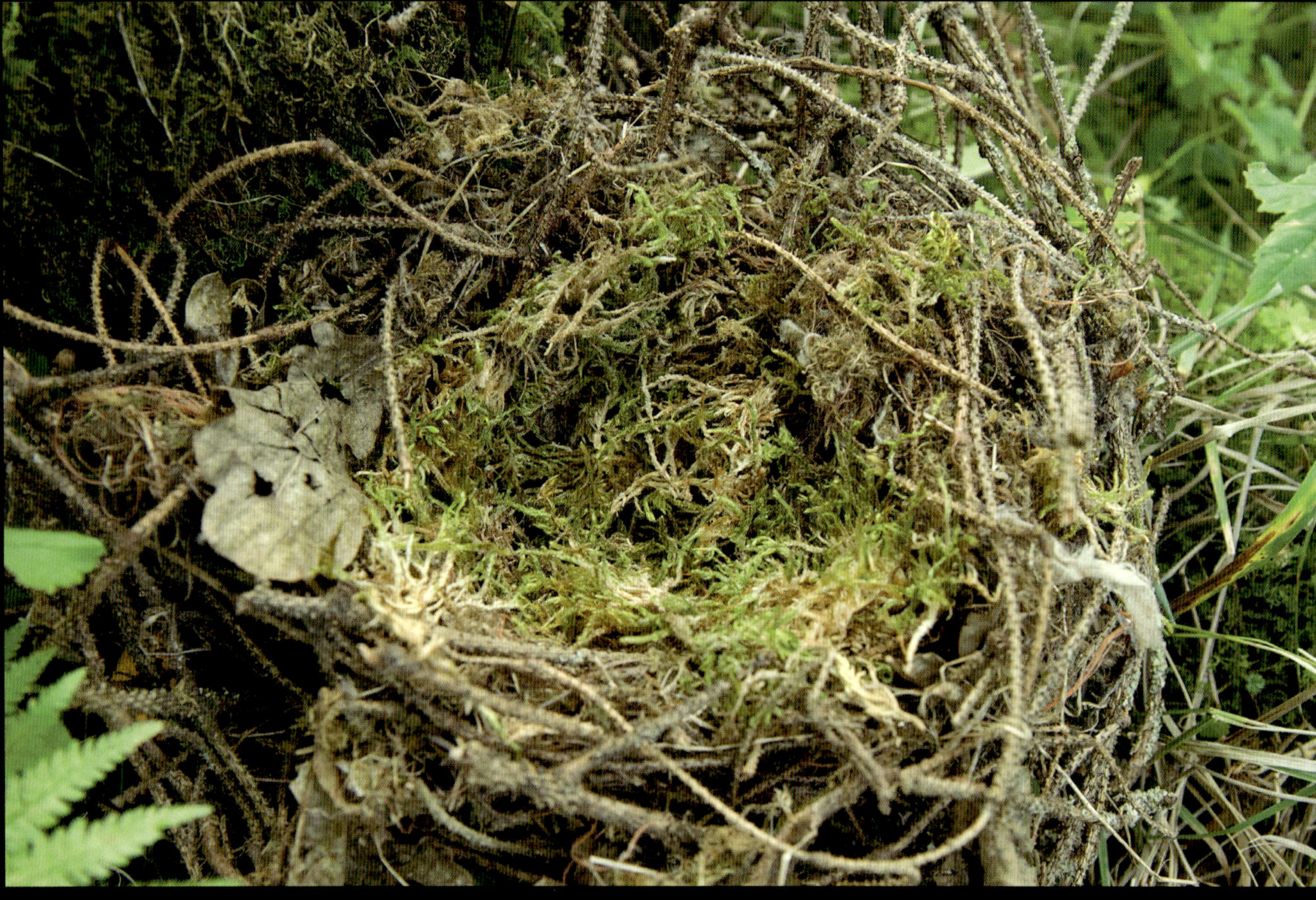

The chase involves rushing around tree trunks, running over branches and leaping from one tree to the next. It is the male pursuing the female, of course, and other males will join the chase to try their luck. Eventually, the female will allow one of the males to mate with her. Males will mate with multiple females in one season, and do not help at all to raise the young.

After a month, the young are born inside the drey. A normal litter consists of three kittens, but this number can vary from just one kitten to as many as six. They are hairless, blind and deaf at birth. This makes them very vulnerable.

Mothers who are nursing their young will have very obvious teats on show. At the beginning of the suckling process they are less obvious, but after a few weeks they become much more prominent. It is this very fact that allows me to determine when I can expect to hear the patter of tiny paws. In the summer of 2013, I suddenly stopped seeing one of the squirrels very often (named "Scooter"). It was strange, as she was a very active individual, and was instead only visiting the hide later on in the evening. It soon became obvious, however, that she was suckling young in her nest. As the weeks passed, she became more active as the kittens needed less attention.

Once they are a little older than a few weeks old, their eyes open and their hearing develops. By this time they have started to grow fur on their bodies, and their teeth also develop. At around seven weeks old, the kittens will begin to leave the drey and explore around the nest tree. At this time they are still suckling and reliant on their mothers, but will be trying more solid foods. By ten weeks of age they are much more independent and will fend for themselves, foraging for their own food.

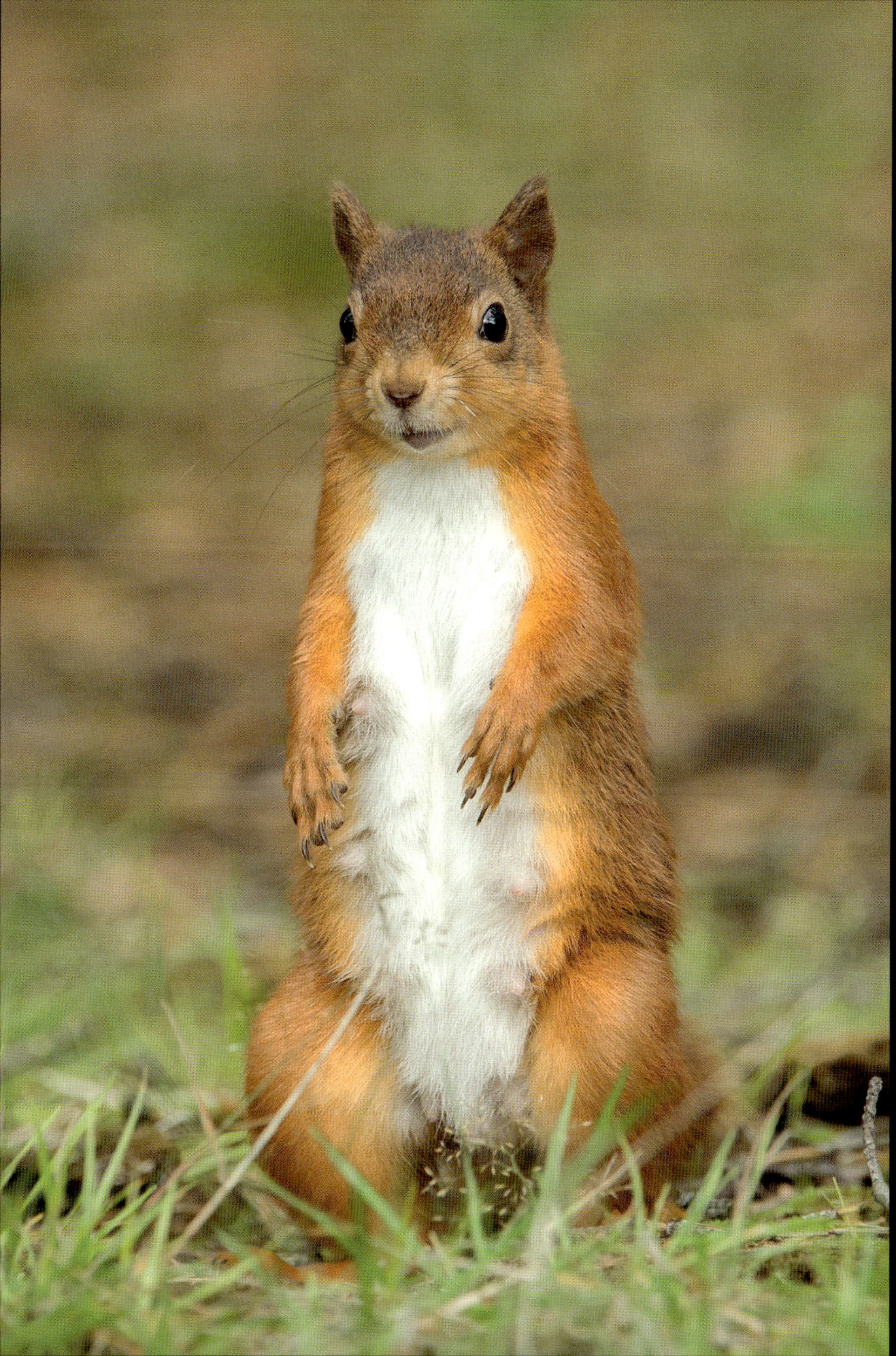

Squirrels may have a second litter, which are born mostly in July. With the supplementary food given to the squirrels that frequent my hide, it is no surprise that the females often appear to be lactating twice during the year (so must have two litters).

It is worth noting, however, that female red squirrels will not breed if they are not of a sufficient weight. If food is scarce and the health of a squirrel is low, reproduction is unlikely to occur.

Left: A female with young back in her drey will have very obvious teats that show she is suckling kittens.
Below: A motion activated trail camera caught these two squirrels together.

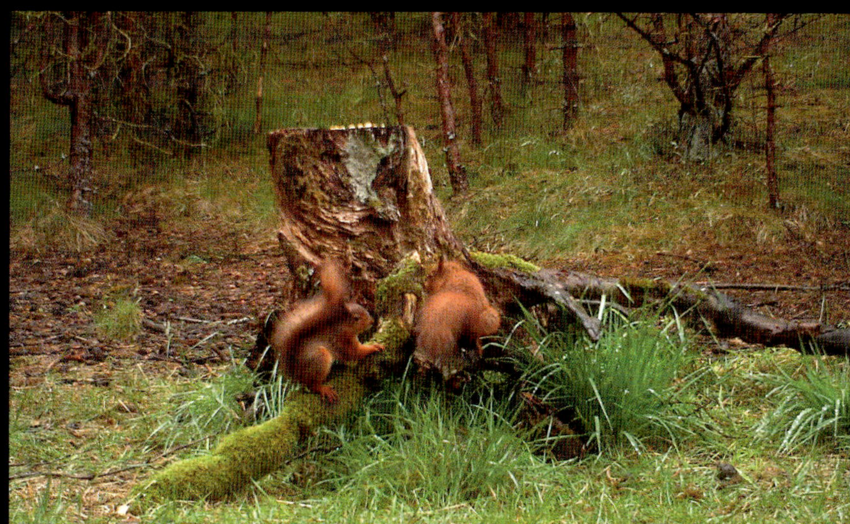

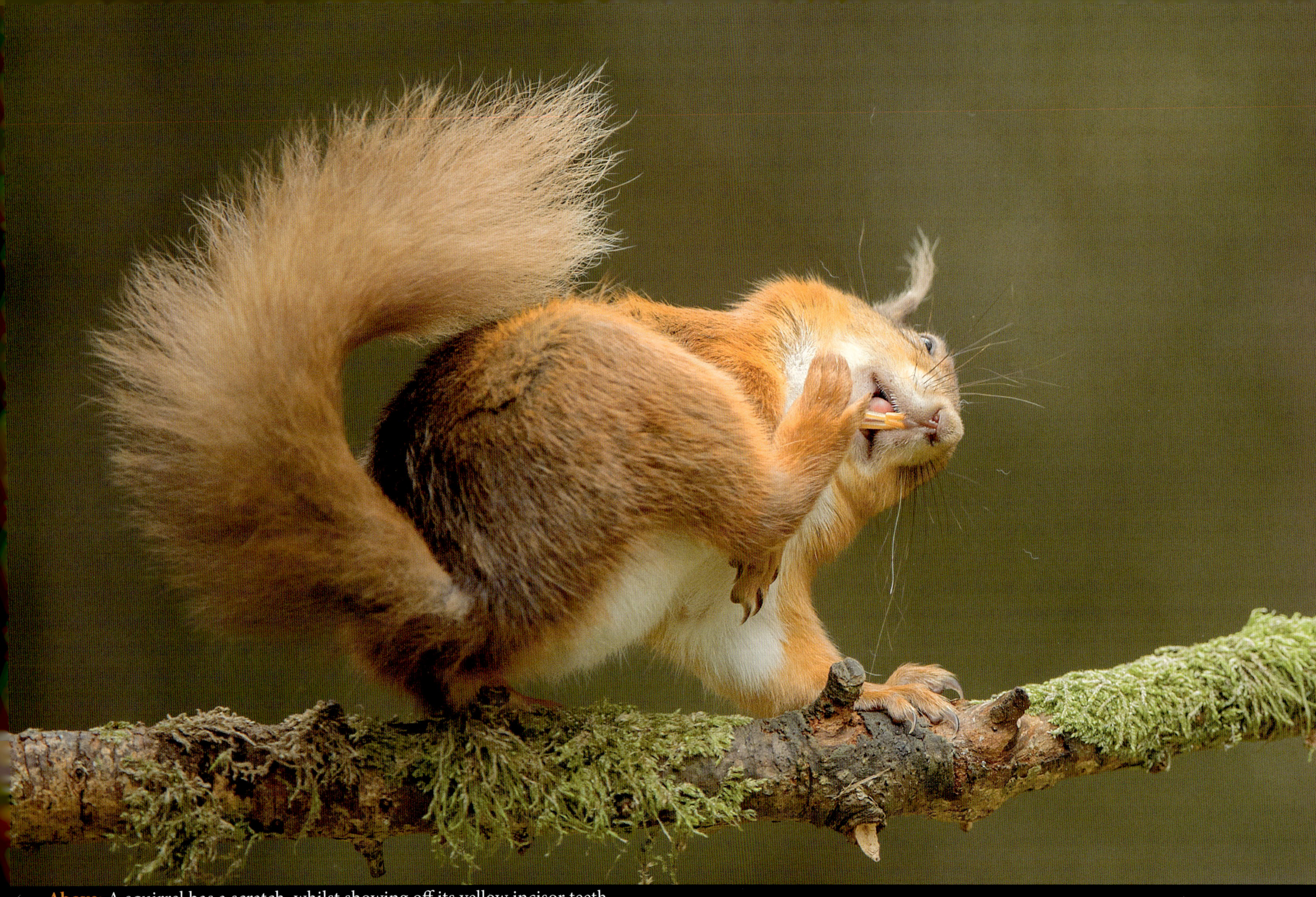

Above: A squirrel has a scratch, whilst showing off its yellow incisor teeth.

Nuts, seeds & other delights Chapter 7

Hazelnuts are the favourite food of a squirrel. The hard shell must be broken into, and this helps to keep the front two incisors sharp. Incredibly, these two teeth are filed down by around two millimetres every week. All rodents have evolved to deal with this problem by having a continuous blood supply to the soft pulp cavity in the centre of the teeth. The result of this is that the teeth continue to grow from this cavity as they are worn away at the tip, just like our fingernails.

The sharpness of the incisors is maintained through biting and gnawing at hard objects. Incisors are yellow in rodents because they are coated with enamel that contains a yellow pigment. However, this enamel is only present on the front surface of the teeth. The pulp cavity in the teeth narrows towards the tip and doesn't quite reach the end, protecting the sensitive cavity from exposure. As a result, the backs of the teeth are worn away more quickly than the fronts, ensuring that they stay as a sharp, angular point.

This explains why when you hear a red squirrel opening a hazelnut, you can hear its teeth gnawing at the shell from quite some distance. Sometimes I know that a squirrel is in the area because I can hear its teeth motoring away, like little bandsaws, at a nut somewhere in a tree.

There was a scene in the original *Charlie and the Chocolate Factory* film where a large group of squirrels were sitting beside dispensers and sorting good nuts from bad nuts. I used to love this part of the film and was fascinated by the animation, which captured the jerky movements of squirrels perfectly. This trait is not a mere myth, as squirrels do in fact know if nuts are good or bad without opening them up.

No, they don't have psychic powers. What they do have is the ability to weigh the hazelnuts. A lighter nut will often have a shrivelled or absent kernel on the inside, and this is discarded in favour of a heavier one. Amazingly, they are most often correct in their calculations. It is a useful skill to have developed, as breaking open the shell requires a reasonable amount of energy. There would be a lot of time wasted if every single nut had to be opened to find a portion of them were worthless.

I get great satisfaction from watching this process. A squirrel will grab hold of a hazelnut between its paws, turning it several times to determine its contents. Sometimes it will find a bad nut and discard it. My observations have proved to me that this isn't just chance, as I have seen one particular hazelnut being discarded every time it is included in a pile of other nuts. Even a week later, the same nut is picked out from the rest and thrown away.

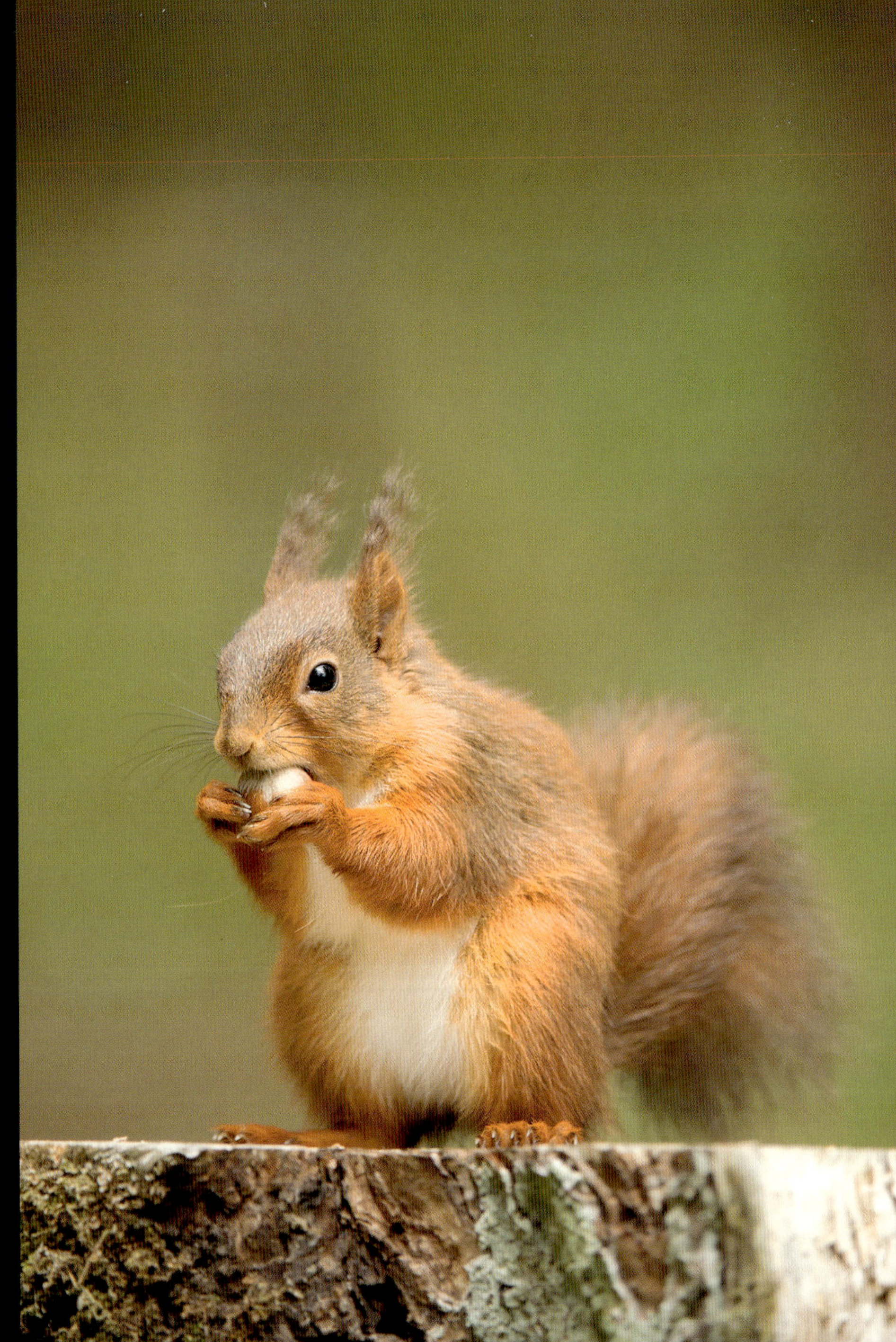

Right: One of the kittens tries to open a hazelnut.
Opposite: Unripe hazelnuts growing on a tree.

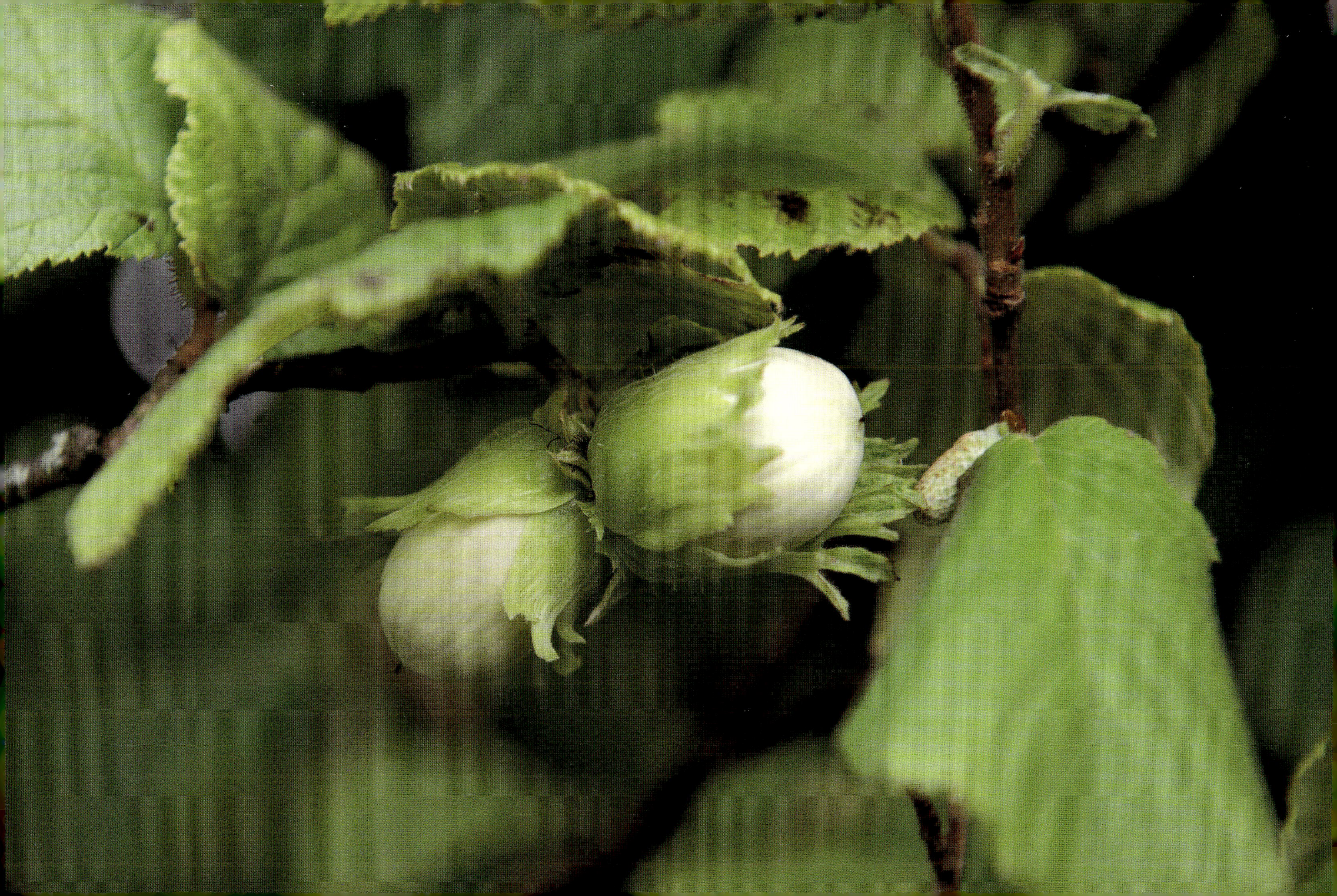

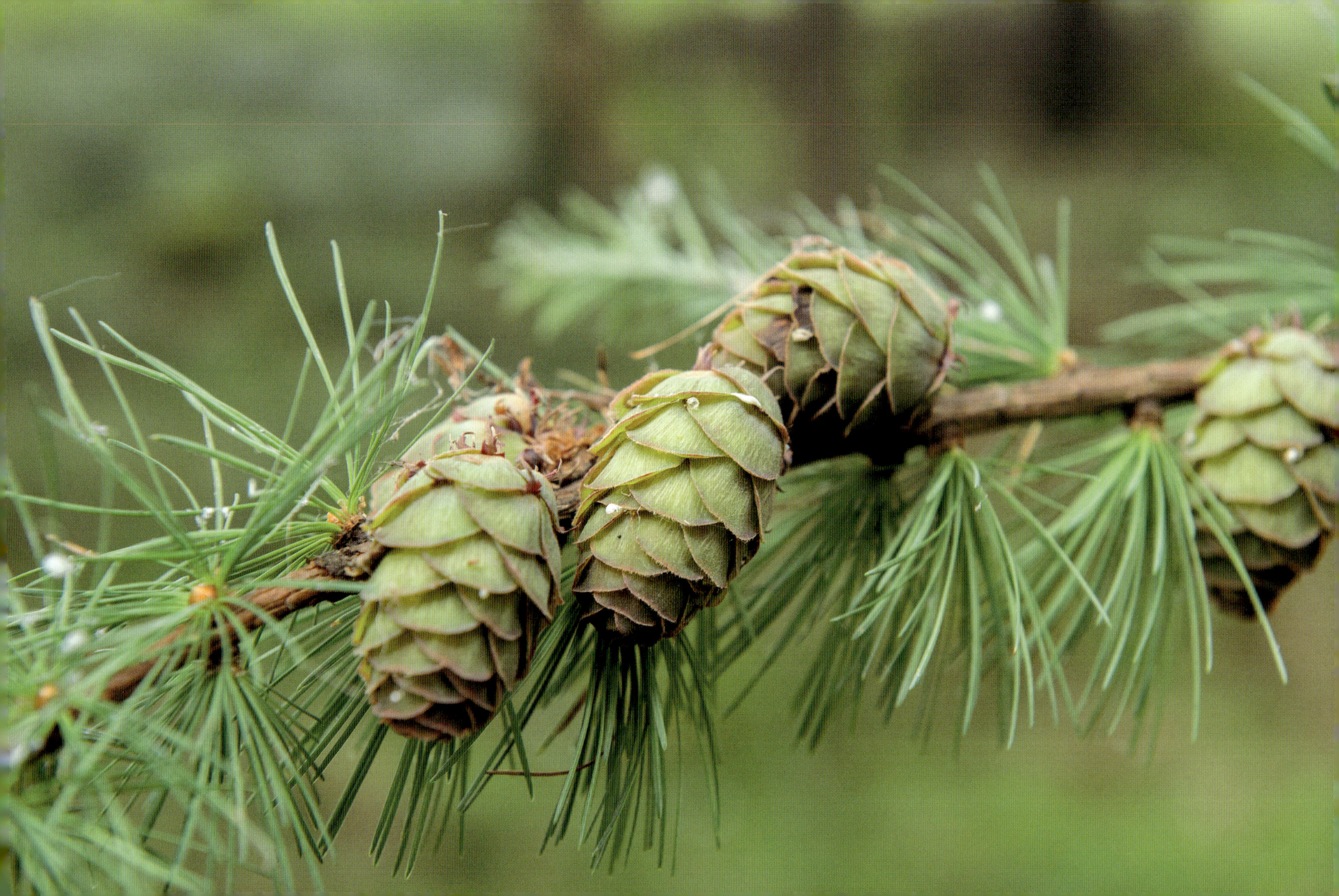

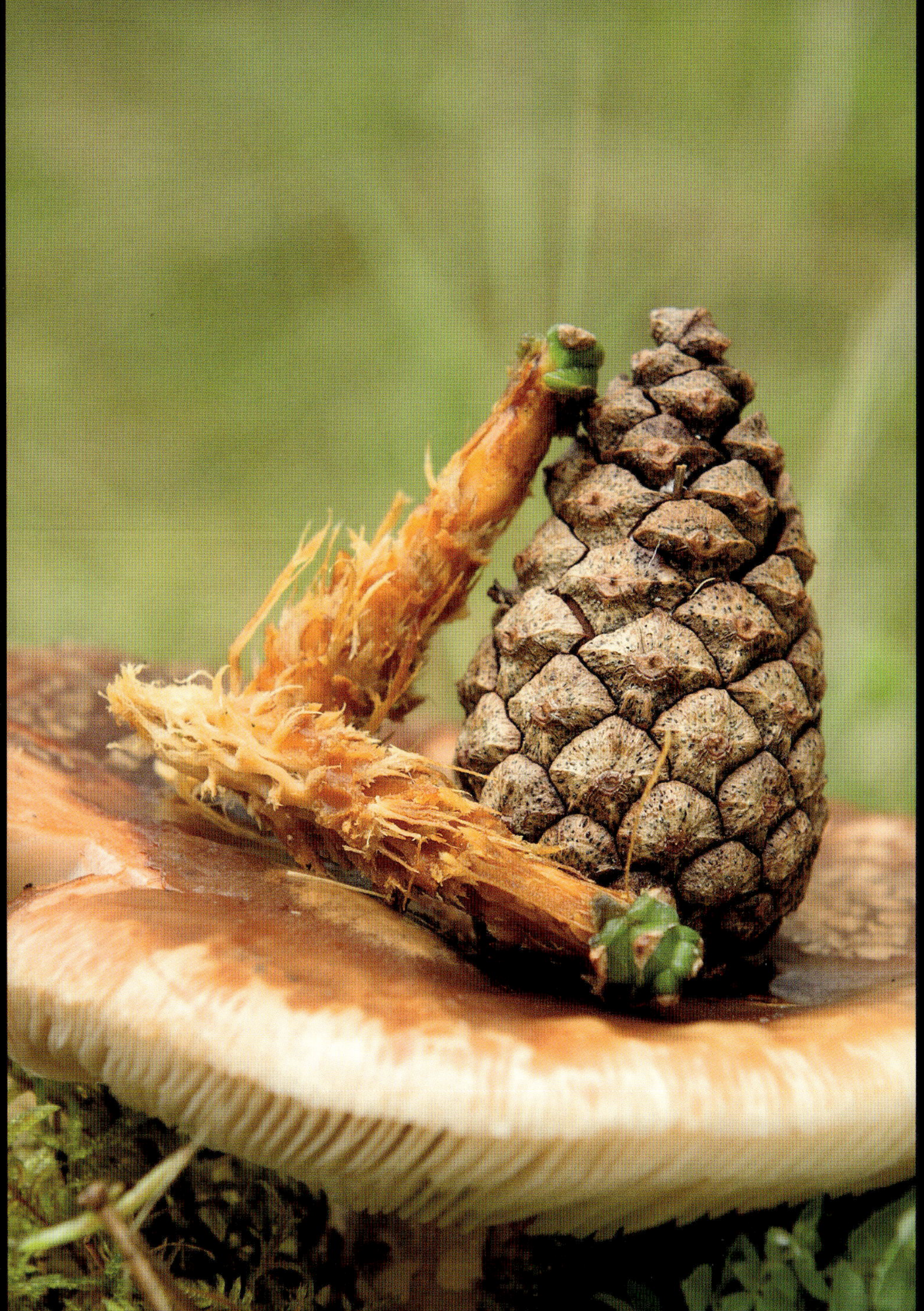

As for nuts other than hazelnuts, red squirrels will eat a variety. This includes beech mast and, as traditionally associated with squirrels, acorns. However, red squirrels do not make a habit of eating acorns as they cannot digest a lot of the tannins inside them. These hard foods provide excellent gnawing opportunities whilst also providing nutrition.

A squirrel's powerful teeth are not just reserved for opening nuts. They are also a great weapon in its arsenal when it comes to prising apart the armour of a pinecone. Inside there is a feast of seeds, but each plate of the pinecone must be removed one by one. Eventually, all that is left is a shredded core. They are then dropped to the woodland floor, providing excellent clues for a squirrel's presence.

Left: Squirrels remove the plates from pinecones when feeding.
Opposite: Pinecones form a staple part of a squirrel's diet.

The list doesn't stop at just nuts and pinecones. Red squirrels will also eat shoots, flowers and sometimes even birds' eggs. The latter is rare as they don't actively seek out bird nests, but it can happen. Our cute, furry friends are even capable of taking baby birds from the nest and eating them, although this is even rarer still. It requires a lot of effort to track down a nest and keep away from the scratching talons of the parent birds. The safer bet is to just stick to nuts; they tend not to bite.

Mushrooms and other fungi supplement the diet of squirrels. Woodland floors are often littered with poisonous mushrooms, which can also be harmful to squirrels. Luckily, they will steer clear of these most of the time. However, it has been known for a squirrel to take a bite from the poisonous fly agaric mushroom.

Right: Beyond a hazelnut's shell there is a tasty kernel to be eaten.
Opposite: Porcelain fungus is one of the many fungi squirrels may come across.

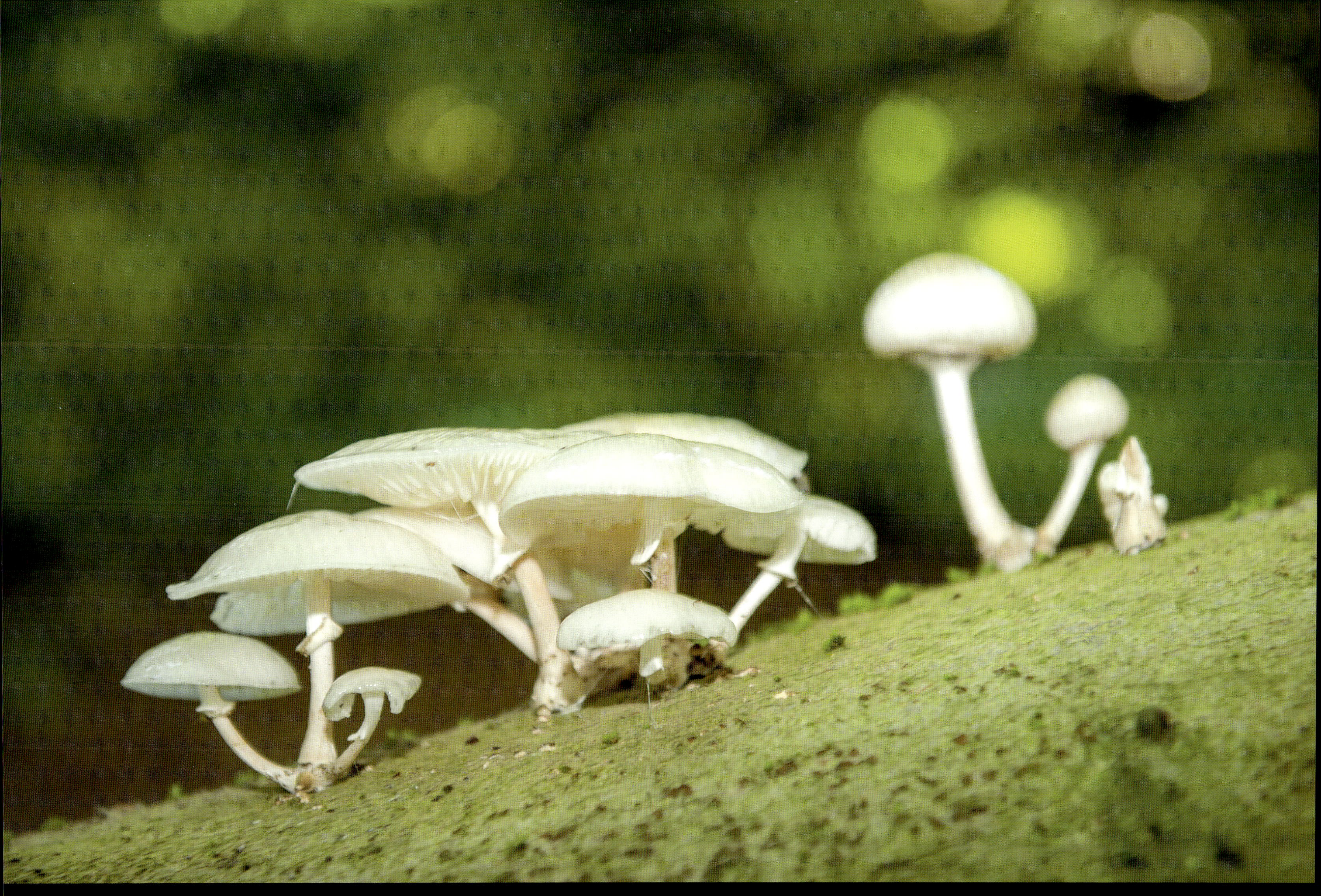

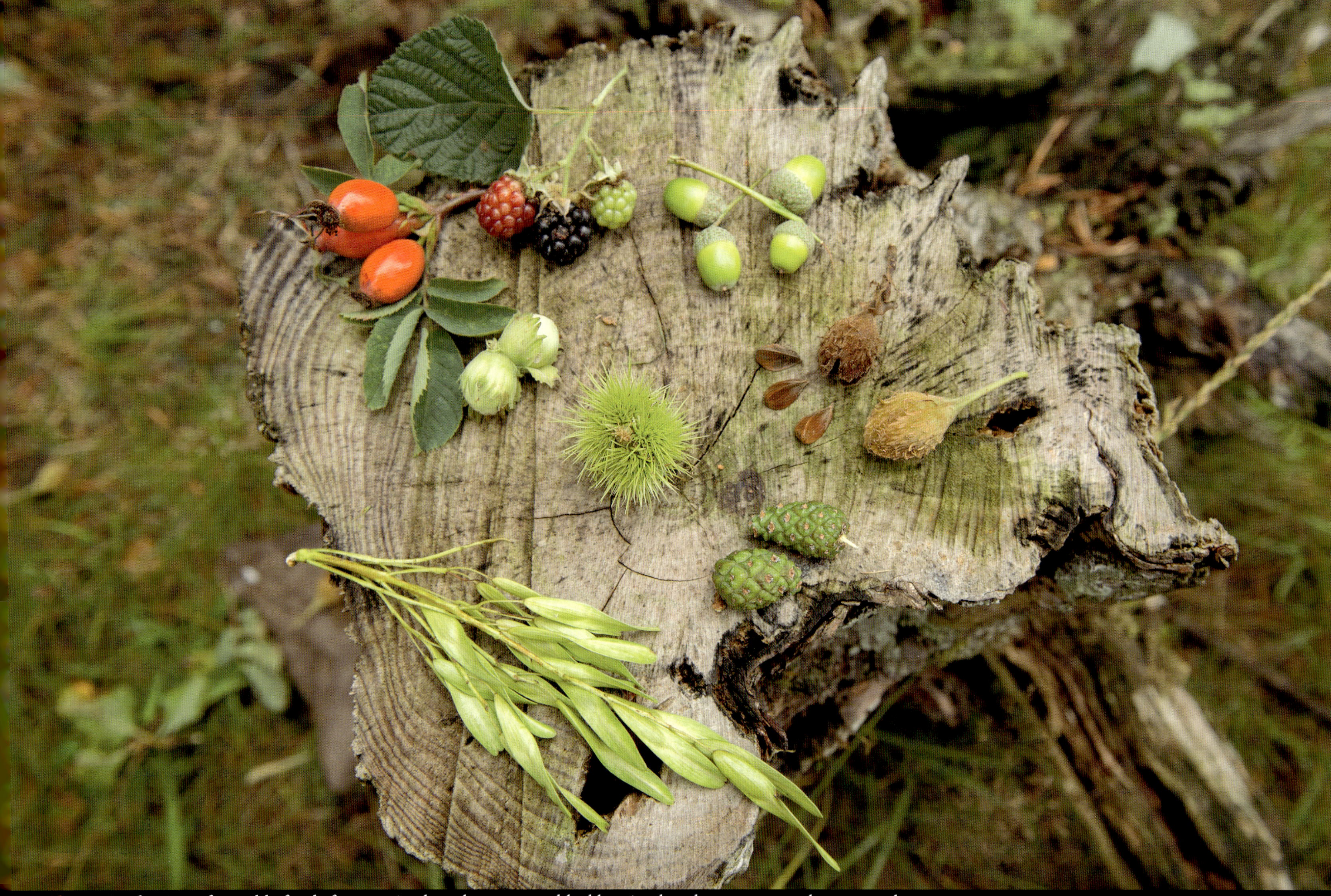

Above: A selection of possible foods for a squirrel, such as acorns, blackberries, beech mast, sweet chestnut and more.

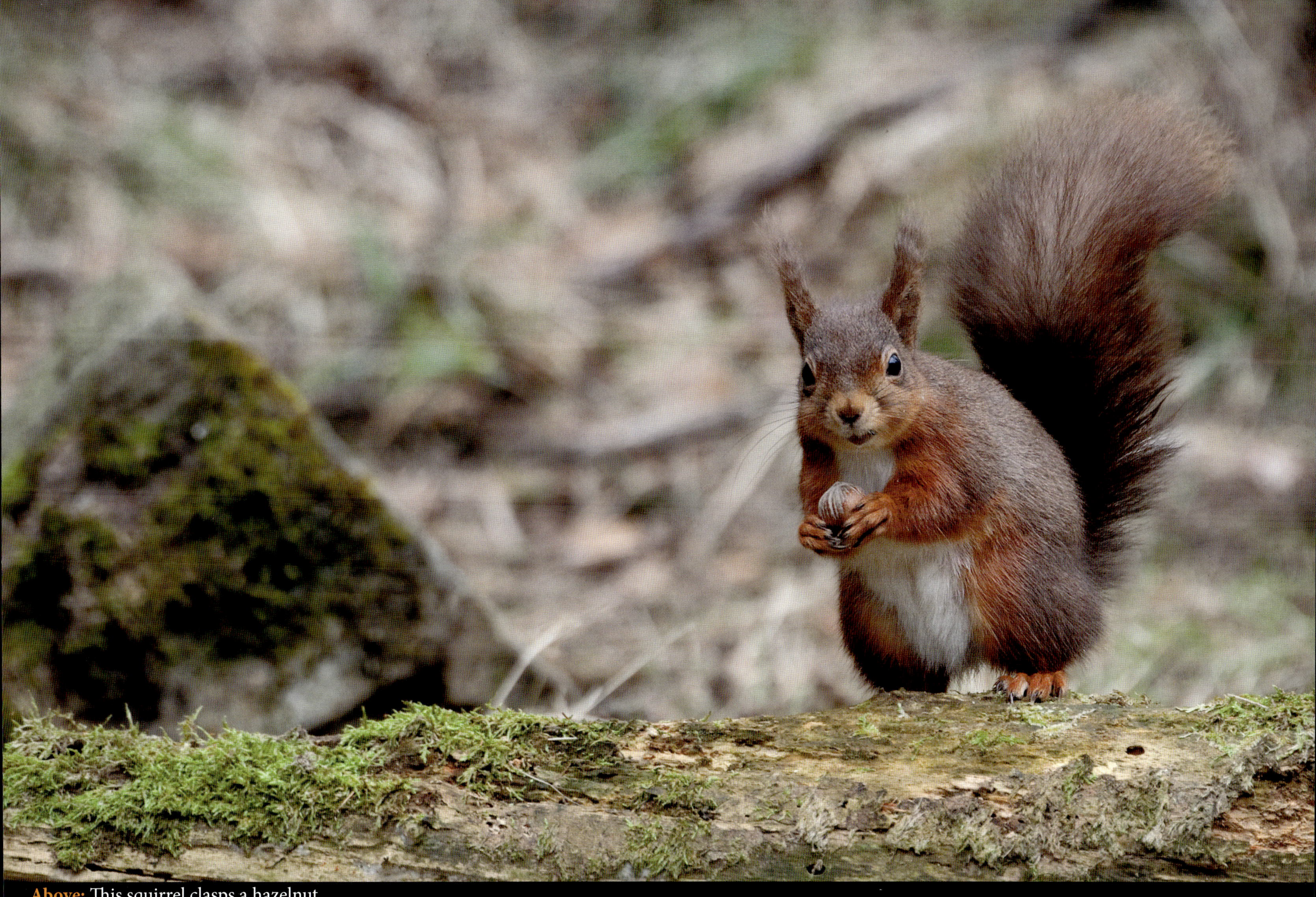

Above: This squirrel clasps a hazelnut.

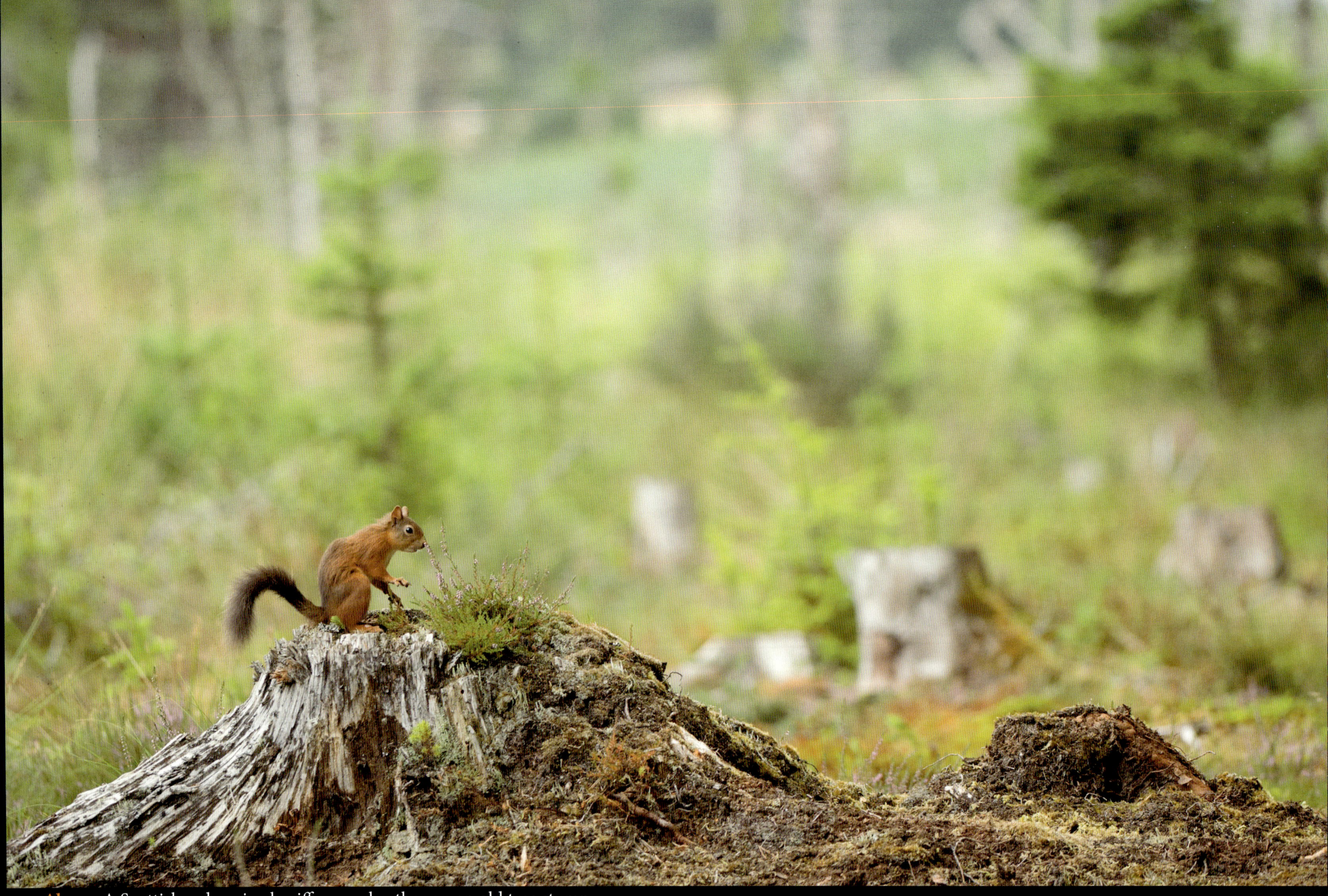

 A Scottish red squirrel sniffs some heather on an old tree stump.

Saving the red squirrel

The best known fact about British red squirrels is that they are under threat from the non-native grey squirrels. Grey squirrels came from North America in 1876, and were released in Henbury Park, Cheshire. As well as this, several other introductions occurred, including one hundred individuals being released in Richmond, Surrey. It is estimated around four million grey squirrels now roam the UK, contrasting with what now amounts to just one hundred and twenty thousand red squirrels.

The main problem with the grey squirrel is that some of them carry the Squirrelpox Virus. Whilst grey squirrels are immune to this, red squirrels are not and suffer a painful death within three weeks of infection. The sight of a red squirrel with its face covered in lesions and scabs is not something anyone wishes to see. It is true that very occasionally red squirrels have been found to have antibodies to the disease, but there is another important issue not often considered by many.

This issue is that the ecological niches of the red and grey squirrels overlap. Ultimately, no two different species can survive within the same niche. Grey squirrels often consume nuts and berries before they have ripened, meaning there is much less food available for red squirrels when the two species coexist. In other words, there is a lot of interspecific competition, and grey squirrels are always one step ahead of the game.

In addition to this, grey squirrels live at much higher densities than red squirrels. That is to say, more greys will live in an area than reds given the chance. This means there are even more mouths to feed, and the natural food sources deplete more quickly. As if this wasn't enough, the physical size of grey squirrels is greater, meaning that they eat a lot more food than the reds too.

Conservation efforts in the UK are very determined to secure the future of one of our most treasured mammals. The national charity *The Red Squirrel Survival*

Trust, a patron of which is HRH Prince of Wales, organise efforts across the UK. *Red Squirrels Northern England* employ a team of rangers in the north of England, and also help to organise several local volunteer groups. Culling is done as humanely as possible, and trail cameras are deployed in a scientific manner to assess the impact this has on red squirrel distribution. These actions keep the grey squirrel at bay until a vaccine is developed.

My mother and I are heavily involved in this conservation effort, and without our work I wouldn't be able to display most of the images in this book. Neither of us enjoys having to do this, but ultimately there are only two options. Either the red squirrel suffers a long and painful death, or the greys are quickly dispatched without knowing much about it.

Those who aren't sure about the cull often say something along the lines of "but it is evolution". The fact is that it is man's fault the grey squirrel is here in the first place, and it is adapted to a harsher environment than ours, meaning that any process of natural selection is unfairly biased. There is but one real option with this issue, and that is to right our wrongs.

Right: A curious squirrel holds a hazelnut between its jaws.
Opposite: This female pauses before scrambling up the tree stump.

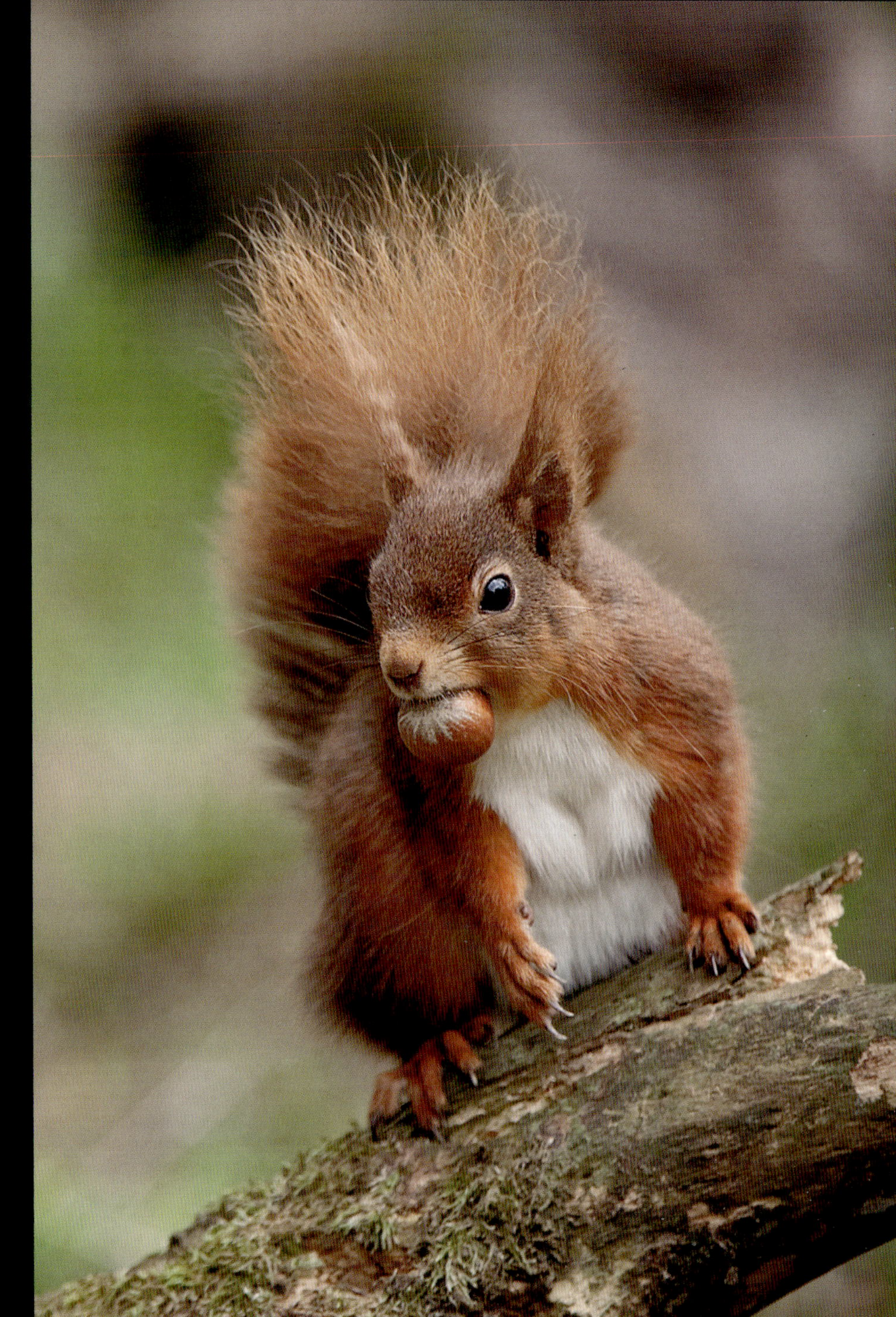

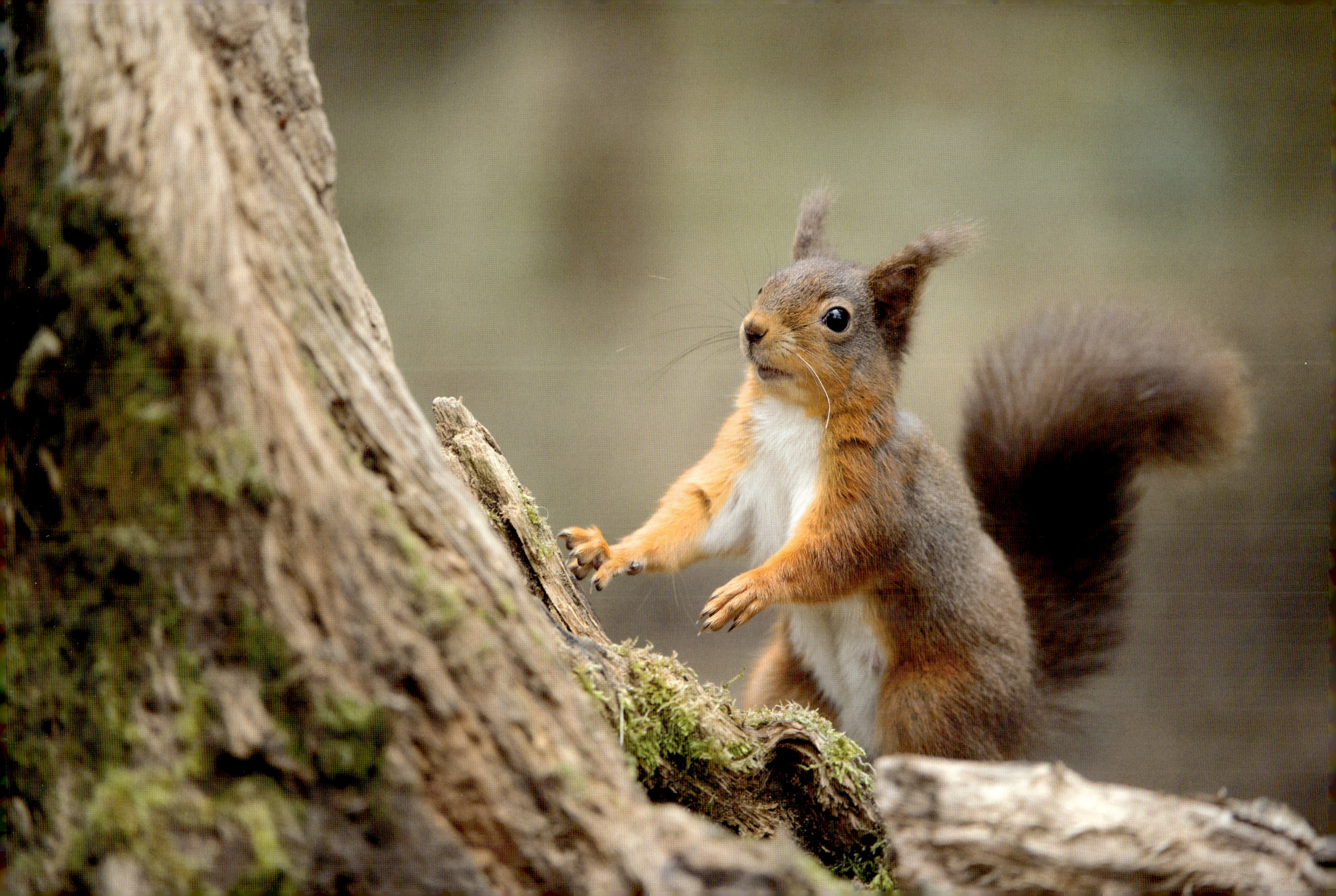

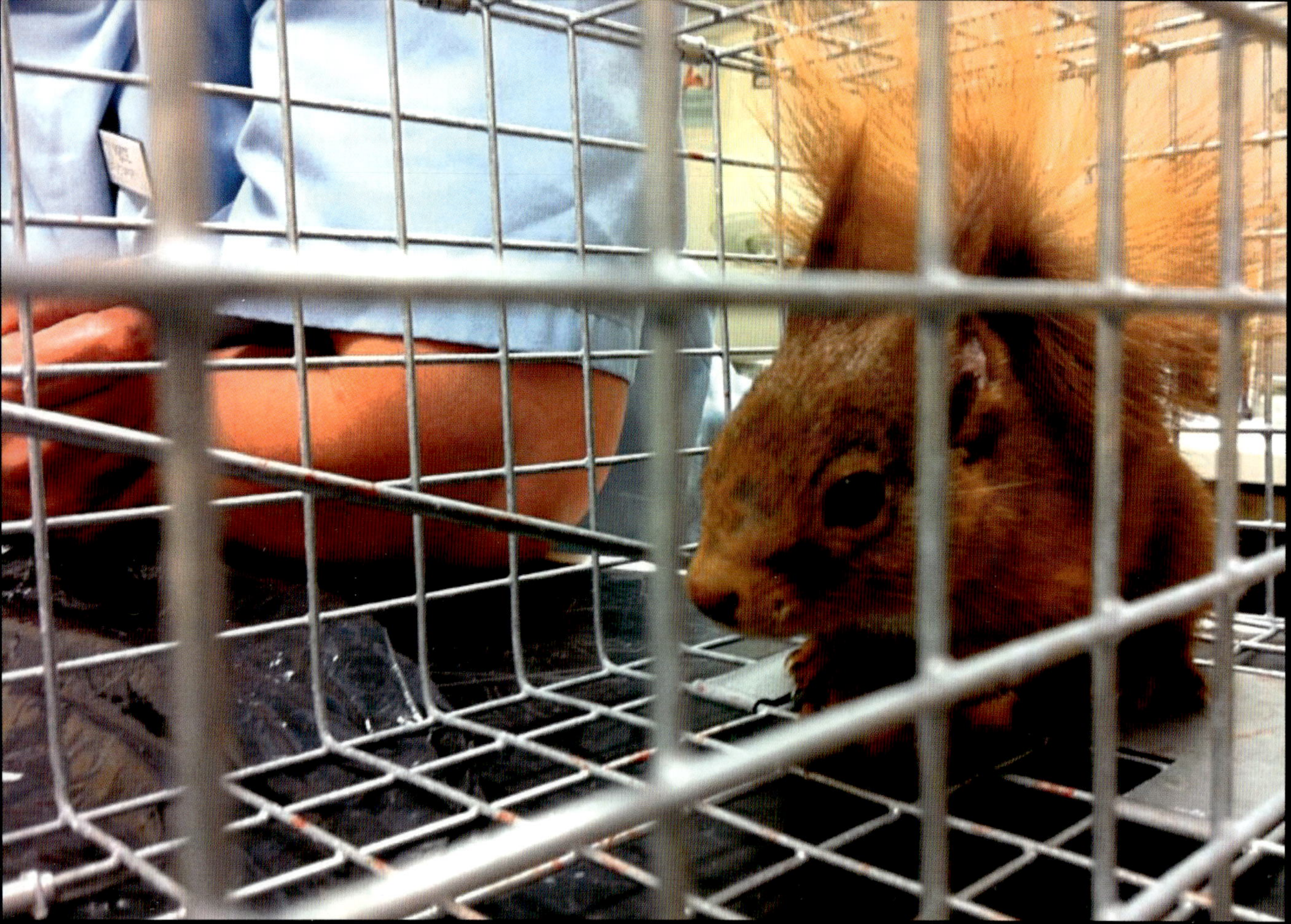

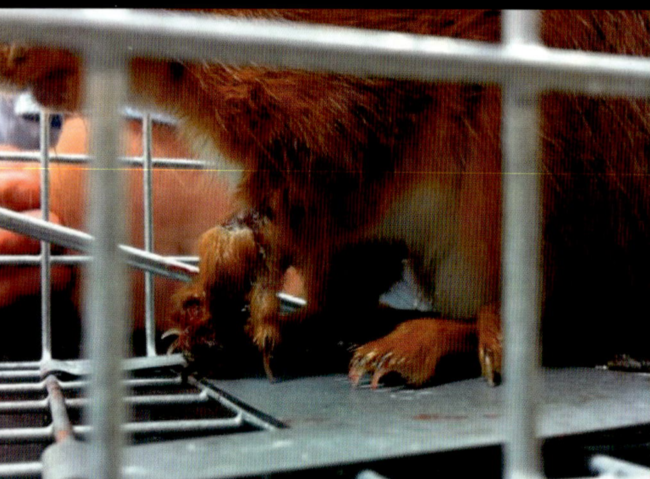

It was spring 2013, and I was once again waiting in the hide. It was a rather lovely morning, with beautiful light and up to four squirrels visiting at once. One squirrel caught my eye however, but not because he was being overly bold. It was quite the opposite, as he was moving slowly and didn't appear to be putting any weight on one of his legs.

Alarm bells began to ring, and I took various images to try and establish what the problem was. On closer inspection, it appeared that this individual had a badly injured paw. I called up two other squirrel fanatics, and we all agreed that it would be worth a trip to the vet.

So the next day I was out setting up four cage traps around the feeding station. It was a hot day, so I was checking them every two hours to ensure no squirrels were stuck inside for very long. I ended up catching four of the five squirrels we had at the time, the last of which was the injured squirrel. This was a good opportunity for me to check the health of the other squirrels too, which is no bad thing.

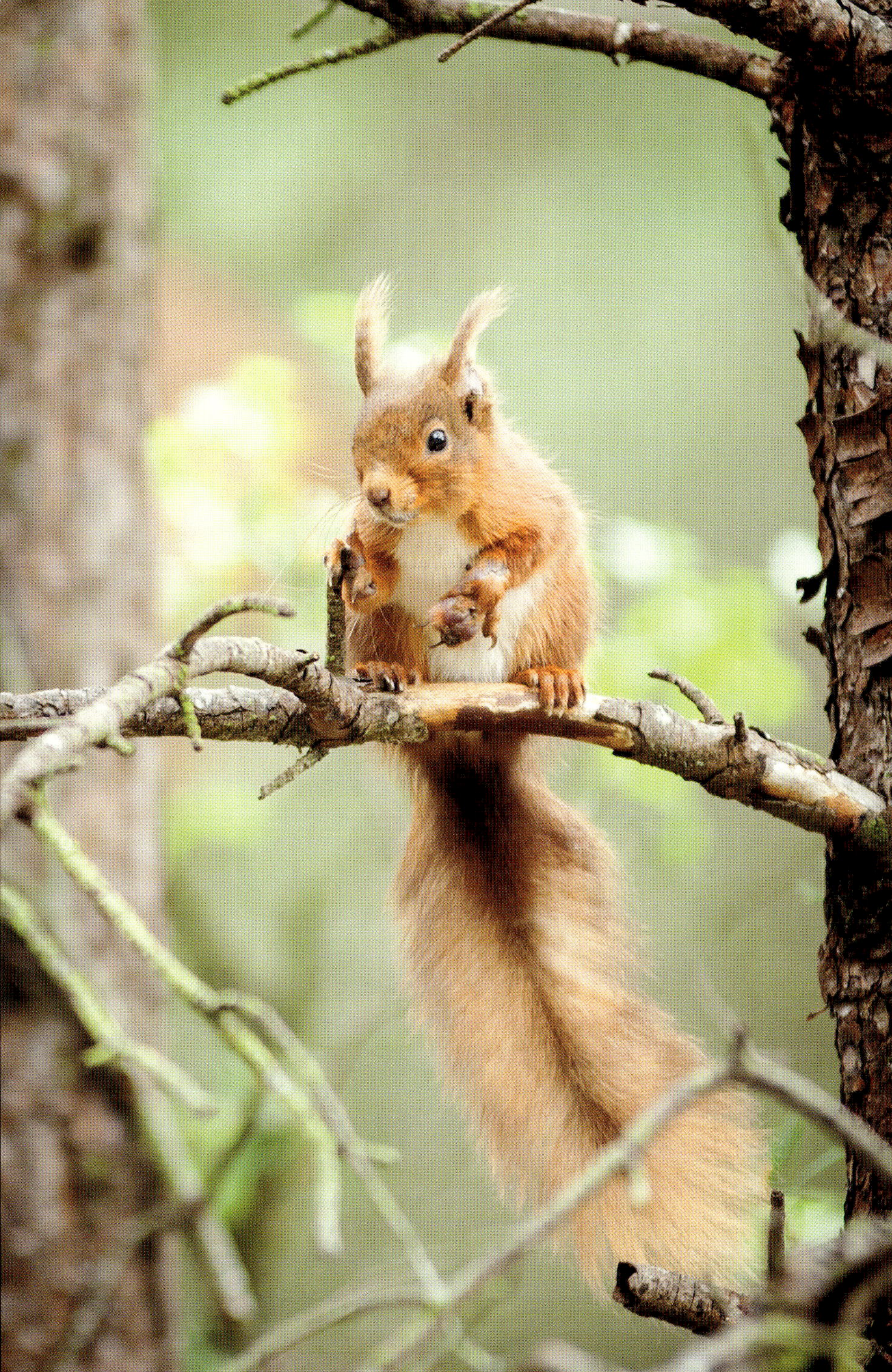

Up close, the injury looked even worse. His paw had swollen and was covered in bad scabs that were spreading up the arm. Thankfully my car had air conditioning, and I was able to keep the environment cool. I placed newspapers over the cage, ensuring that the squirrel was kept in the dark so it remained calm.

The local vet allowed us an emergency appointment, which was very fortunate. After examination, we came to the conclusion that the injury must be from barbed wire or some similar material. After a quick shot of long-lasting antibiotics, the squirrel (now named "Lucky") was released back into his wood.

Unfortunately, this release coincided with the annual shift in red squirrel populations. Many of my favourite squirrels moved out of the woodland in search of new territories, being replaced by a new group. This meant that I didn't see what happened to Lucky in the end, but hopefully he made a full recovery.

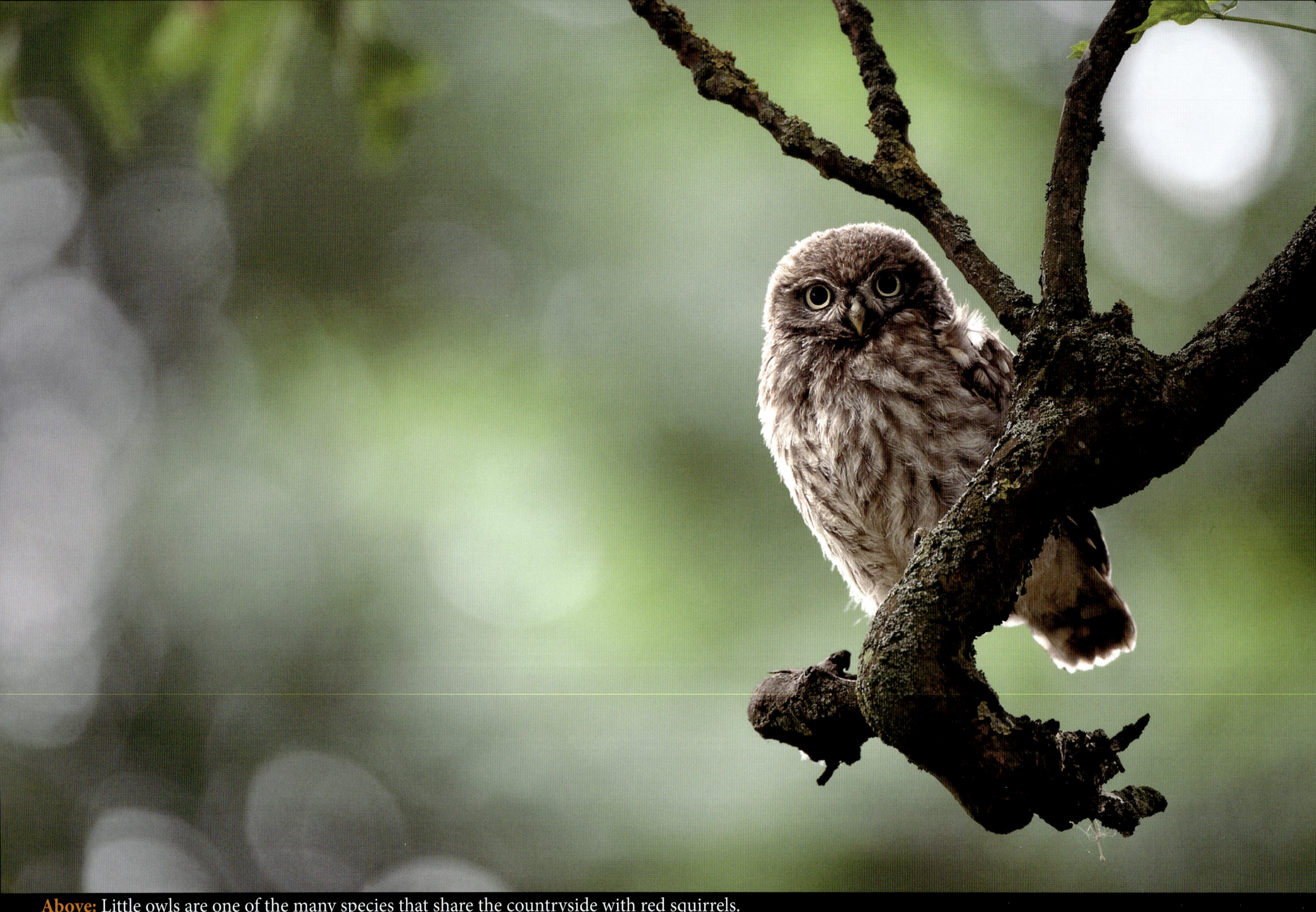

Above: Little owls are one of the many species that share the countryside with red squirrels.

Chapter 9

Branching out

The ecosystems within woodlands are held together with such delicacy by a number of participants. Each organism plays its own special role in keeping its environment stable, and this is the reason that we often hear of ecosystems coming under threat from the removal of just a few species.

When I'm not in my red squirrel hide, I like to capture a wide range of different species. Every animal comes with its own challenges, and I will often spend long periods in a hide without seeing anything. However, a species that has bucked this trend is the little owl. Having located a family of little owls nesting in an old barn in the local farmer's field, I acquired the necessary permission and set up my tent hide underneath a big oak tree outside the nest. I left the hide there for a couple of weeks to ensure they became fully accustomed to its presence, and then waited inside with my camera.

An hour passed and I had seen no movement at the nest entrance at all, so naturally I began to wonder if they were aware that I was there. Then, looking out of the small window to my left, I noticed an adult little owl sitting on a branch staring directly at me. Suddenly, as if by magic, the entire family began to appear around me. The juveniles began to call, nagging their parents for food, and one shoved the original adult off its beautifully gnarled branch. It was at this moment that I captured one of my favourite photographs, and all within an hour or two of my first session.

However, there are extremes at both ends of the spectrum. I travelled to Scotland to photograph the elusive pine marten, and spent fifteen hours in a hide each day waiting for them. Unfortunately for me they clearly had better things to do, and I didn't get one sighting. The pine marten, whilst being an incredibly beautiful creature, is the only mammal in the UK capable of catching a squirrel in the tree canopy. They are built for similar agility to the squirrel, and are capable of moving quickly through the trees.

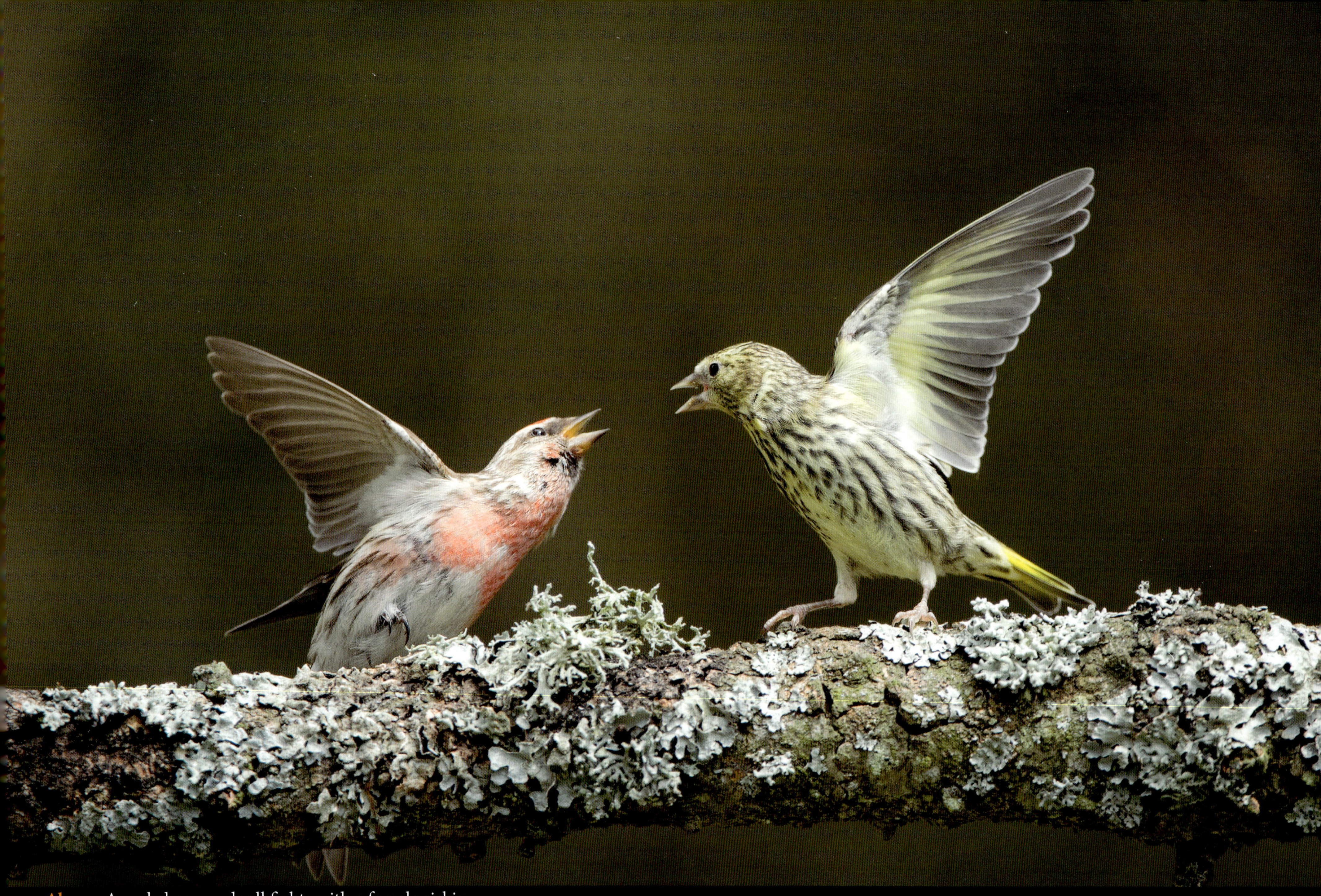

Above: A male lesser redpoll fights with a female siskin.

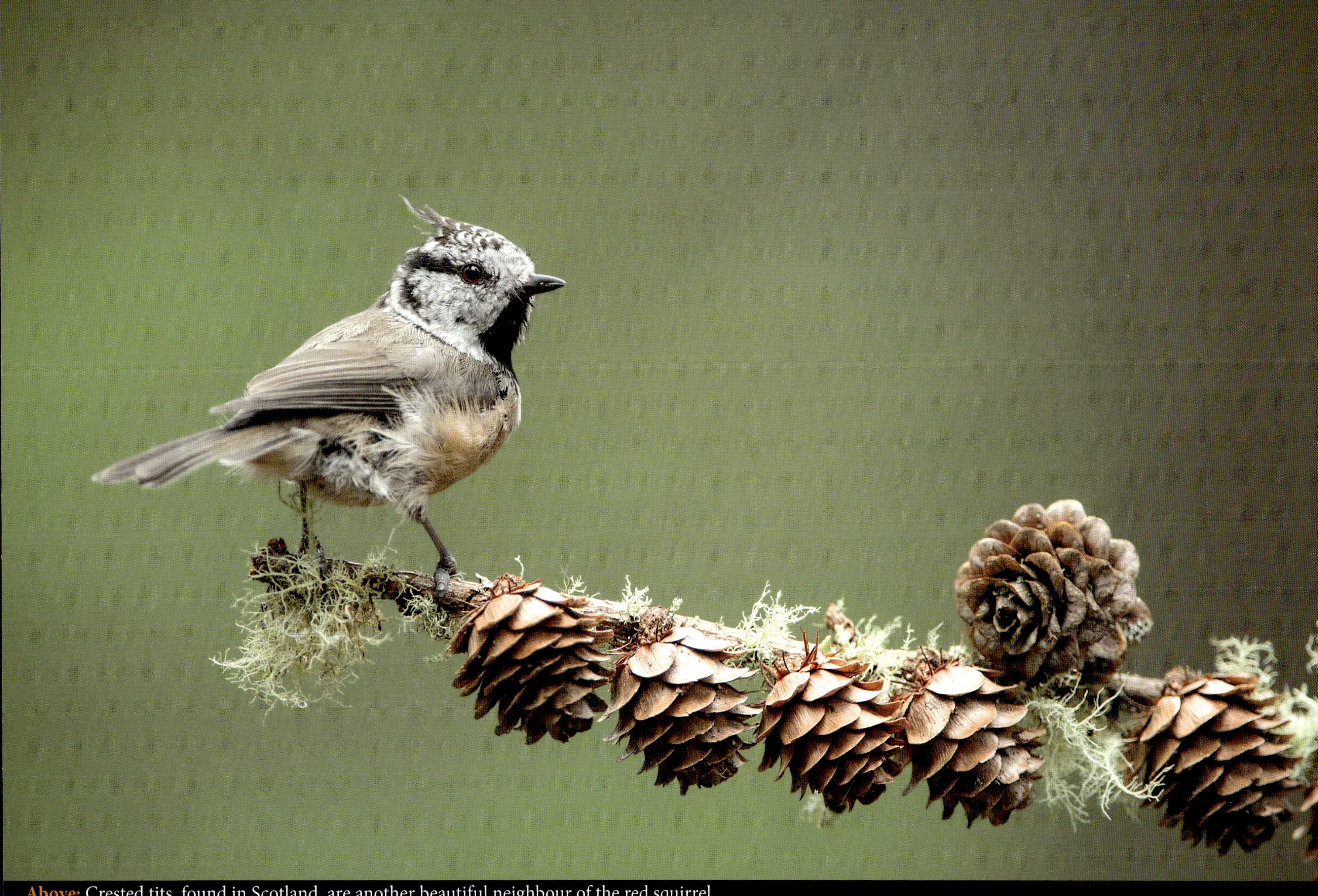

Above: Crested tits, found in Scotland, are another beautiful neighbour of the red squirrel.

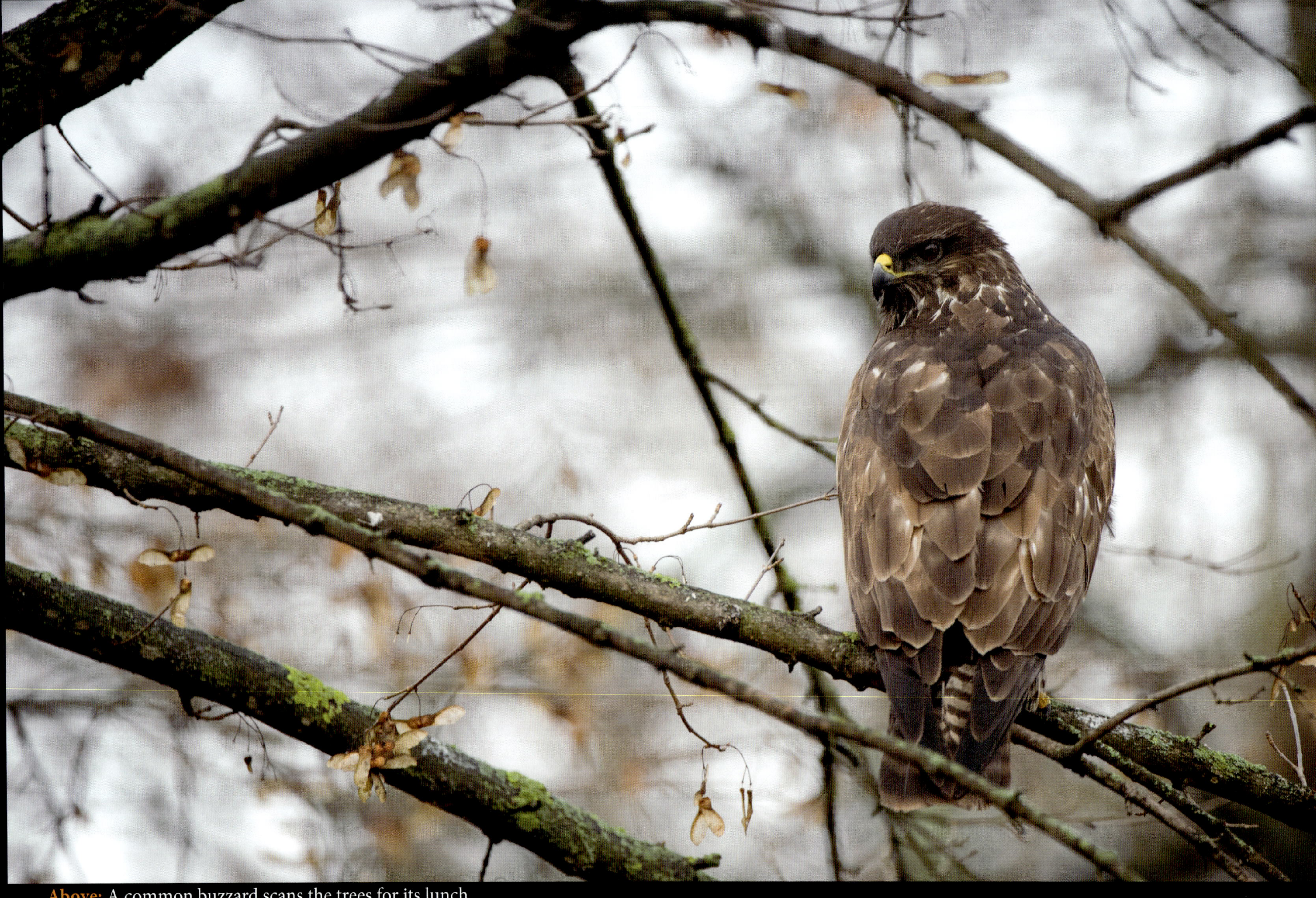

Above: A common buzzard scans the trees for its lunch.

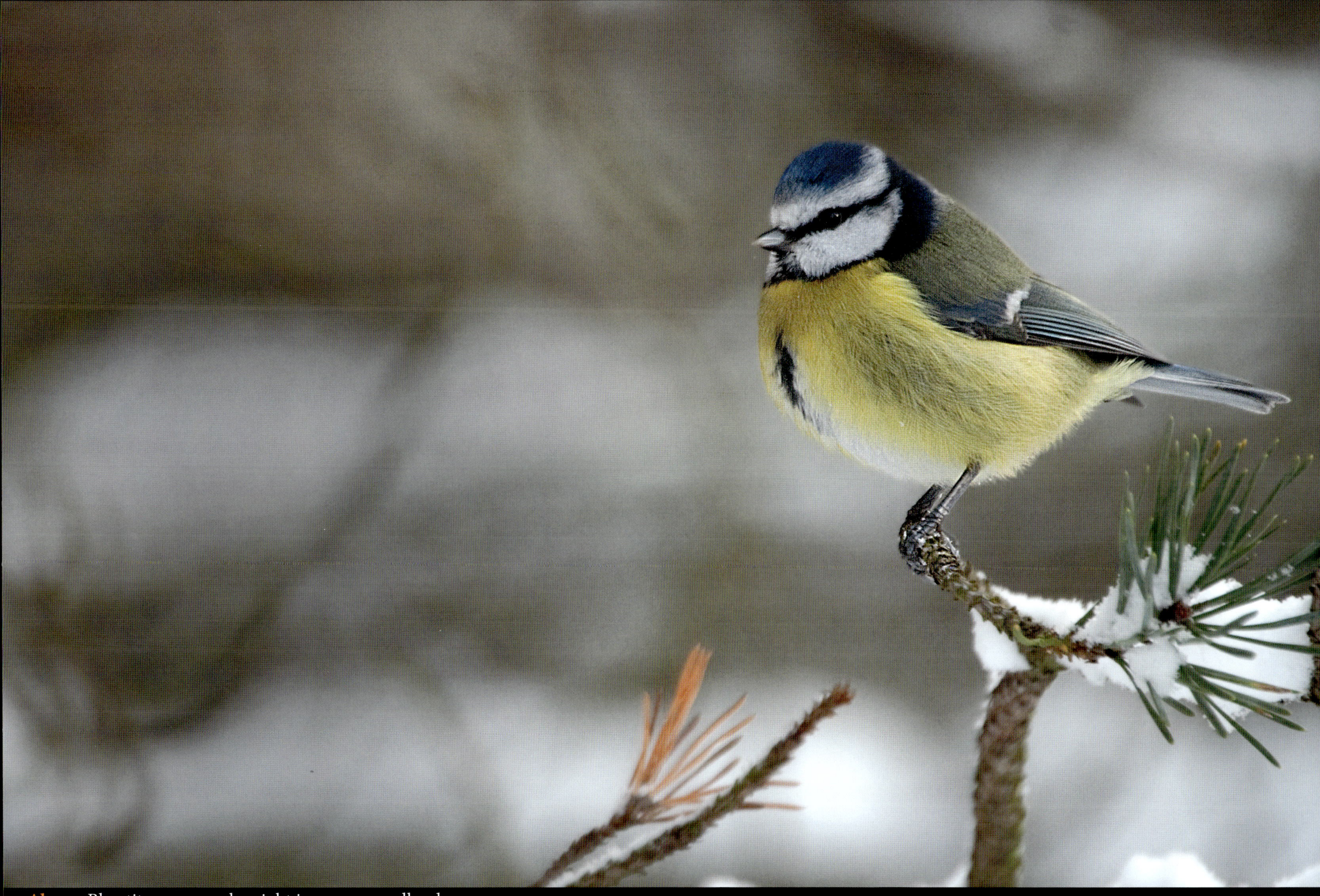

 Blue tits are a regular sight in many woodlands.

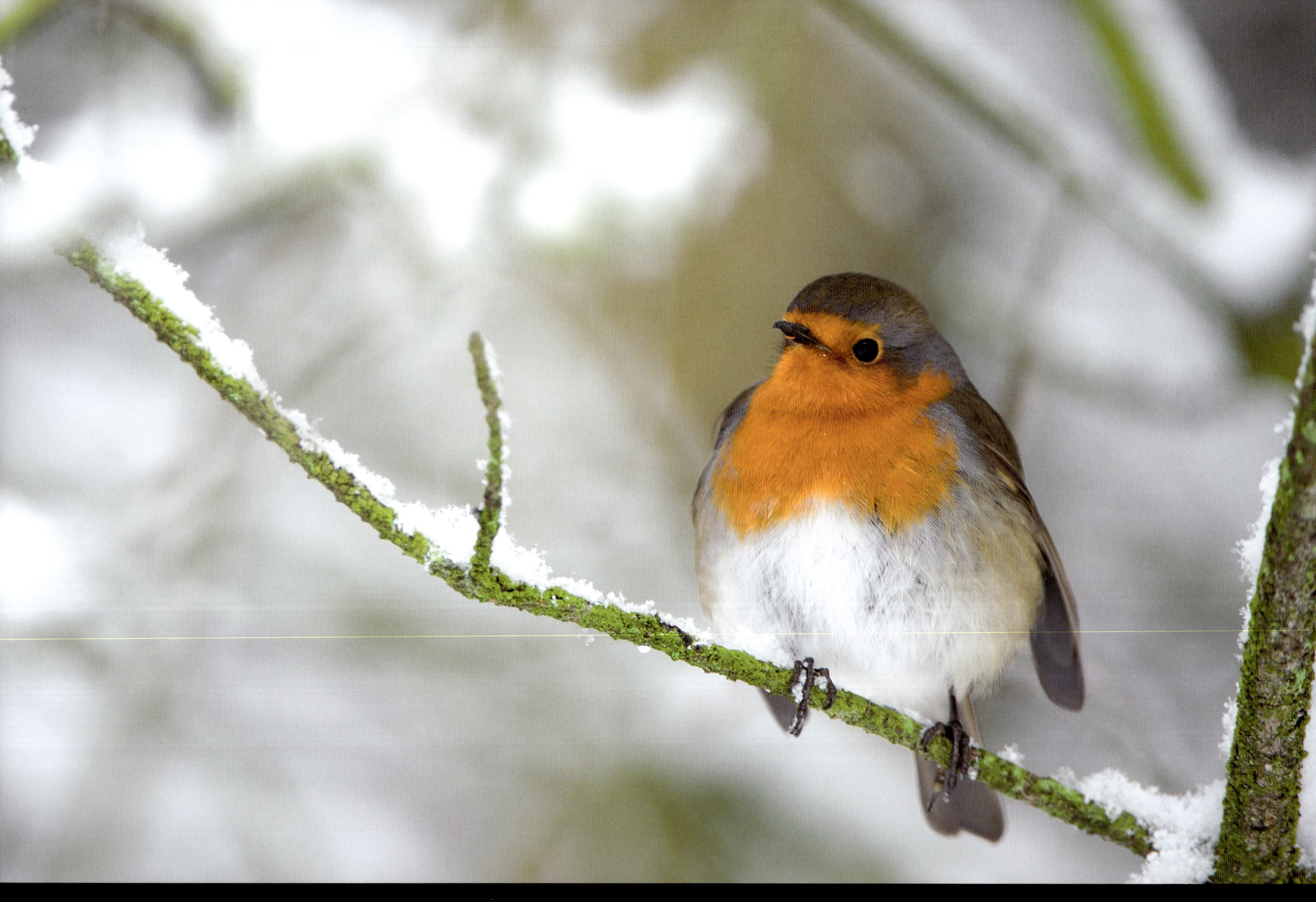

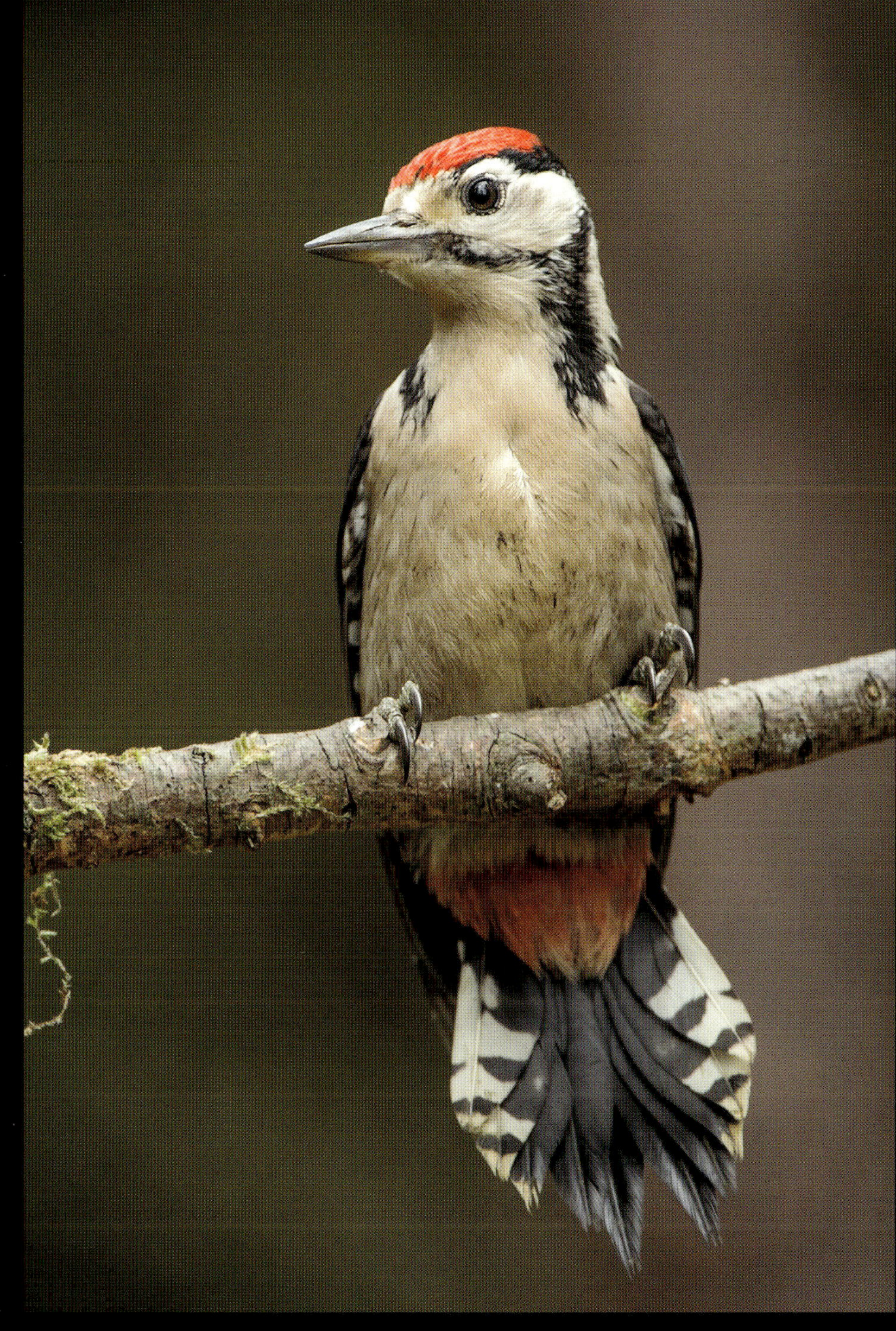

This is not seen as a problem, because any casualties at the hands of a pine marten are sustainable. Pine martens are native to the UK, so any predation is part of the overall balance. In fact, they rarely eat red squirrels and will feed more on other small mammals like voles. The red squirrel spends much more time in the tree tops than grey squirrels, which are more likely to feed on the ground, and for this reason pine martens are likely to be a helpful ally to the reds. If the comeback of the pine marten continues, grey squirrels will need to watch their backs.

Other predators of the red squirrel include the goshawk and the common buzzard, but again casualties are a rare occurrence. Buzzards are notoriously hard to photograph. Even when they are hovering and screeching above you, as soon as you move towards them or step out of your car they will glide away effortlessly. Using roadkill, I have baited areas for months in an attempt to photograph them. A trail camera would show me that they were coming down to feed, but as soon as I stepped into my well-hidden hide they would be nowhere to be seen. On one occasion a buzzard did begin to circle downwards to the pheasant carcass laid out for it, but at that exact moment a quad bike roared through the field and scared it away. That is the challenge of wildlife photography though, and it makes it all worth it once you succeed in capturing the image you are after.

Left: Juvenile great spotted woodpeckers have a red cap.
Opposite: Robins are territorial birds and will sing all year round to ensure their territories are maintained.

A variety of other woodland birds visit my hide in Northumberland.
When the squirrels are busy elsewhere, I am able to enjoy
photographing everything from great spotted woodpeckers to
goldfinches. Whilst the smaller birds may move very quickly, it does
provide an excellent opportunity to train my reflexes on the shutter
button. Capturing them fighting over the prime position near the
bird feeders is time consuming and results in plenty of out of focus
images on the memory card, but it can become quite addictive.
Woodpeckers are slightly slower in flight but are extremely skittish,
and a single twitch of the lens will often cause them to disappear.
The juvenile birds, identified by their red cap, have proved more
bold around the hide than the adults.

In Scotland, some squirrels have to share the tree tops with what
would seem an unlikely companion. Capercaillie are huge birds of
the grouse family and can be seen to roost in the tops of spindly
pine trees. The markings on their tail feathers fascinate me, and
I have seen images of some with what looks like Chinese writing
scrawled on them. These impressive birds make an incredible call
when trying to gain the attention of females. It is very hard to
describe, but it consists of various different pitches. Parts of their
call are so deep that humans cannot hear it, but it is these tones that
allow it to carry across large distances. They are aggressive birds
when lekking, so I would think that any sensible squirrel would
keep its distance and find some other trees to climb up.

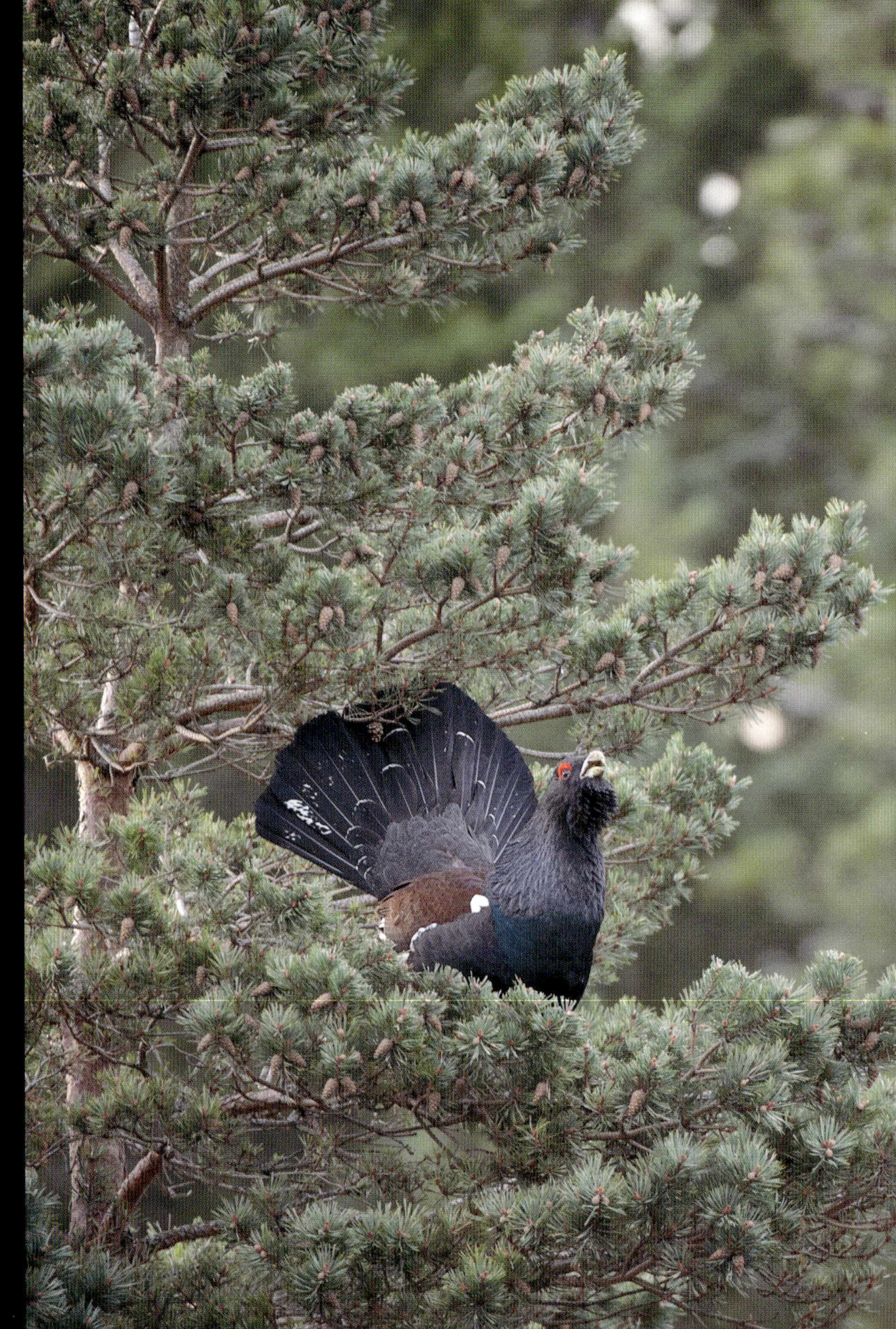

Right: The large capercaillie displays from the top of a pine tree.
Opposite: Males put on a fantastic display to attract females.

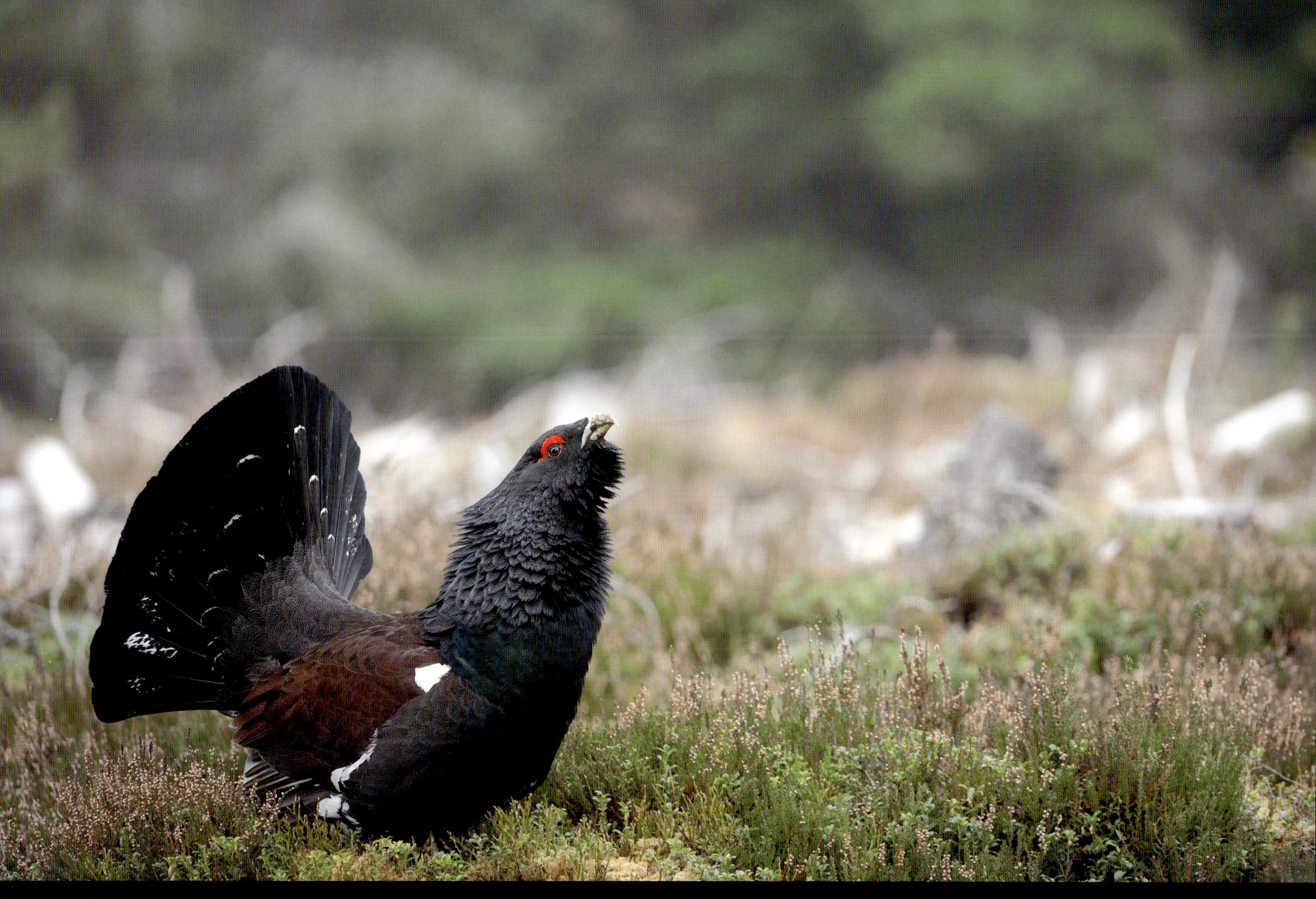

Roe deer are a classic woodland mammal. They move silently, with
their ears pricked to alert them of approaching predators. When I
was younger, I went looking for roe deer in Kielder Forest with a
ranger. It was very early in the morning, and we had just arrived at
a clearing deep inside the forest. We were walking quietly along a
track, and spotted a beautiful buck around a corner. We dropped
to the ground, allowing us to remain hidden from the deer. It was
standing in the middle of a stream in an almost fairytale setting.
Sometimes, at home, I spot a deer moving through the woodland,
but it is a rare sight for me.

Right: An adult little owl. Could this be the juvenile I saw previously all grown up?
Opposite: The roe deer is another mammal that shares woodlands with red
squirrels.

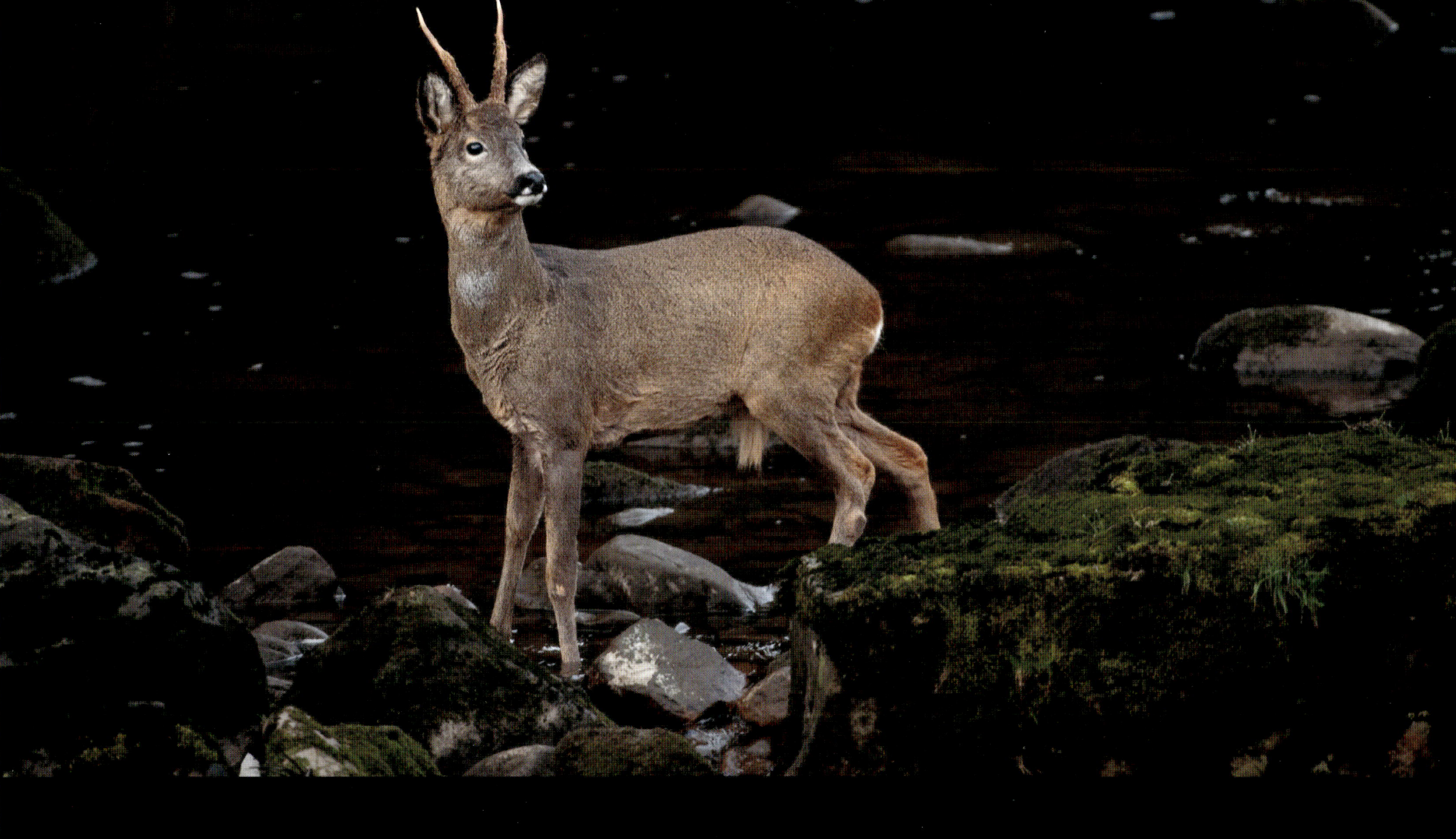

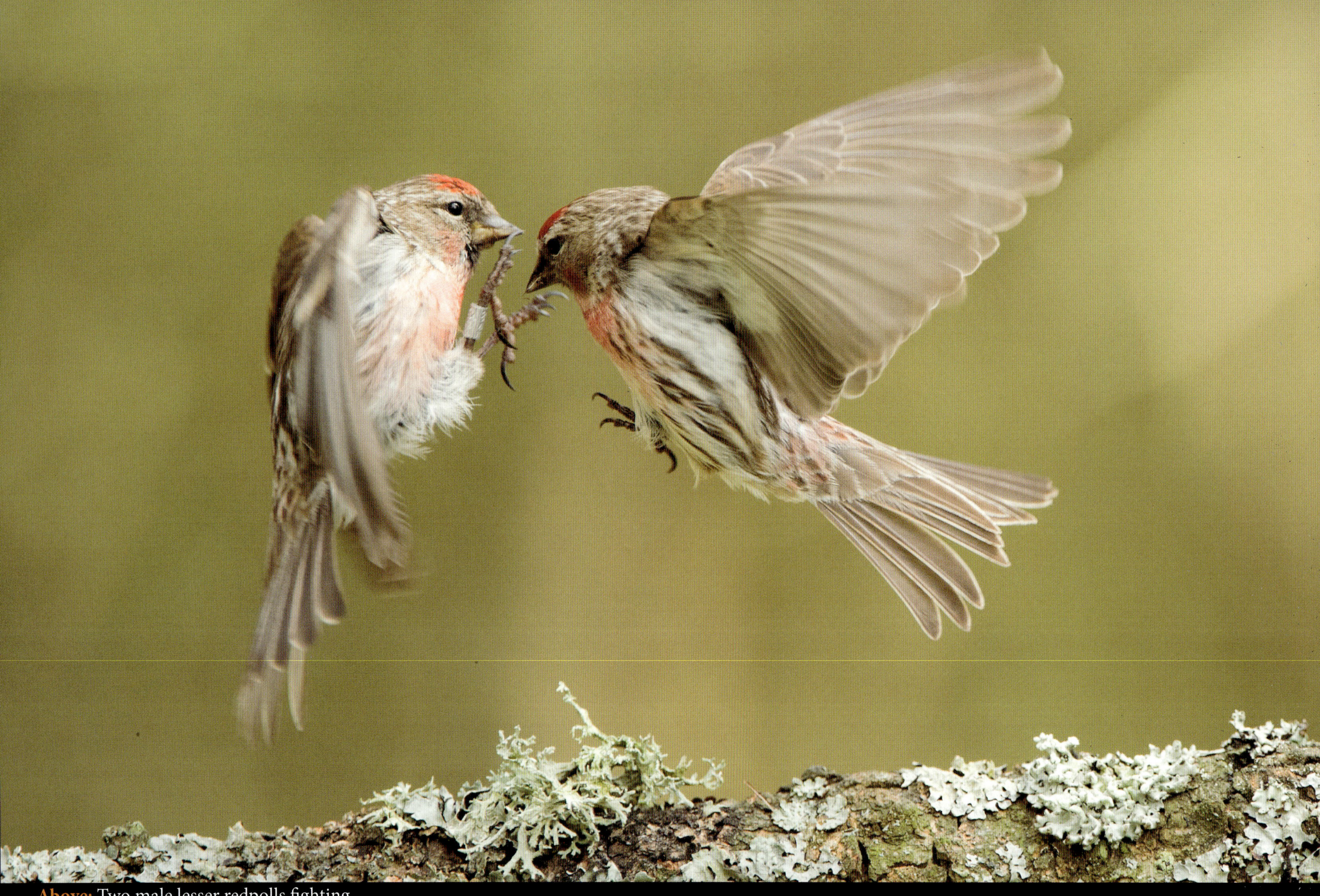

Above: Two male lesser redpolls fighting.

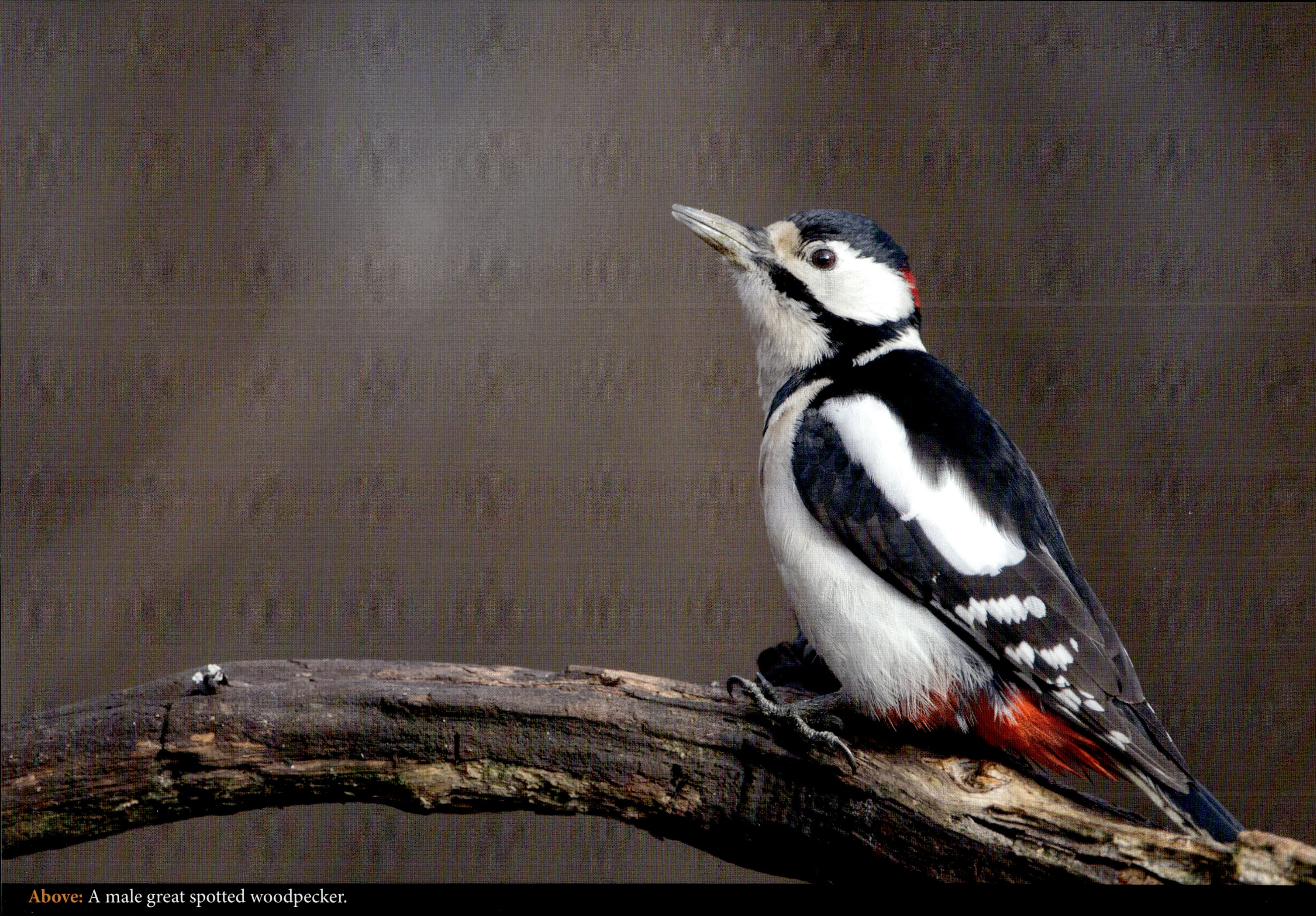

Above: A male great spotted woodpecker.

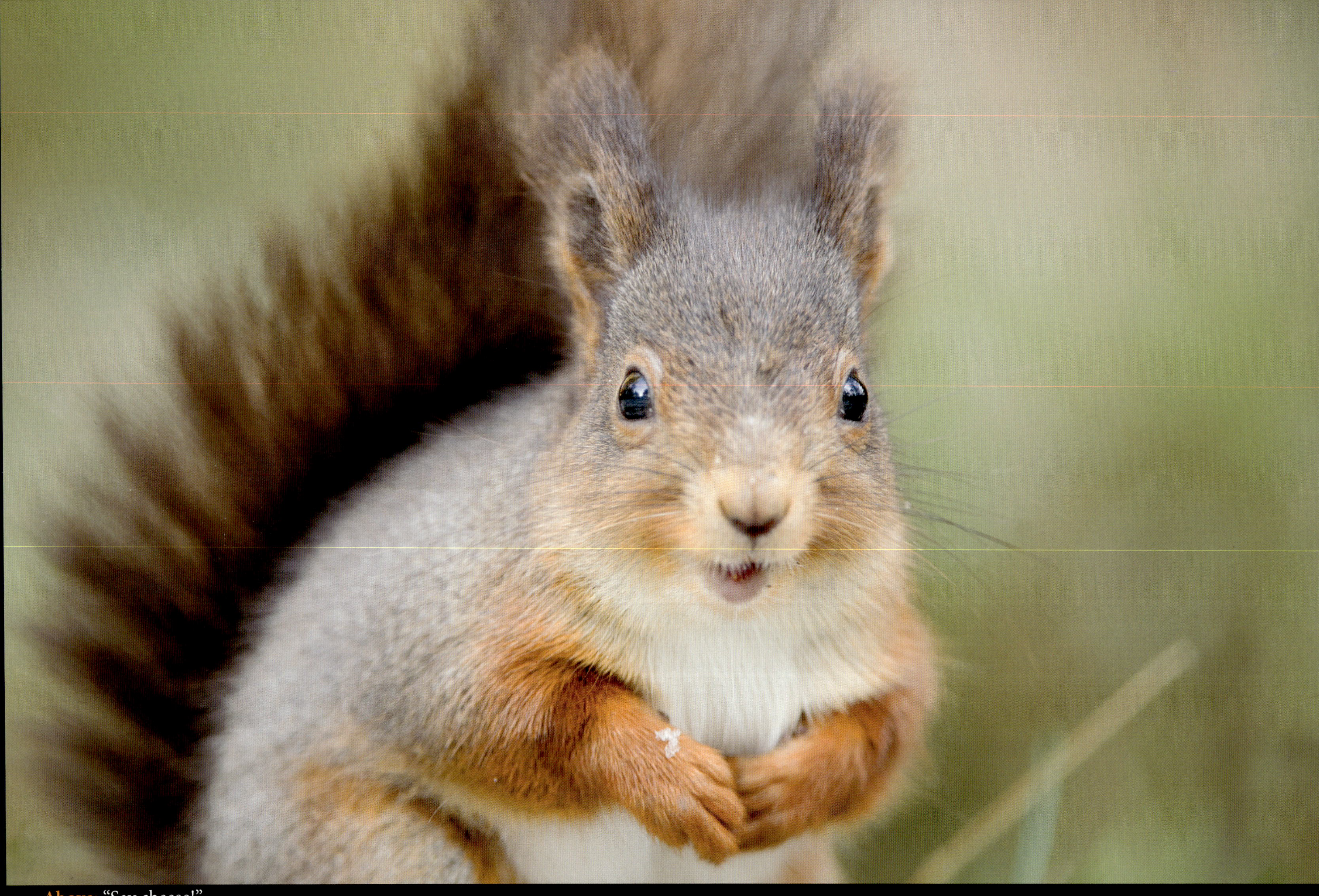

How to find squirrels

I am often asked where to find red squirrels, which is not surprising since they are such charming animals. The major difficulty is finding a location, since they are no longer as numerous as they used to be. In England, the best places are in Northumberland. Kielder Forest is the best bet, as it is the last major stronghold we have, which holds twenty five percent of the UK's red squirrel population. Otherwise, traveling further north to Scotland should also provide good opportunities.

If you are lucky enough to have regular access to a spot frequented by red squirrels, it is worth setting up some feeders. Squirrel feeders are not too expensive and can hold a reasonable amount of food, whilst also sheltering it from the rain. They are boxes with clear fronts and hinged lids, allowing the squirrels to lift it open and grab a nut. I remember seeing an image of a red squirrel sitting inside one of these feeders, with another squirrel sitting on the lid and trapping it inside.

These feeders should be secured to the side of a tree, since reds are more comfortable at heights than on the ground. If a grey squirrel does turn up into the area, you must remove the feeder and disinfect it to avoid transferring Squirrelpox Virus. Until the grey has been removed, you should scatter the food around instead to prevent the two species from using the same surfaces on a regular basis.

The next job is to decide what you are going to feed them with. The ideal food is hazelnuts, as they are very good for them. They are reasonably costly if you are feeding them a lot, but it is worth it to keep their diet healthy. Other possible foods include raw peanuts (definitely not salted or any other type), but you should mix these with other nuts. Only feeding a squirrel with peanuts could cause calcium deficiency, so occasionally treating them to a slice of apple will help keep a balanced diet. If you can find a deer antler, hang it on the side of a tree as this provides them with an even greater source of calcium.

I find that the squirrels love sunflower hearts too, although these shouldn't be purposefully given in large quantities as they are very oily. Sometimes I think they love them too much, because they will often sit below the bird feeders filling up on all the seed that the birds have discarded below. So instead of eating all the tactfully placed hazelnuts, they would just take a couple and then leave because they were full up. To combat this issue I bought a bird feeder that had a tray fitted to the bottom. The birds waste an awful amount of seed, and the tray catches all the bits they drop. This

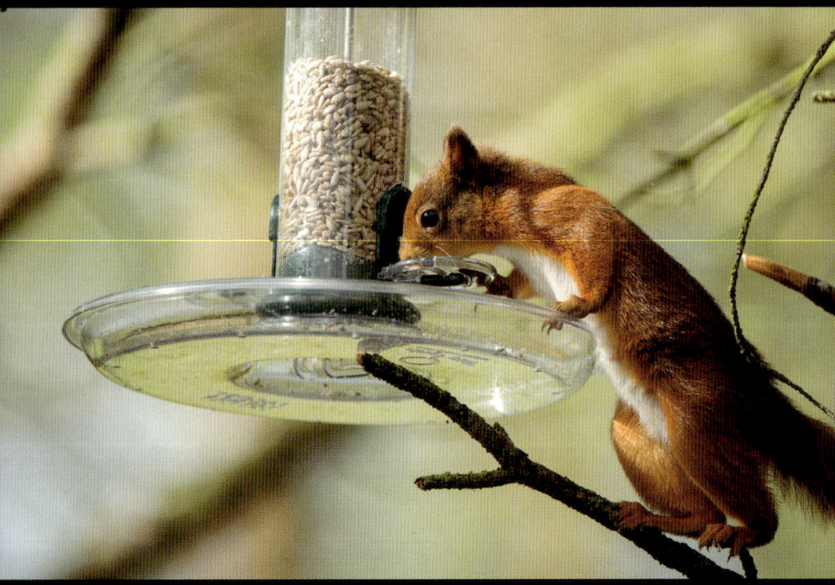

Above: "Scooter" overcomes my cunning plan.
Right: "Blondie" stares down the lens.
Opposite: Foraging amongst primroses.

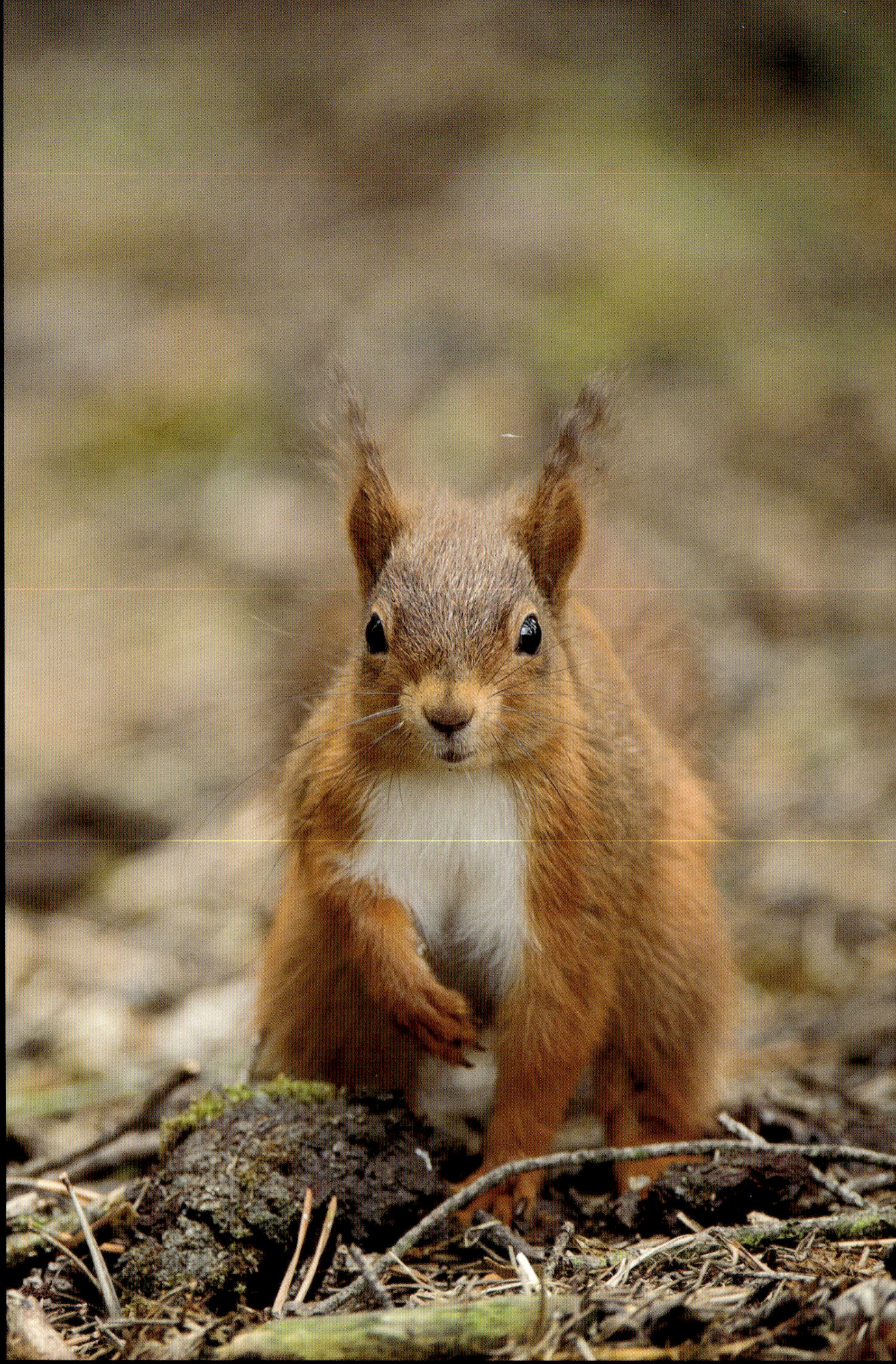

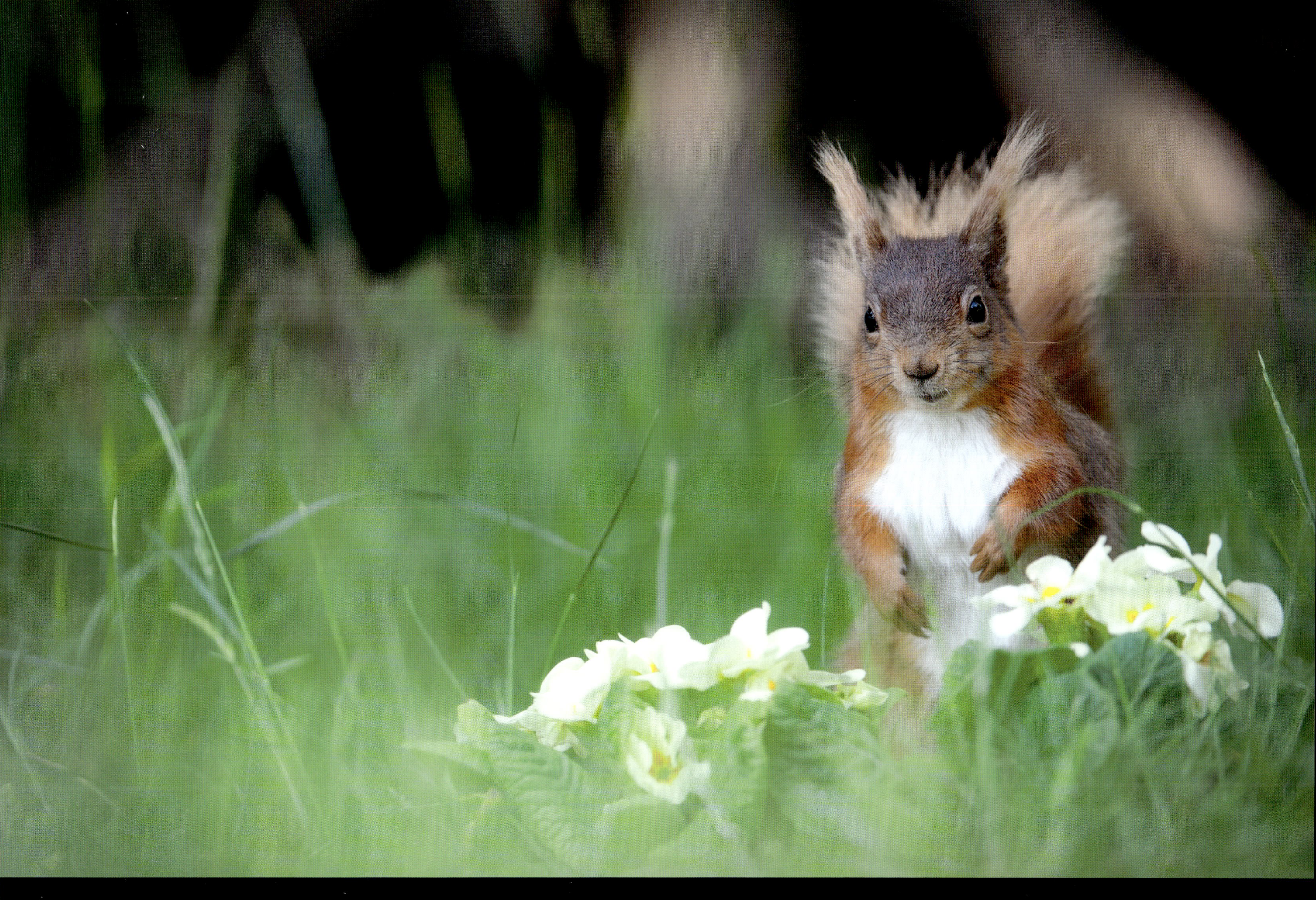

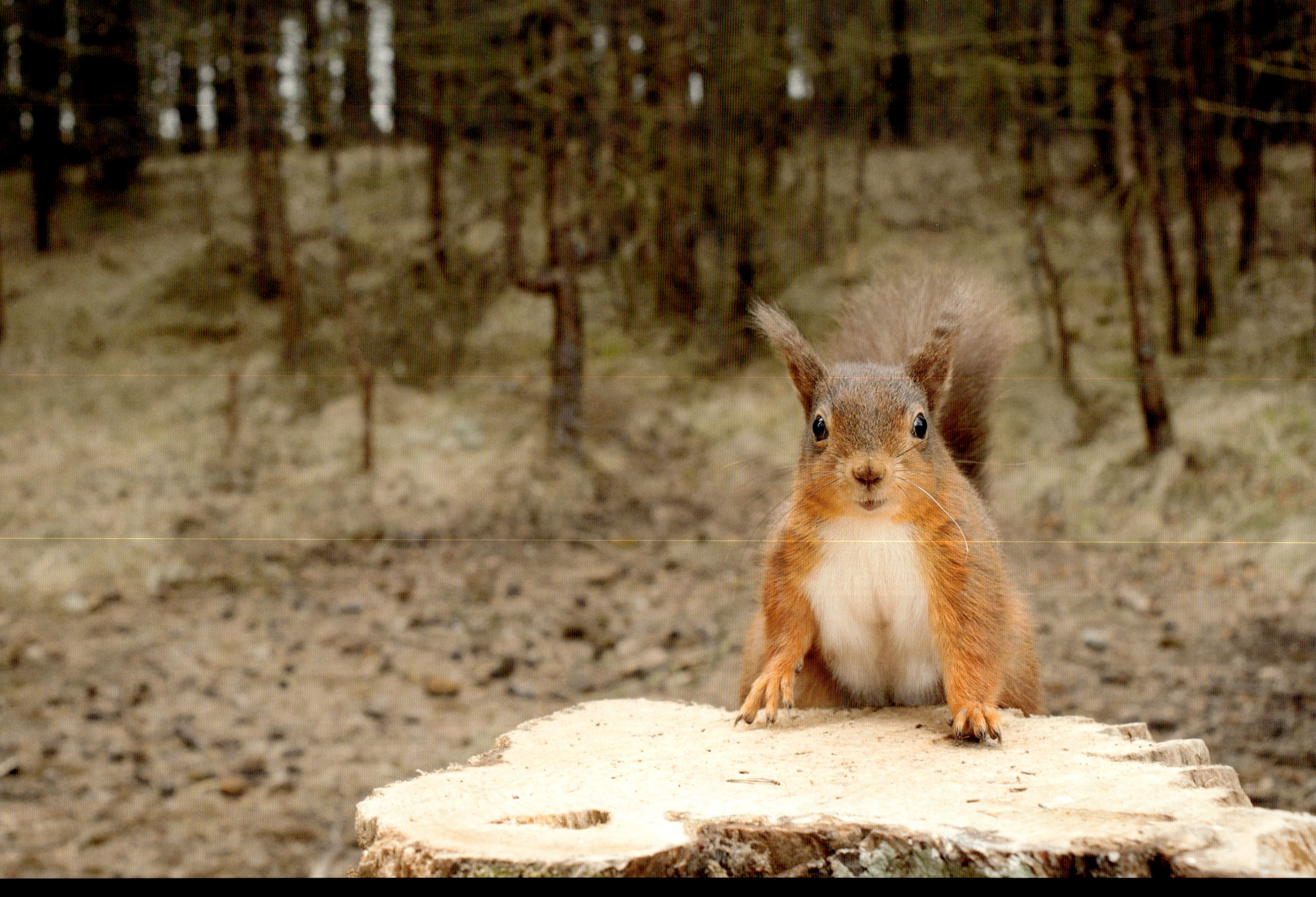

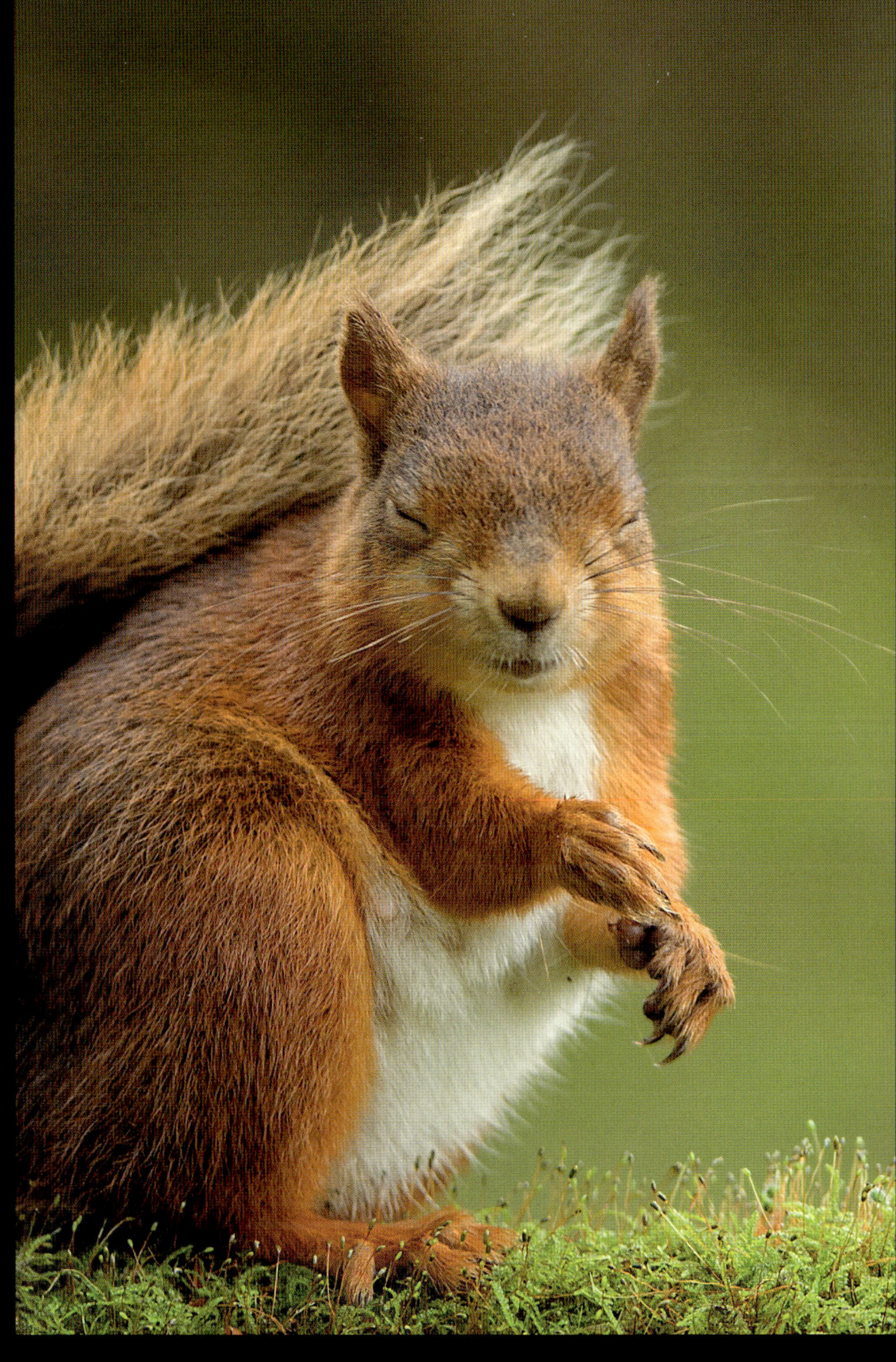

worked for a week or so, until the squirrel worked out that it could jump from the side of a tree onto the bird feeder and munch away from there.

If there are squirrels in the area they will find the nut feeders, as they are foraging animals. A pop-up tent hide provides cover for you whilst you are photographing. This is what I use, and it means that any sudden movements are hidden from view. The squirrels know I am there, as they can see through the opening, but as long as I stay in the hide they are not bothered by me.

Woodlands are scattered with fallen trees, logs and mossy rocks. These all make for excellent images. Placing hazelnuts around the new props will entice the squirrel to explore around the more photogenic areas that this will create. This is different to using a

Left: Sometimes it gets a little tiring being the star of the show.
Opposite: Waiting at the dinner table.

static feeder, because the squirrels are forced to be constantly on the move. With a feeder on the ground, they are sat in one place with their head in a dispenser, causing them to be in a more vulnerable position.

With time, you will begin to learn their behavioural patterns. This is invaluable information, and with it you can predict movements and start to capture images that others may miss.

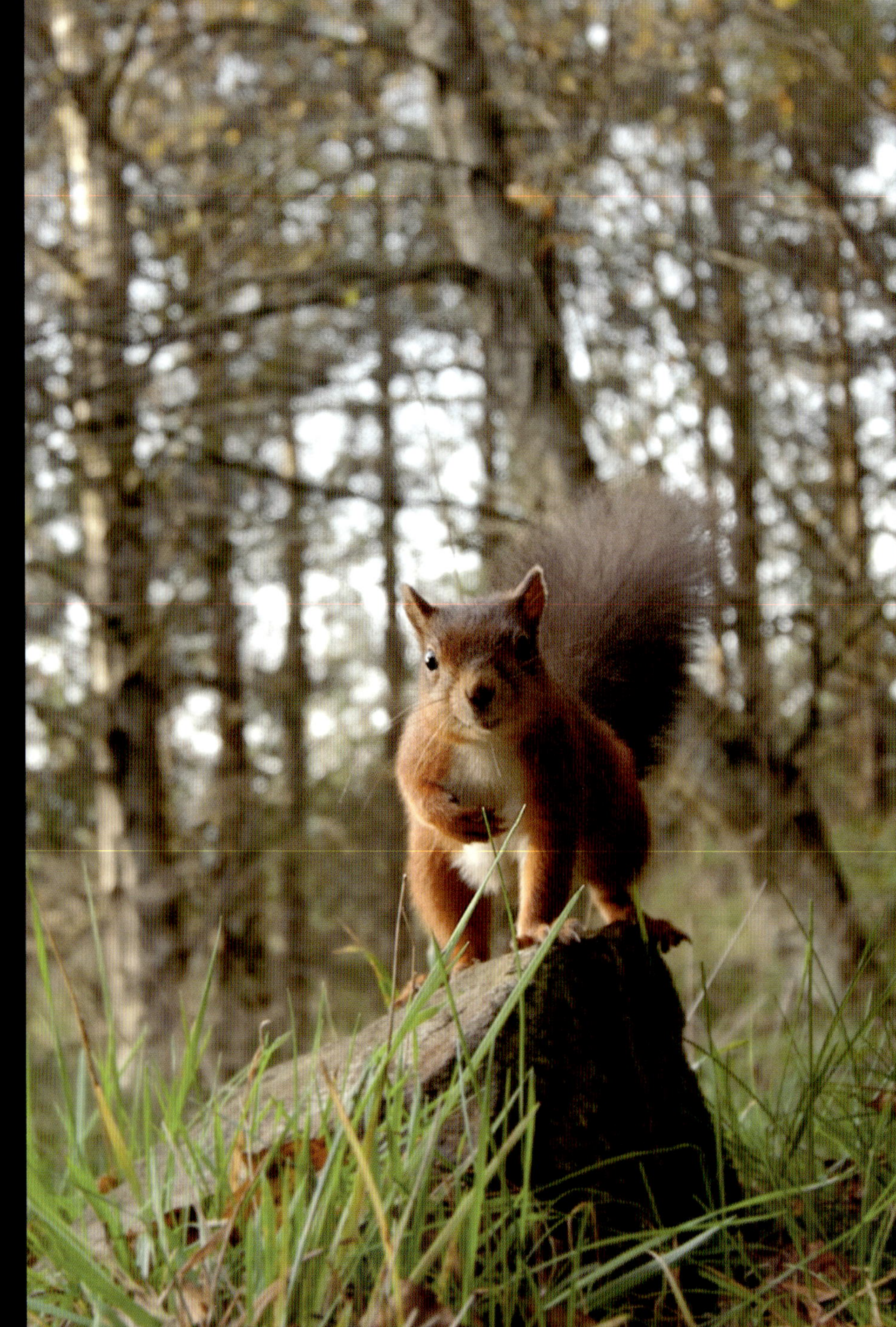

Right: Squirrels often clutch their chests when surveying their surroundings.
Opposite: The bushy tail is shown off in this image.

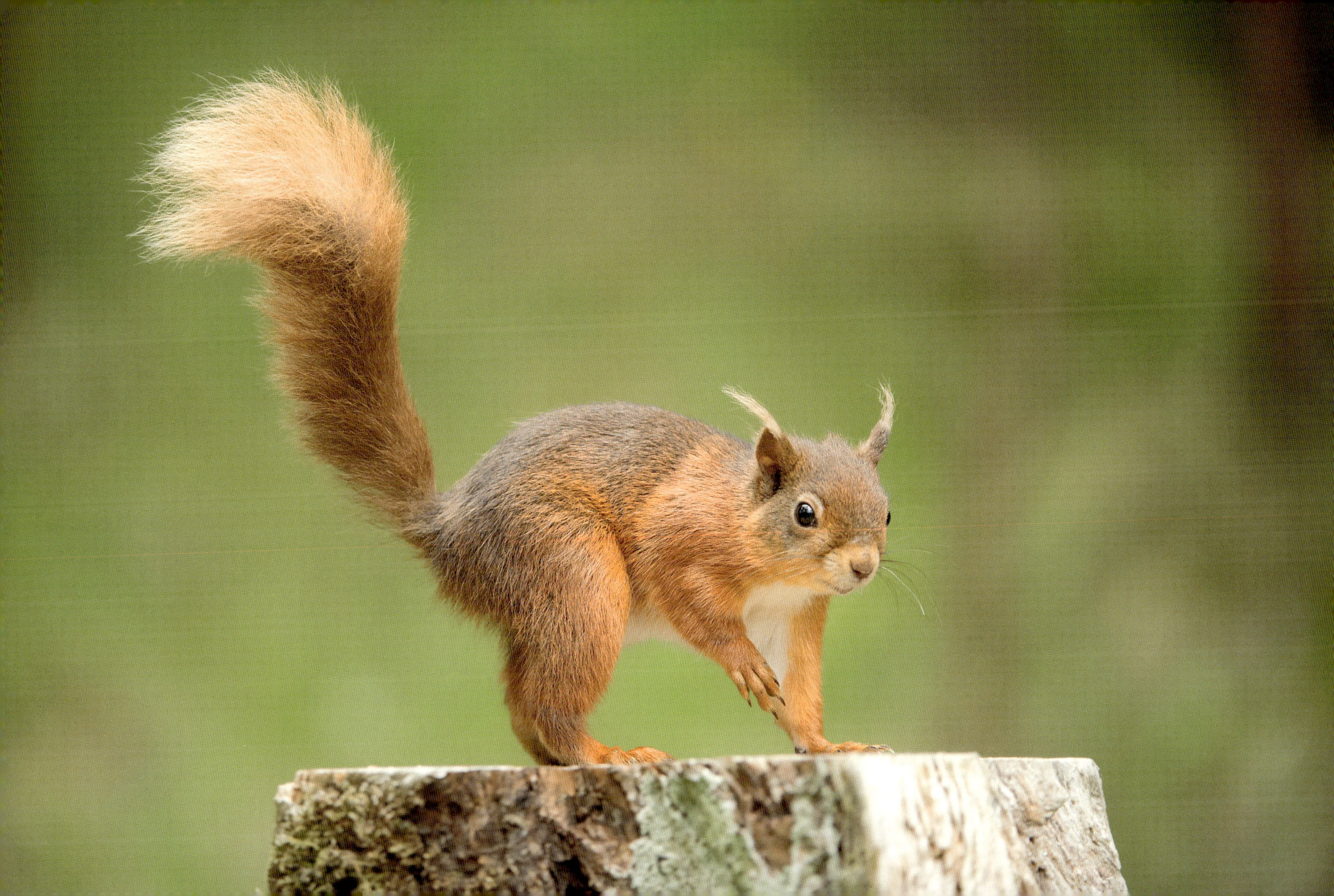

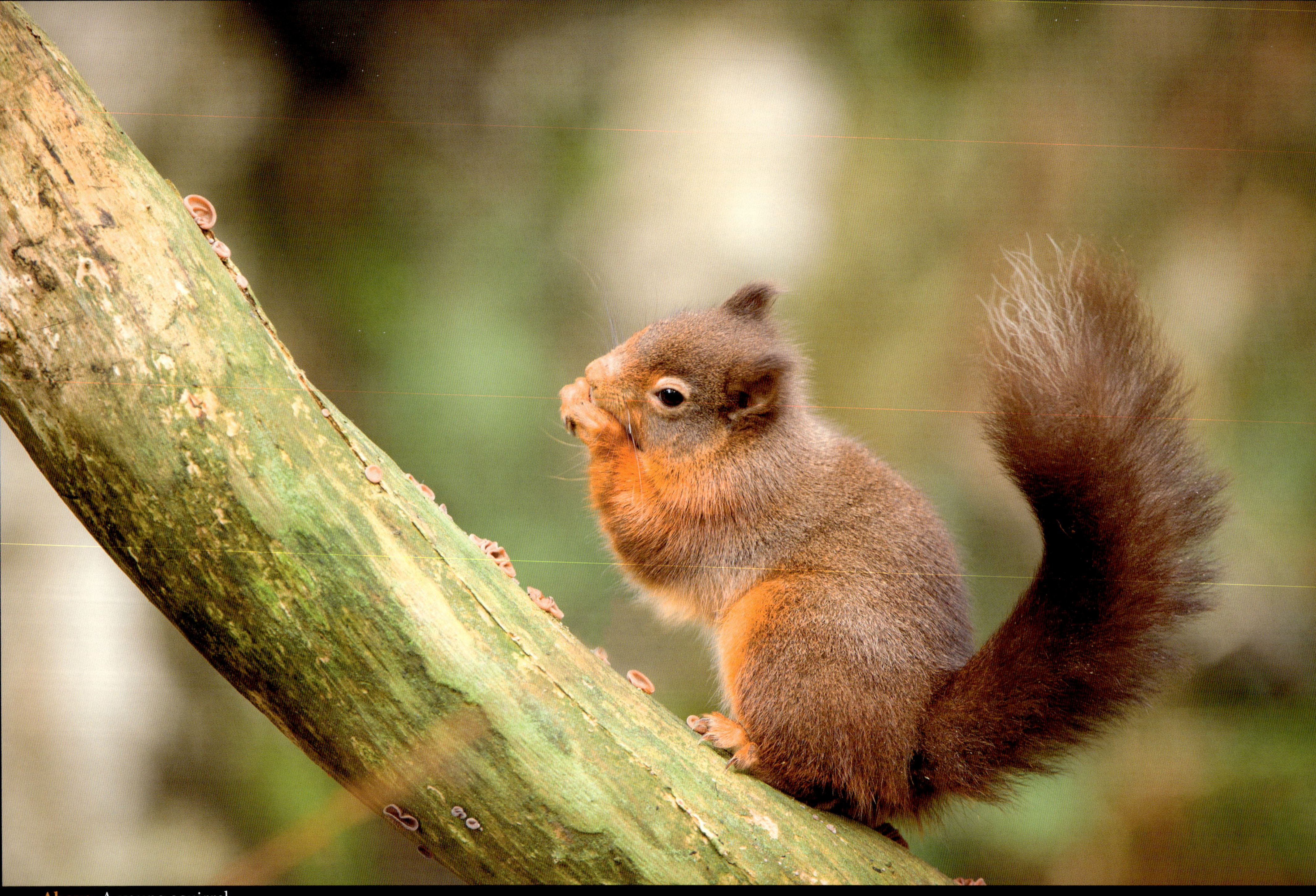

Above: A young squirrel.

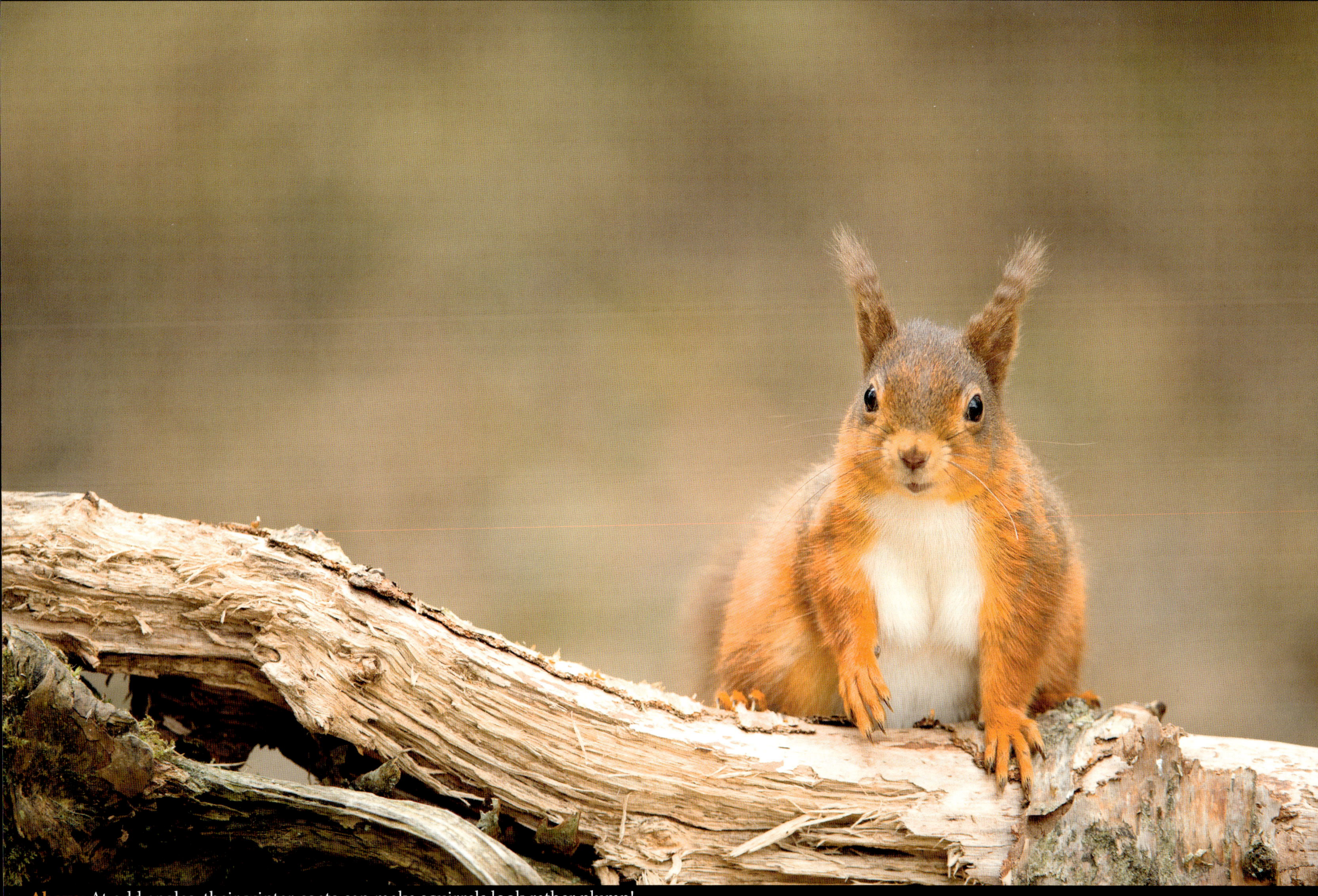

Above: At odd angles, their winter coats can make squirrels look rather plump!

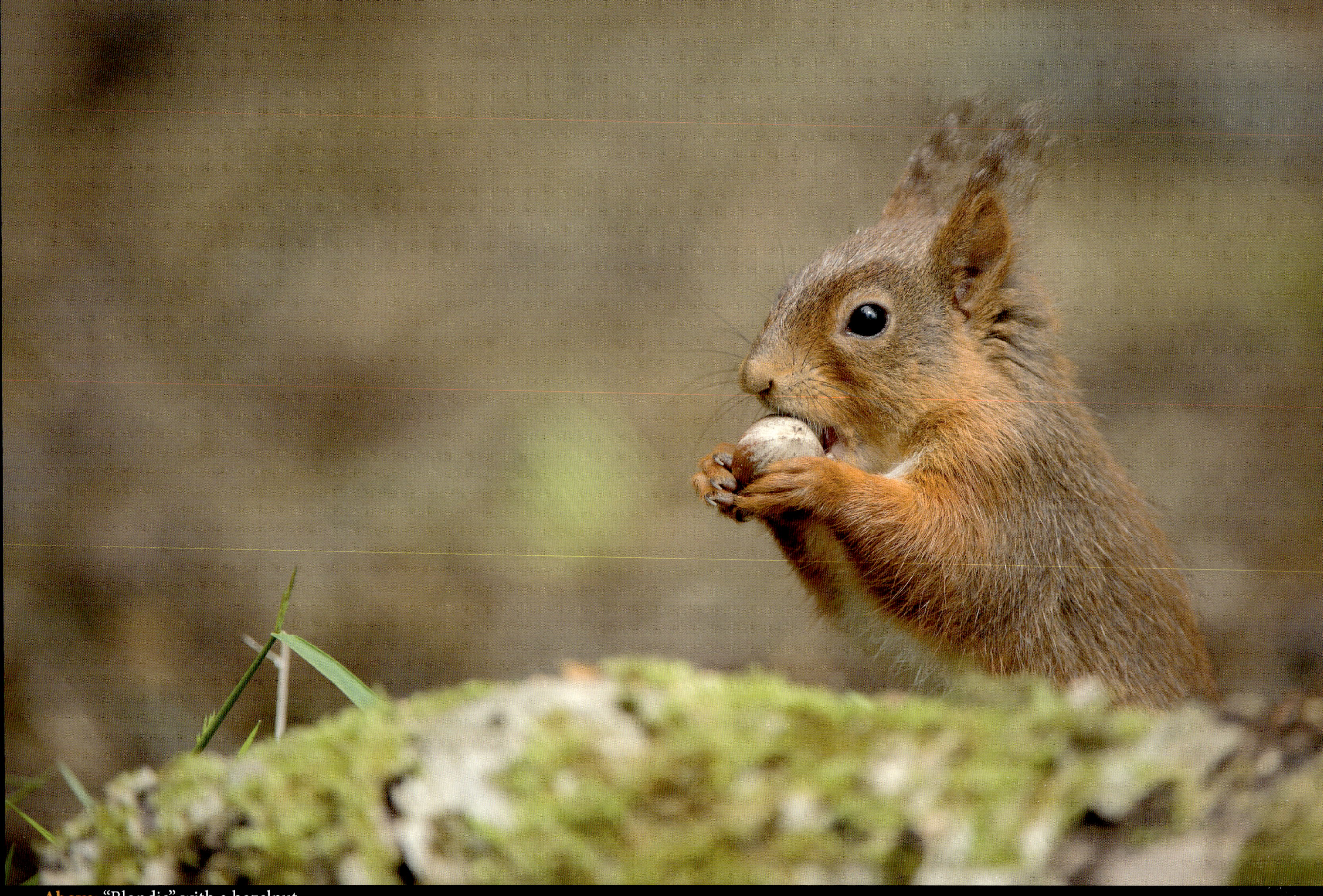

Above: "Blondie" with a hazelnut.

Looking ahead

The future for red squirrels in Britain is uncertain. Public support for conservation efforts to save them is continuing to grow, and if this trend is maintained the odds are much more manageable. If you live in a region where red squirrels are present, you can help by reporting sightings of red and grey squirrels to *Red Squirrels Northern England*.

I hope that I will always be able to sit and watch red squirrels, and not have to flick through old photographs of distant memories. It will be a very sad day if they are ever declared extinct in the UK. It is less widely known, but grey squirrels are becoming a problem for reds in other European countries too. Vaccines and grey squirrel contraceptives are the way forward, in my opinion, and hopefully one day a solution will have been reached.

Public opinion and understanding of wildlife has increased greatly over the years. Now many more people empathise with the difficulties the animals we share our planet with face. This is thanks to people such as Steve Backshall and Sir David Attenborough, who are in a position where they can share the treasures of this world with a wider audience.

It is easy to depress yourself reading all the horrors of rapid deforestation, oil extraction, overfishing and the many other environmental issues we have today. I worry that it is the easier option for those in positions of power to ignore these issues and leave them for someone else to fix. As long as we continue to hold nature close to our hearts and look after our planet, these problems will slowly begin to sort themselves out. Simply getting involved with a local wildlife charity can make a huge difference to the ecosystems in your region.

When I am older, I would like to be able to look back at this book and find that red squirrels are once more a common sight within Britain's woodlands. Wouldn't that be a good day.

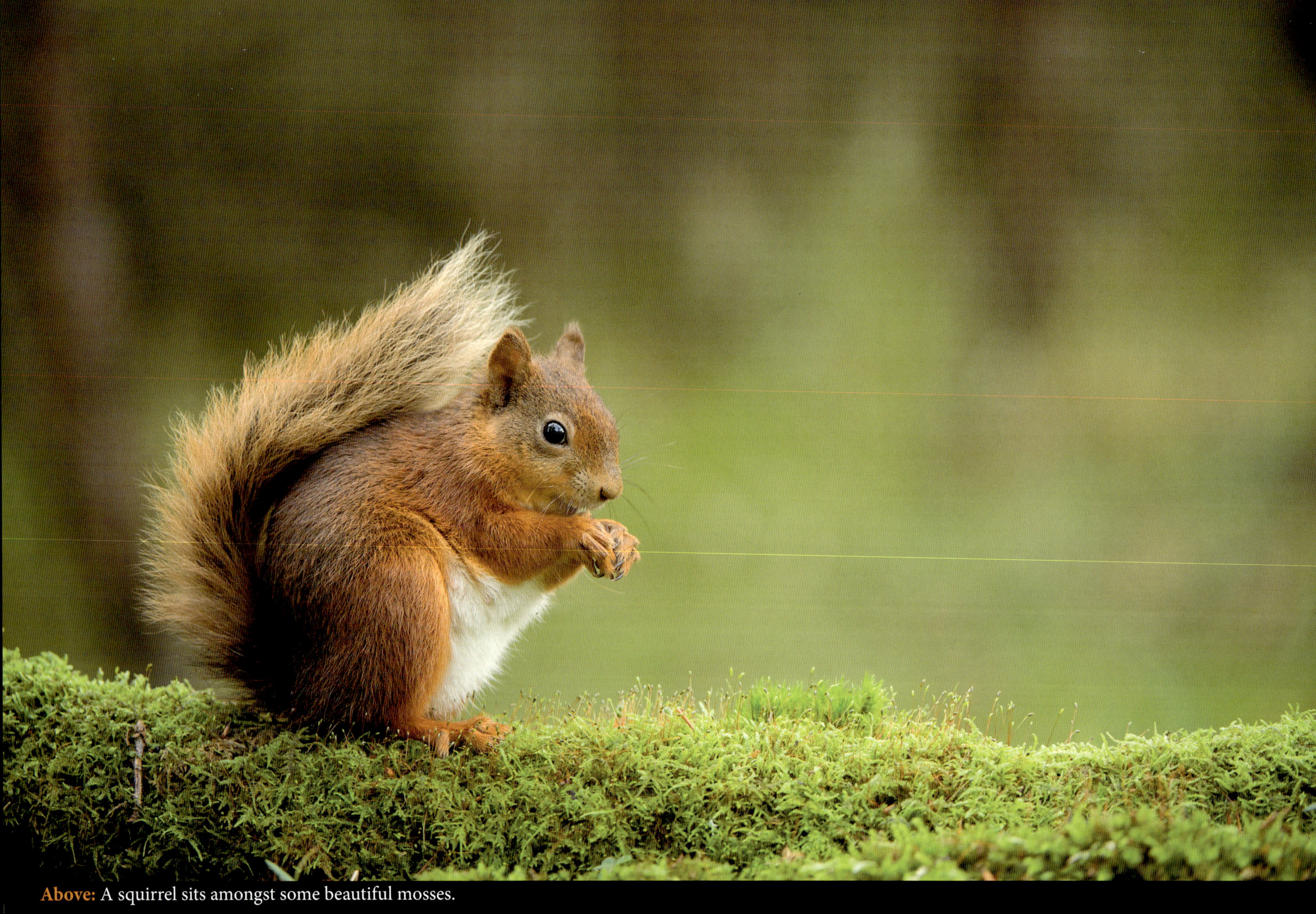

Above: A squirrel sits amongst some beautiful mosses.

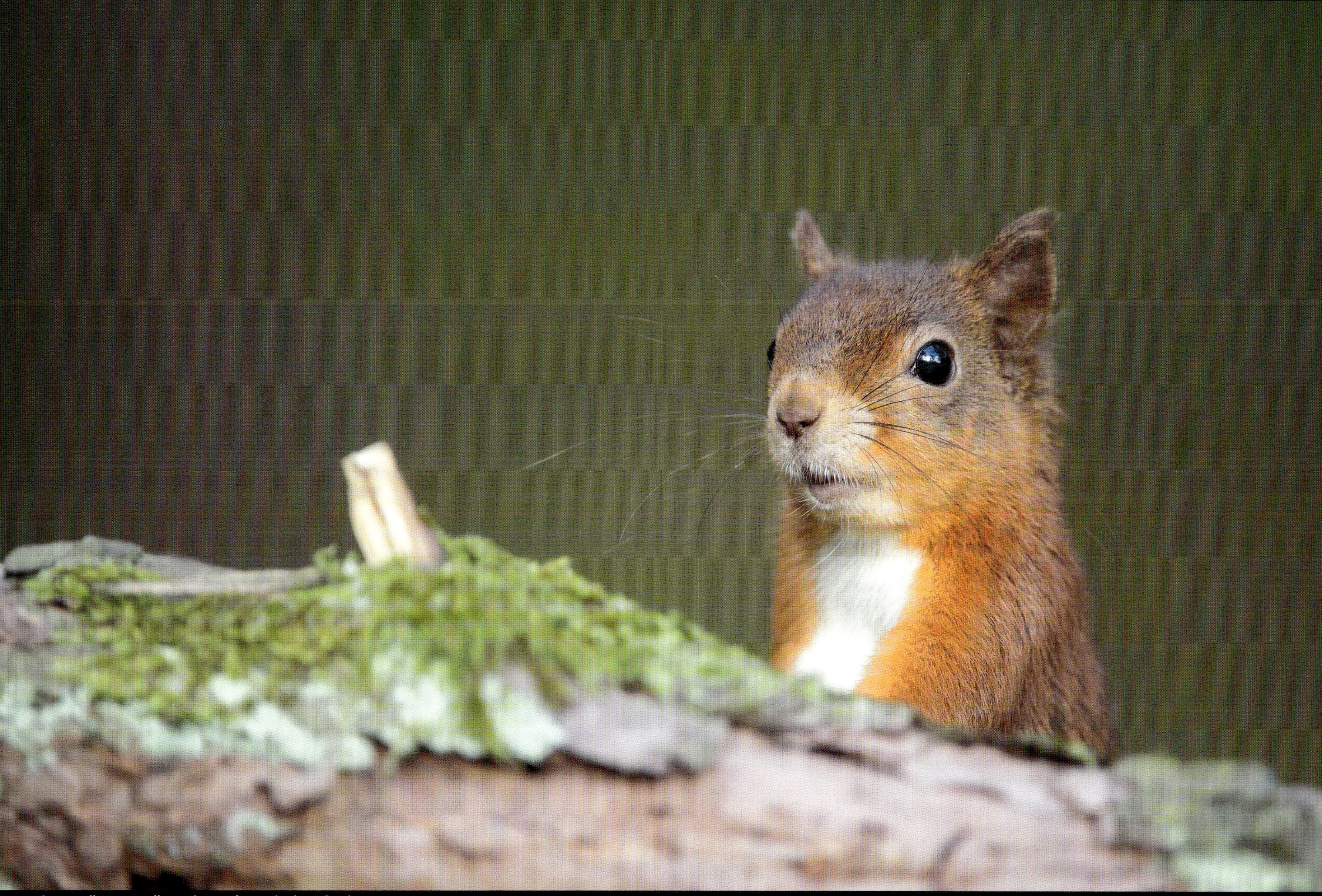

Above: "Scooter" peeking from behind a log.

Photographic technicalities

Most of this book has been free of camera related jargon, but it wouldn't be right to not include some details about what goes on behind the lens. All of the images in this book are photographed using a DSLR camera, as I haven't ventured into the world of film photography (although I do remember having a Bart Simpson film camera when I was little). As far as the "Nikon vs. Canon" argument goes, I am a Nikon man.

I shoot on a full-frame sensor as it provides a better quality image when shooting in low light. This is very helpful as I spend a lot of time photographing in woodlands. The downside of this is that you lose some reach, but I like to think of this as a challenge to get closer to wildlife using my fieldcraft skills.

My hide is a great asset. It is camouflaged and portable, meaning that I can set it up wherever I want and adjust it if the angle isn't perfect. Sometimes stalking through the undergrowth isn't the best way to photograph a certain subject. Red squirrels are a great example of this, as they move very fast and cover a lot of ground very quickly. By using a hide, I let them come to me and display much more natural behaviour. Chasing after a squirrel often results in it being high up in a tree and chattering at you.

It is not necessary to have all the top equipment to be a wildlife photographer. Many of my most popular images were taken on a Nikon D80, which is by no means the best DSLR camera out there. Better equipment does, of course, bring benefits, but it is not the be-all and end-all for getting a good image.

A pleasing image is often accompanied by good lighting. I can no longer count the amount of times a potentially good photograph has been ruined by poor lighting. Trees inconsiderately casting a shadow over the subject's face are particularly irritating. But this is part of the reason that I find myself spending so many hours in a hide, as eventually the conditions will be perfect. I think that, for most things, the best light comes when the sun is overcast by clouds. These clouds act like a giant diffuser, spreading a softer light over the scene.

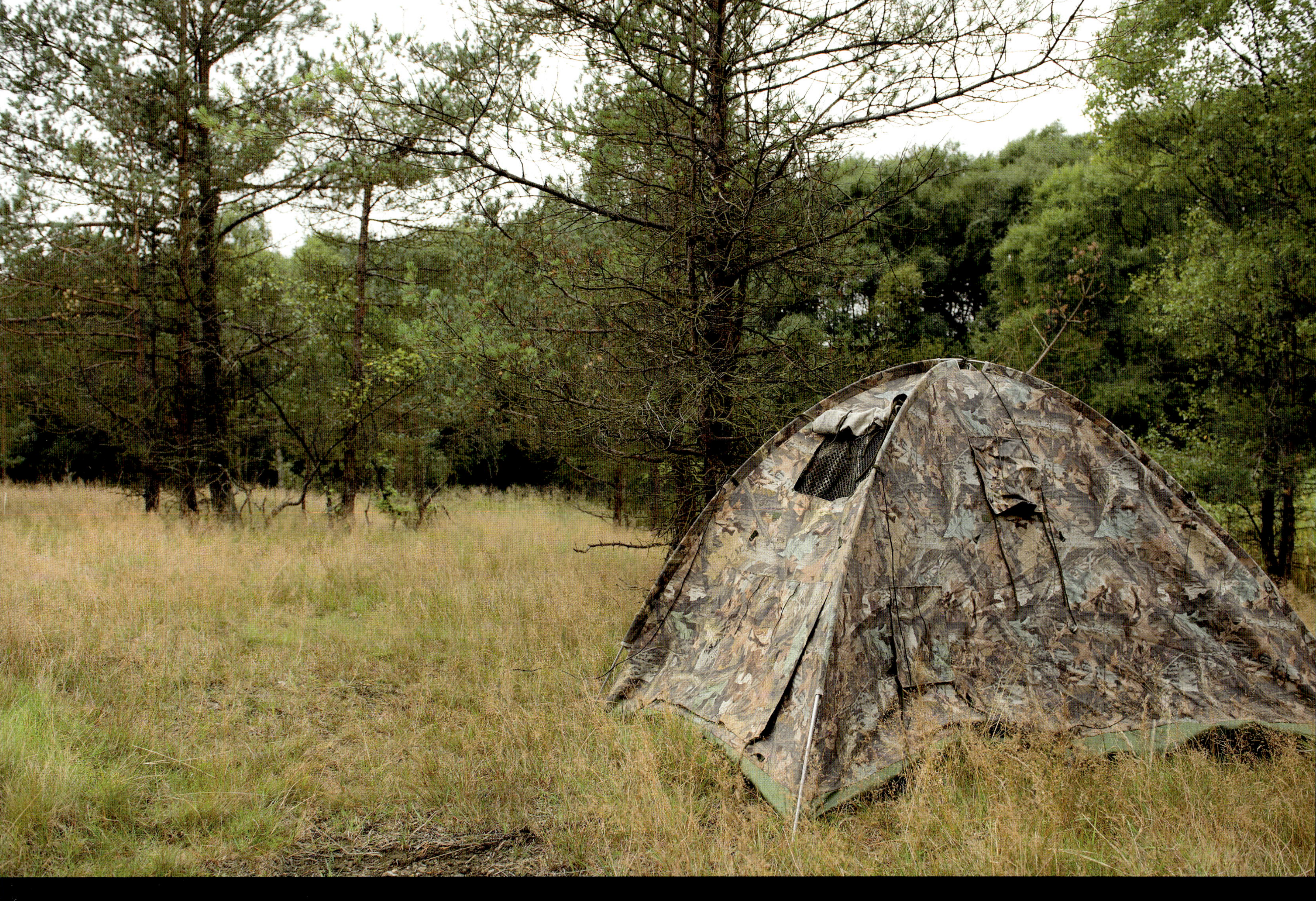

I would also like to thank the **Wardle family** who, although they probably haven't thought about it in this way, have had a huge influence on my photographic career. Without their kind permission to allow me to work on their land for the last six years, I wouldn't be doing what I am doing today.

Hilary Kristensen and **Gemma Wilkinson** have been working closely with me since we first came up with the idea of this book. Thank you both for your support, and especially to Hilary for having so much faith in this production.

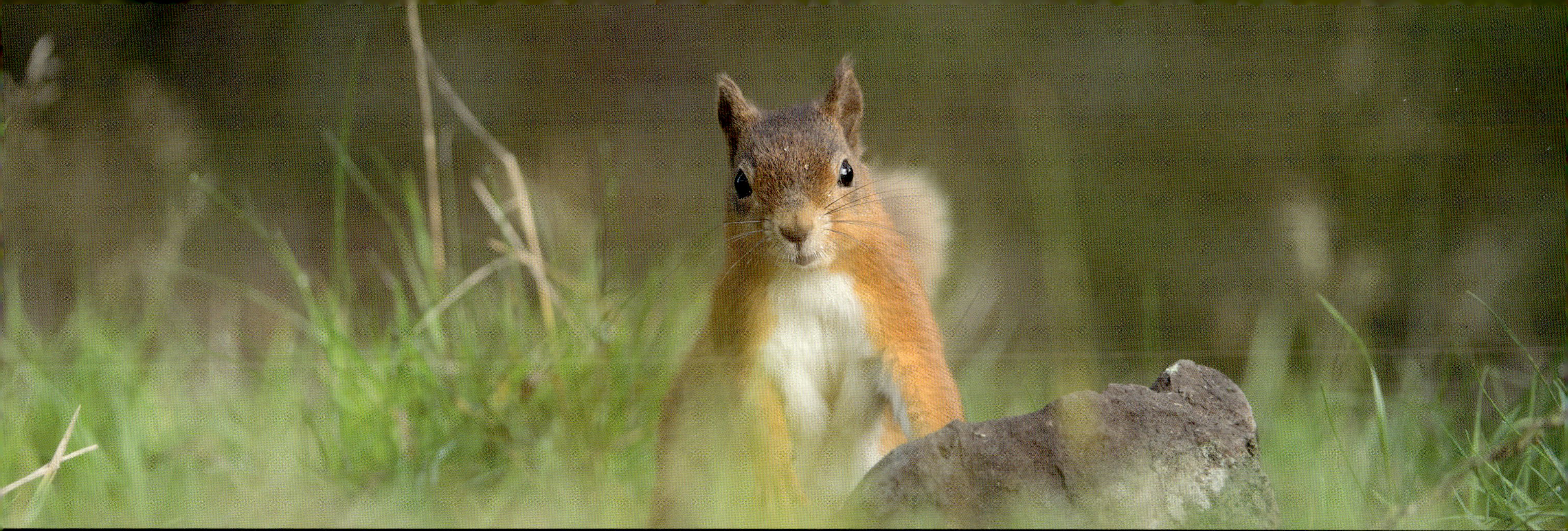

Finally, I would like to thank the following people for their generosity in pledging money to help with the printing costs of this book:
Brian Kloetzel & Chelsea Sparta, Martin Fletcher, Katrin Glaesmann, Ann Chapman, Lilian Rasmussen, Teresa Doherty, Alan Fearon, Anthony Symonds, Jamie & Paul Wyver, Sue-Ellen Smith, Matt Berry, Anne Lawson, Jane Lewis, Angela & Phil Livingston, Margaret Murphy, Elizabeth Thomas, Elaine Westall, Don & Lorna Woodward, Russ Valentine, Hannelore Maier, Julie Bailey, Andrea Ballhause, Hazel Blakeley, John Bousie, Wendy Brewis, Gizem Erdoğan, Amanda Galbraith, Adam King, Dirk Köst, David Leslie, Michelle Milburn, Diana Nicholls, Julie Quinn, Marc Read, Clare Robson, Anne & Patrick Rochford, Patrick Sheard, Julian Smalley, Suzanna Snow, Simon Stephenson, Tom Swift, Clare Wilson, and Peter & Joy Wilson.

References

Whilst I have learnt a lot about red squirrels through my own studies, my knowledge does not match those that have dedicated many years to researching the red squirrel. The following books have been used as valuable references:

Squirrels by Jessica Holm (Whittet Books, 1987)
The Eurasian Red Squirrel by Stefan Bosch & Peter W. W. Lurz (Westarp Wissenschaften, 2012)

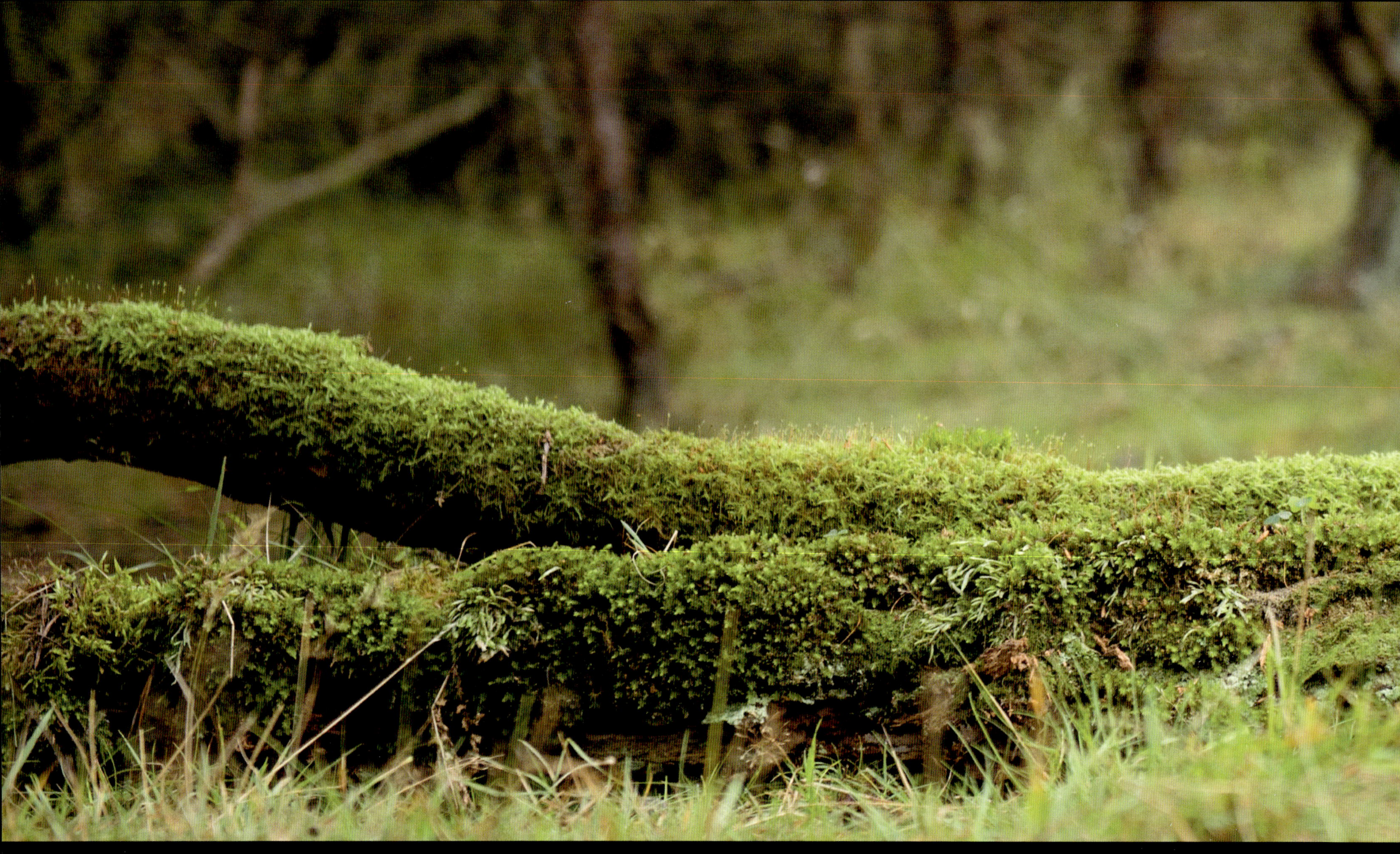

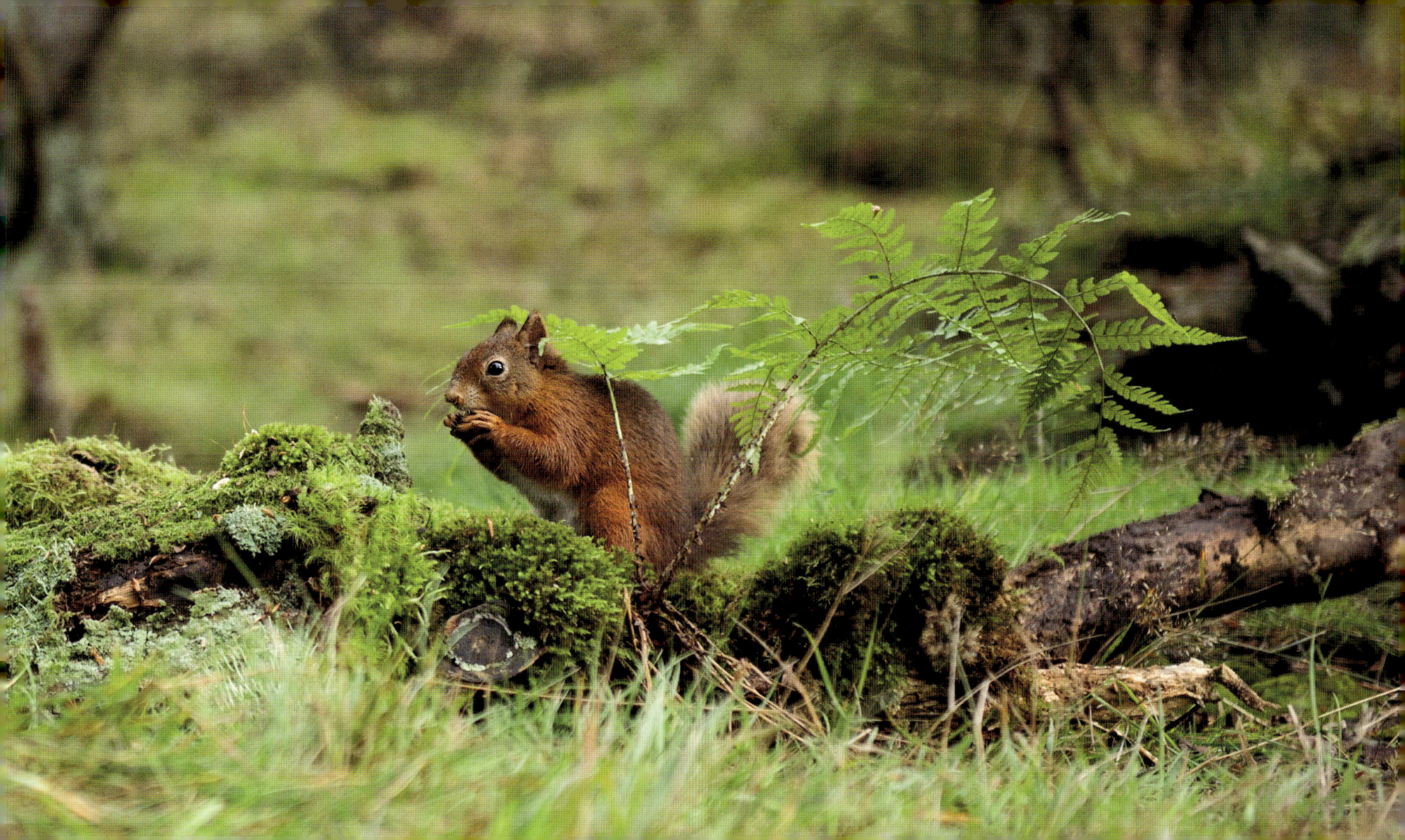

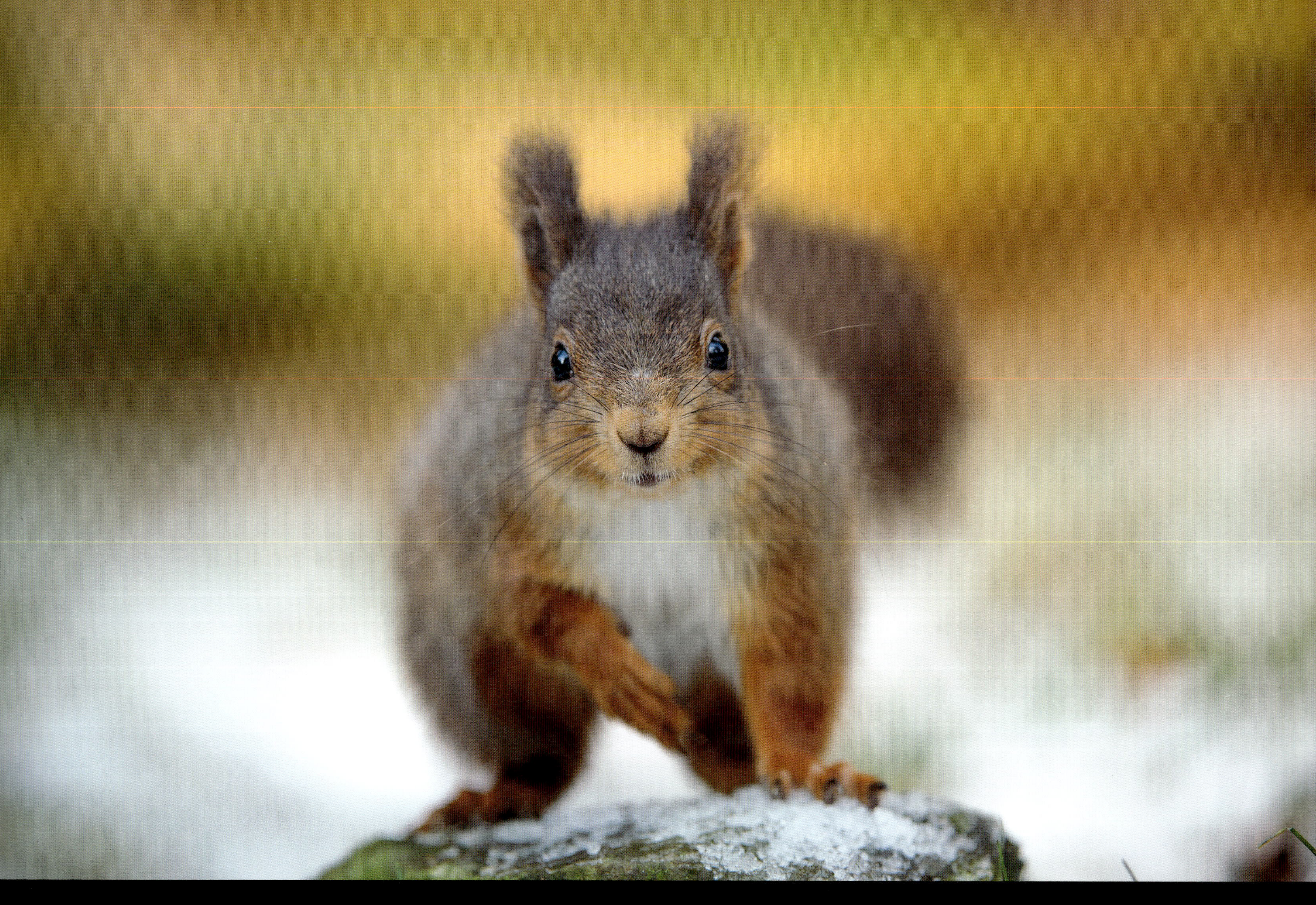

www.willnicholls.co.uk